LEARN HOW T
- FUN & EA



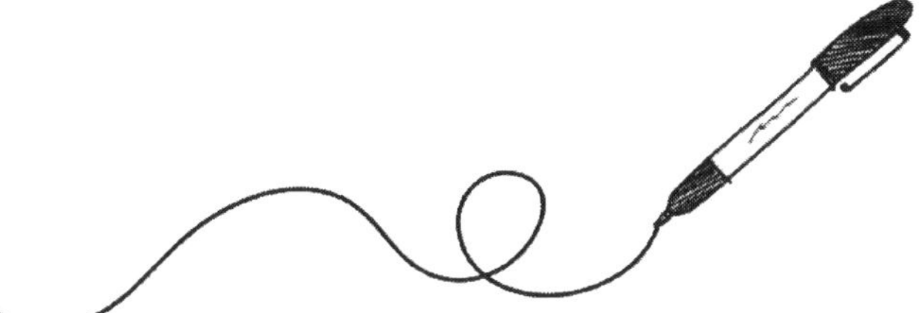

# 1007 DRAWINGS to Sketch in 5 Minutes or Less.

(For **Kids** and **Adults**; With **Three Difficulty Levels**)

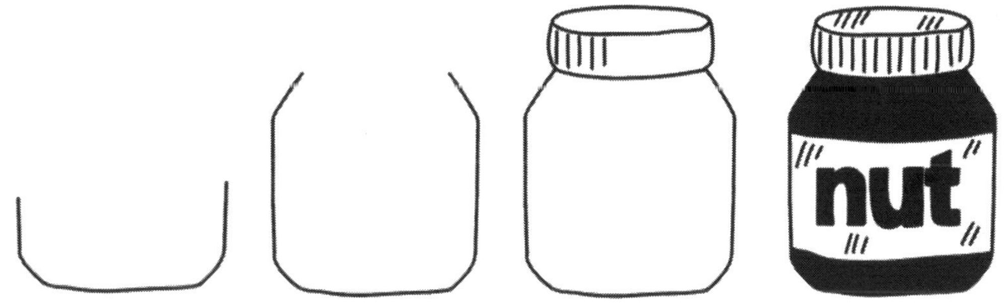


Amanda Piniecka

*Instagram: amy_pini*
*www.amandapiniecka.com*

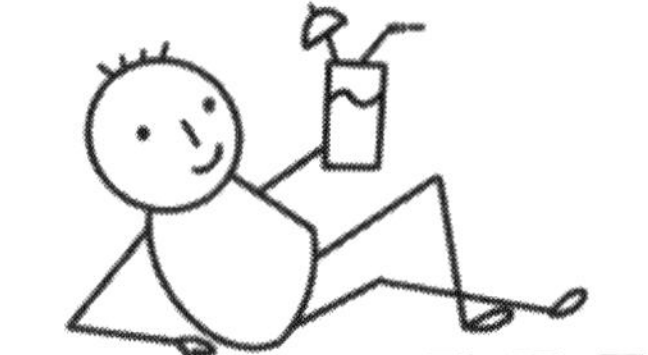

**Disclaimer and legal notice**



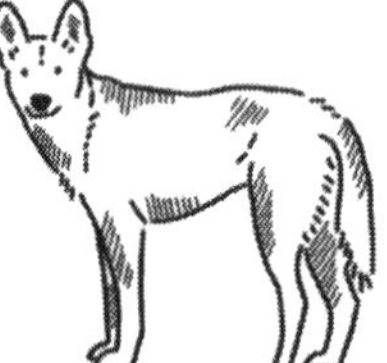

**ISBN: 978-9493264052**

# CONTENTS

# WELCOME

This book shows you **step-by-step** how to draw literally any object or creature in **less than 5 minutes** - even if you're a complete beginner or firmly believe you are missing the "talent".

We have divided our **1007 images into 2 different levels of detail.**

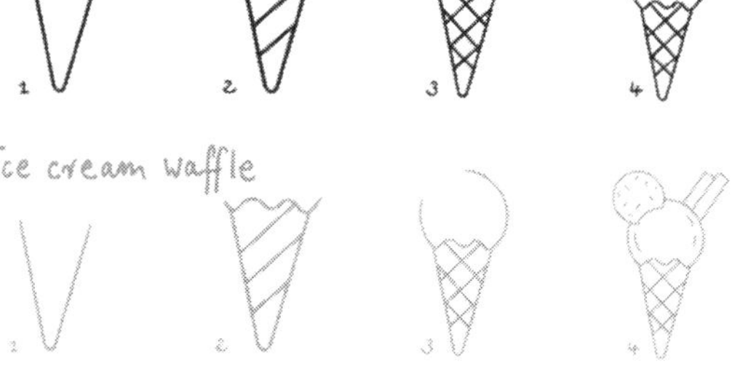


and **3 difficulty levels** (characterized by small circles).

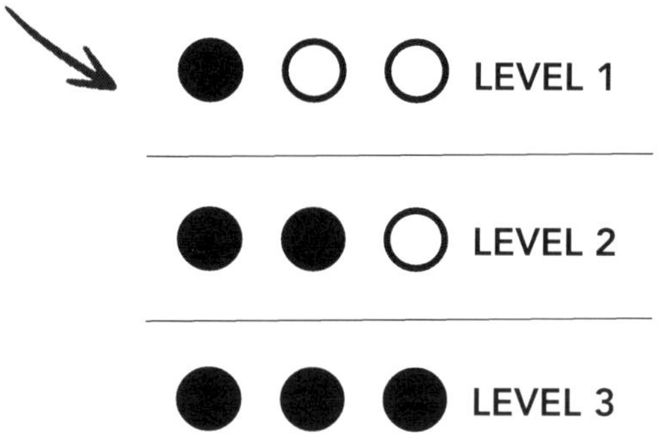


To help you see the **new strokes added at** each step, I've **slightly hidden** the **previous steps.**

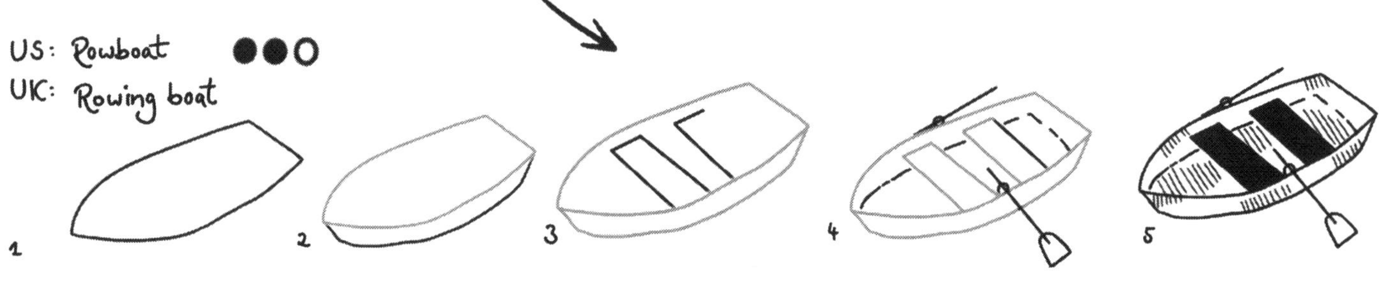


It will take **5 to 7 days** for your brain to get **used to** the **motor demands.** You'll notice how drawing becomes easier and easier, even if you've lacked any previous experience. Basically, drawing inanimate objects with simple corners, curves and lines is easier than drawing detailed plants, animals, and people. For this reason, **I recommend you to start with the objects first**, so that you're better warmed up for the more challenging chapters.

**Ready?**

**Have fun drawing!**

Amanda Piniecka

# WARM-UP

With **basic shapes** like **circles** and **squares,** combined with **lines** and other details (like colors and patterns), you can draw just about anything. Here are some examples of basic shapes with which you can start every illustration. Work through them to gain confidence in drawing basic shapes. Then go to the step-by-step instructions for drawing simple things like a chair, a phone, an apple and more.

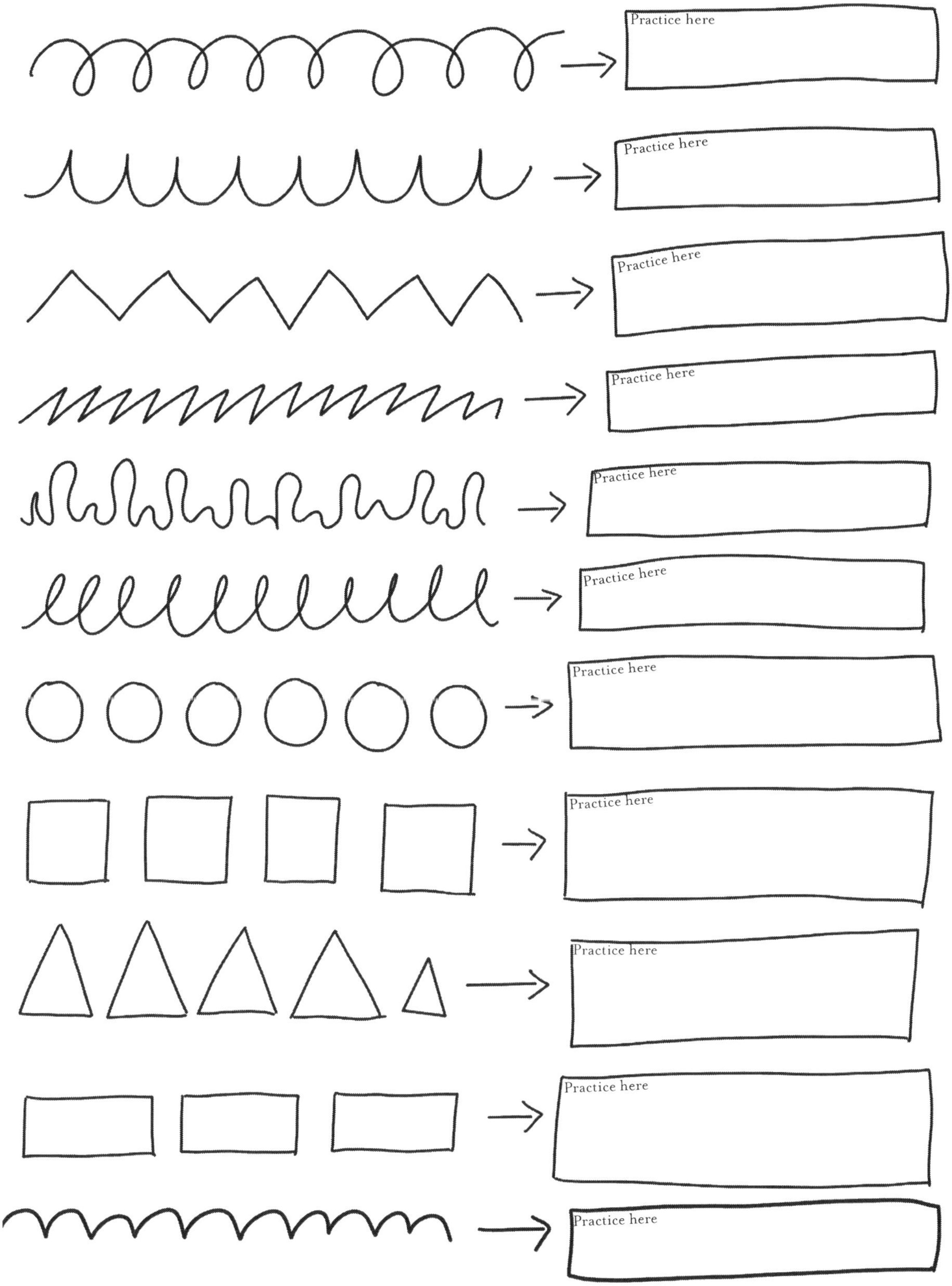

Practice here

Practice here

Practice here

Practice here

Practice here

Practice here

Practice here

Practice here

Practice here

Practice here

Practice here

# BASIC SHAPES

The best way to practice drawing spatial objects is to look at as many items as possible, find the basic shapes in them, and then draw them. Dare to take on complex tasks, even the **most difficult objects** consist of **simple basic shapes.**

***Finally, some three-dimensional shapes follow, so that drawing the sketches will be even easier for you right away***

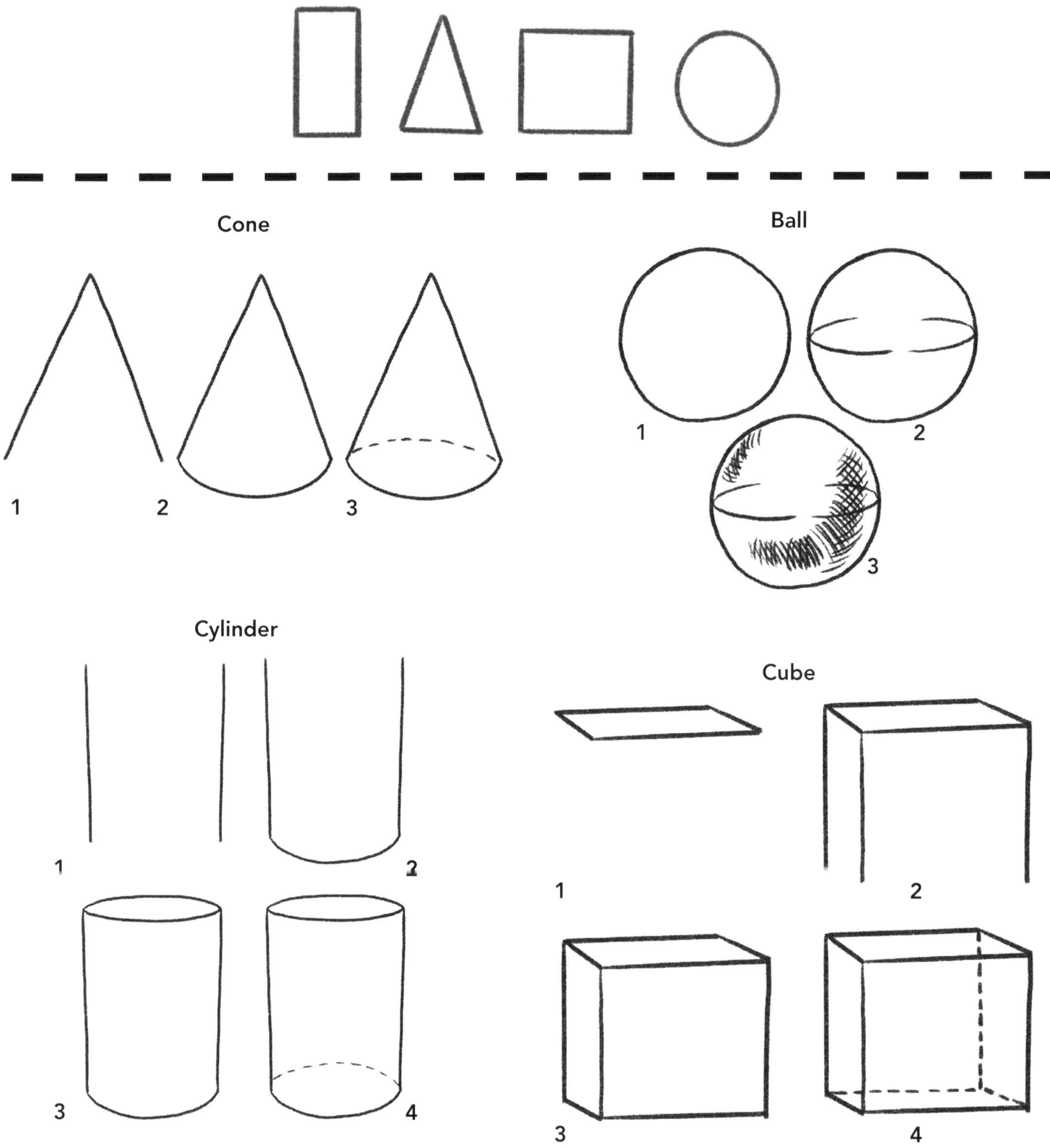

**If you want to copy something that you see in 3-dimensional form in front of you, just close one of your eyes to see the outlines and details more easily.**

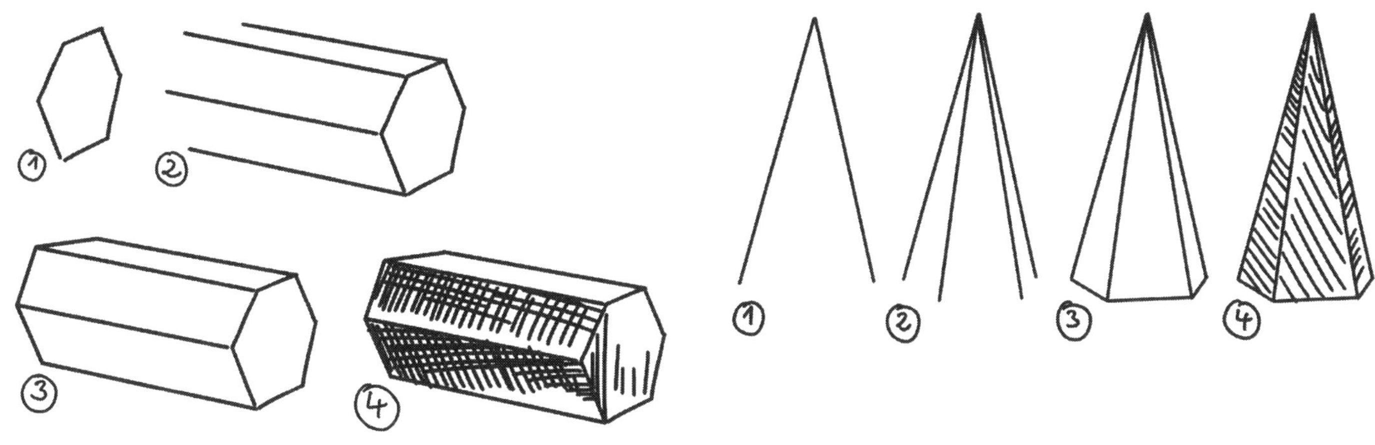

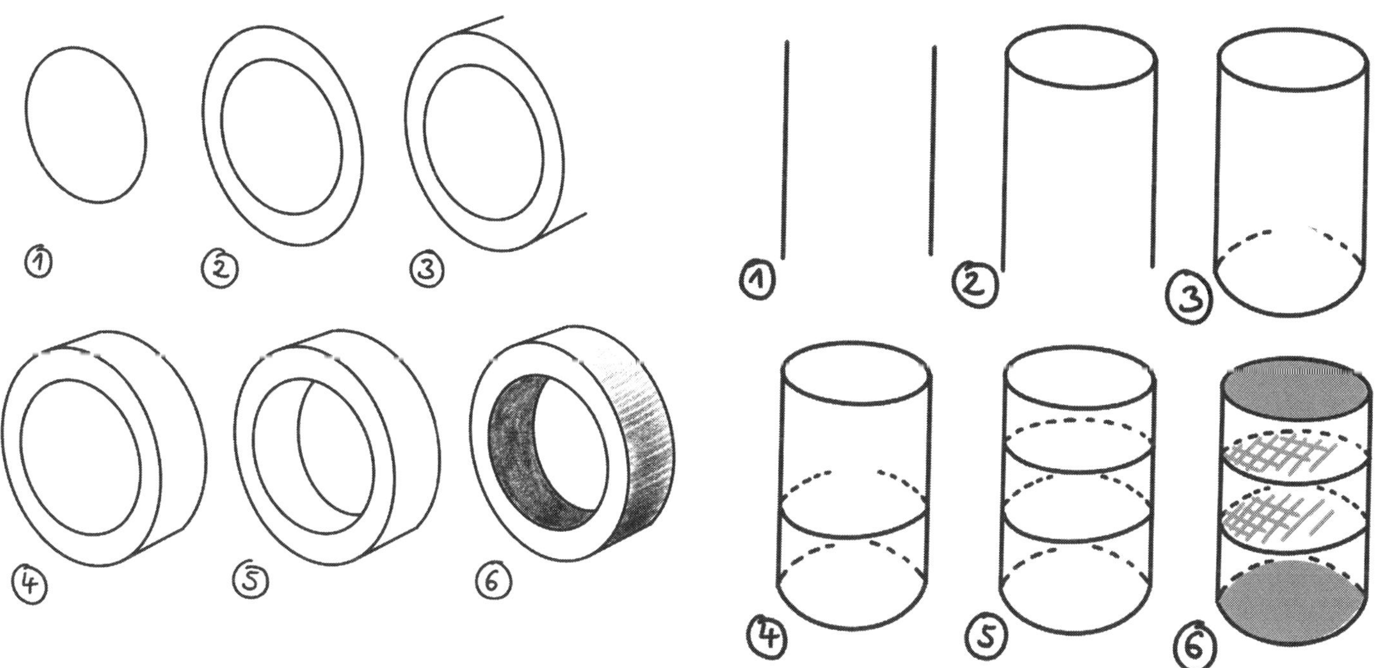

**Got warmed up? Let's get started with the drawings!**

# ITEMS

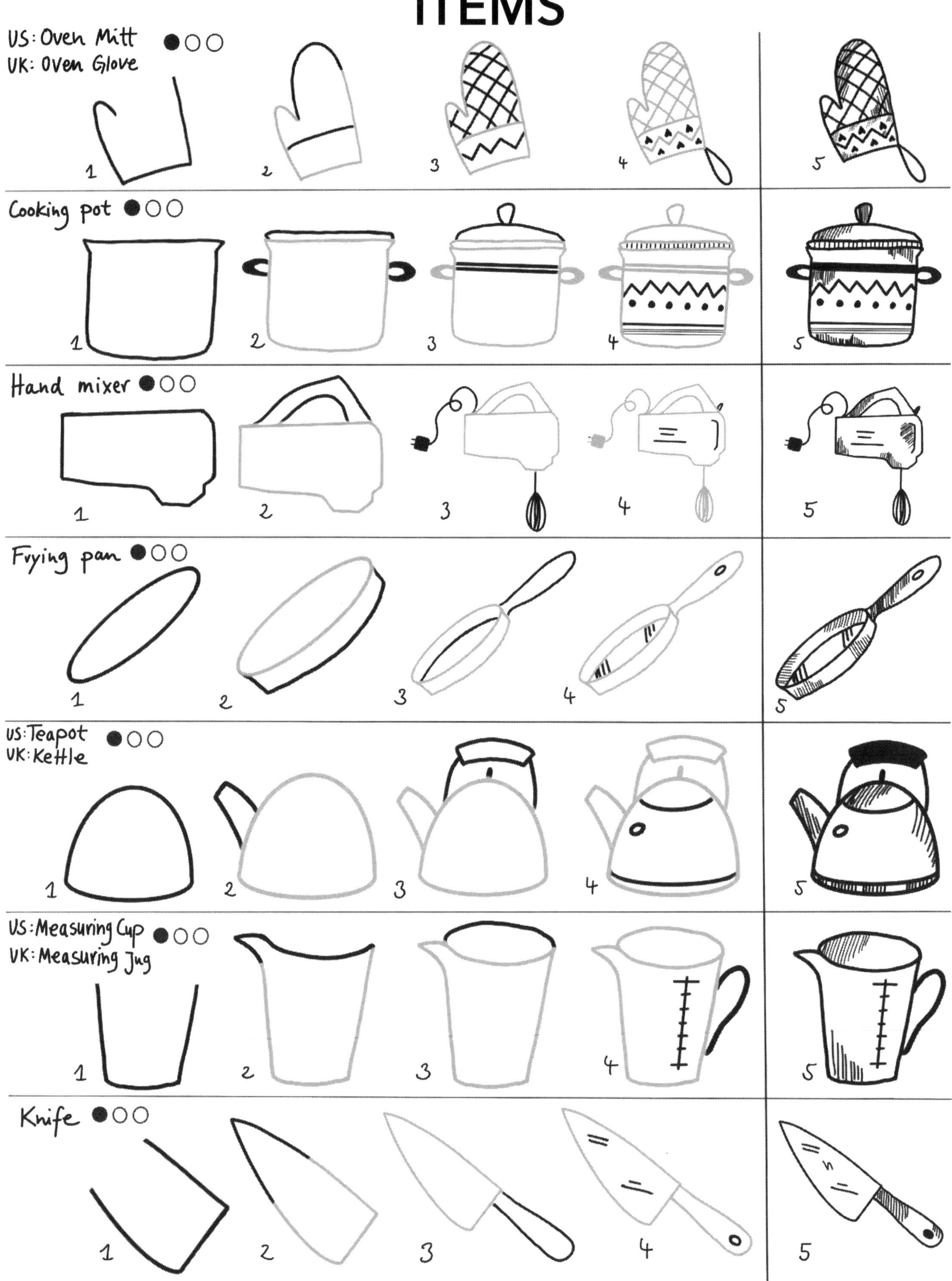

US: Oven Mitt
UK: Oven Glove
1
2
3
4
5
Cooking pot
1
2
3
4
5
Hand mixer
1
2
3
4
5
Frying pan
1
2
3
4
5
US: Teapot
UK: Kettle
1
2
3
4
5
US: Measuring Cup
UK: Measuring Jug
1
2
3
4
5
Knife
1
2
3
4
5

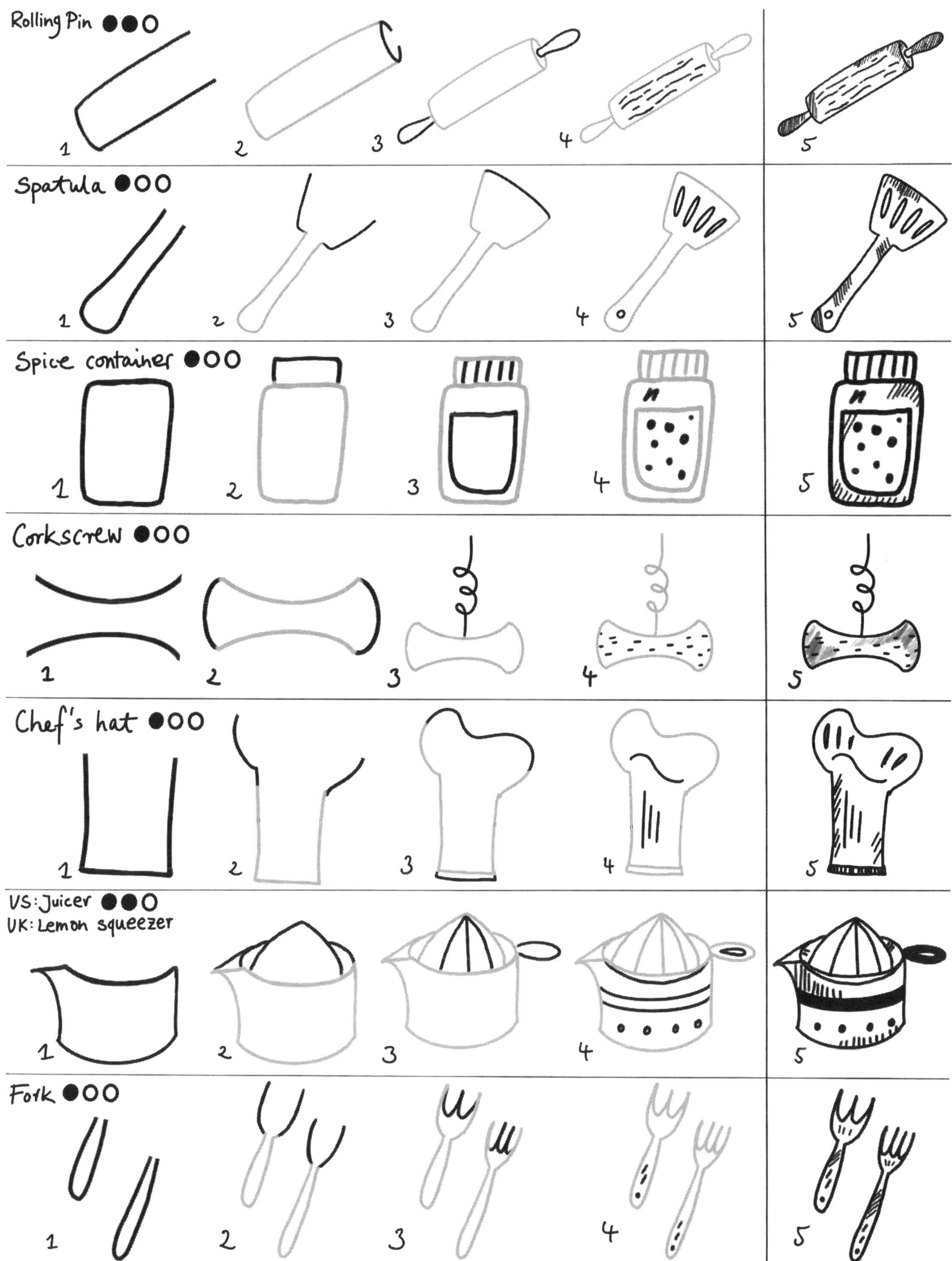
Rolling Pin
1
2
3
4
5
Spatula
1
2
3
4
5
Spice container
1
2
3
4
5
Corkscrew
1
2
3
4
5
Chef's hat
1
2
3
4
5
US: Juicer
UK: Lemon squeezer
1
2
3
4
5
Fork
1
2
3
4
5

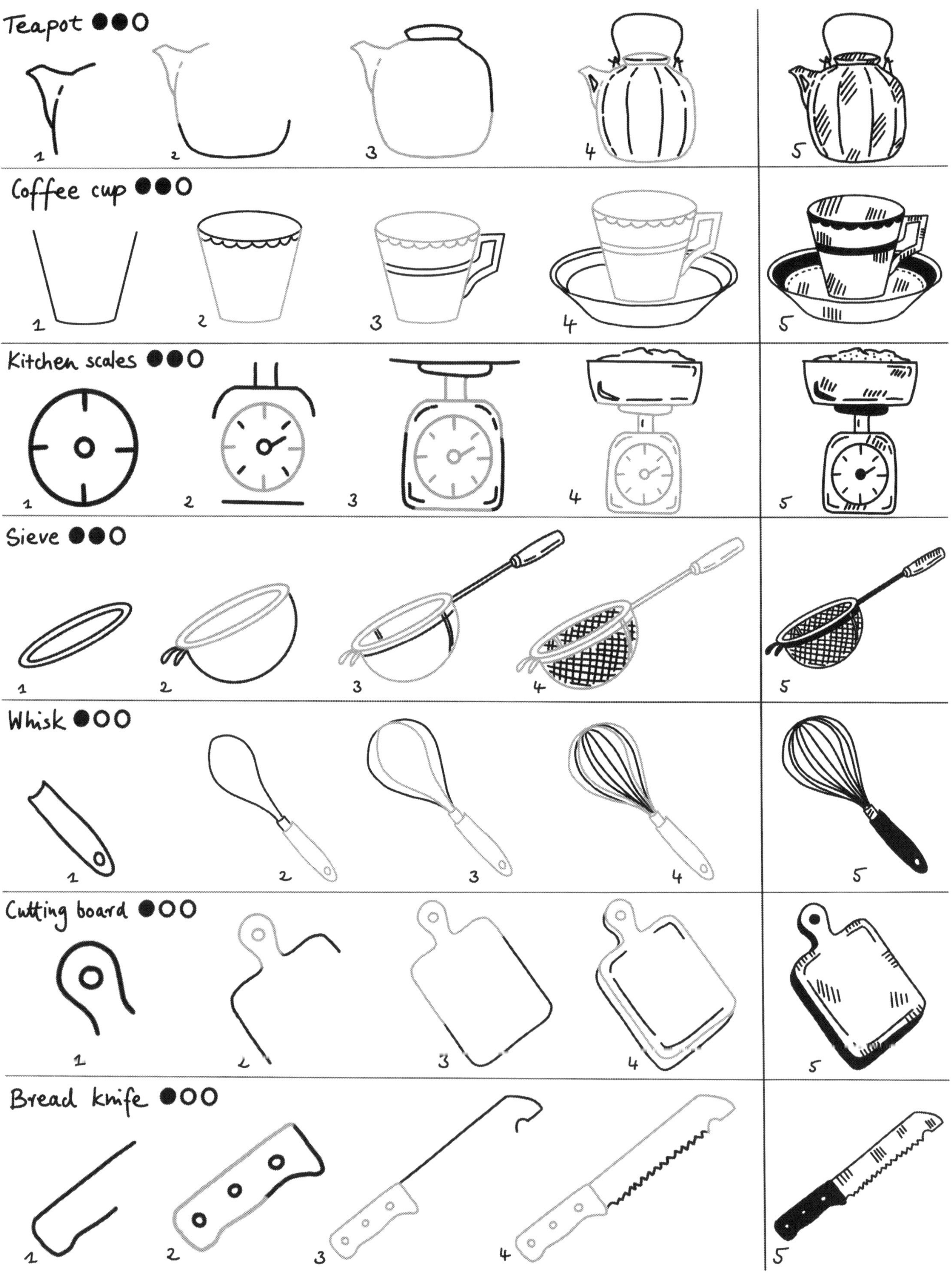
Teapot
1
2
3
4
5
Coffee cup
1
2
3
4
5
Kitchen scales
1
2
3
4
5
Sieve
1
2
3
4
5
Whisk
1
2
3
4
5
Cutting board
1
2
3
4
5
Bread knife
1
2
3
4
5

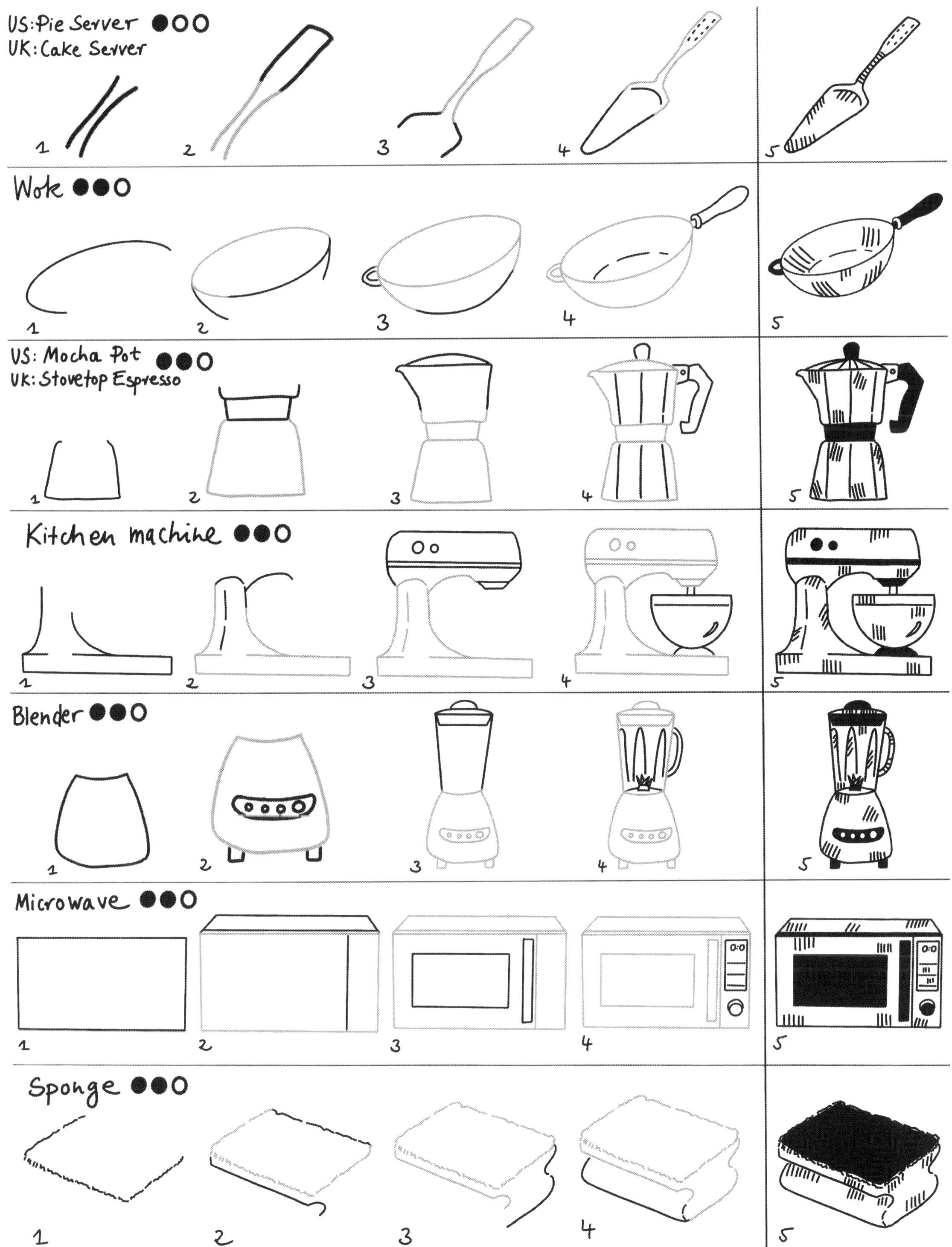
US:Pie Server
UK:Cake Server
1
2
3
4
5
Wok
1
2
3
4
5
US: Mocha Pot
UK: Stovetop Espresso
1
2
3
4
5
Kitchen machine
1
2
3
4
5
Blender
1
2
3
4
5
Microwave
0:0
1
2
3
4
5
Sponge
1
2
3
4
5

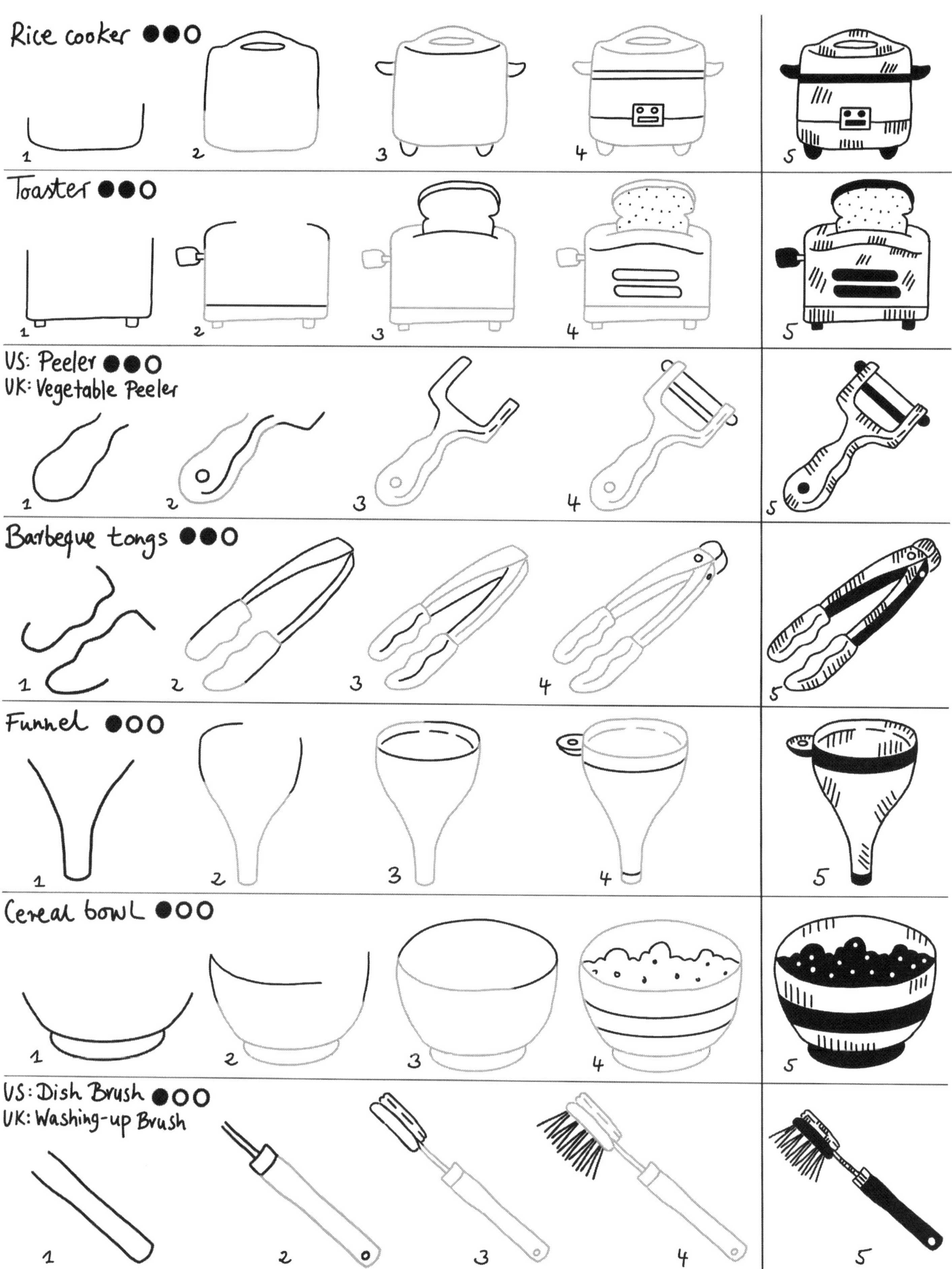
Rice cooker ●●○
1
2
3
4
5
Toaster ●●○
1
2
3
4
5
US: Peeler ●●○
UK: Vegetable Peeler
1
2
3
4
5
Barbeque tongs ●●○
1
2
3
4
5
Funnel ●○○
1
2
3
4
5
Cereal bowl ●○○
1
2
3
4
5
US: Dish Brush ●○○
UK: Washing-up Brush
1
2
3
4
5

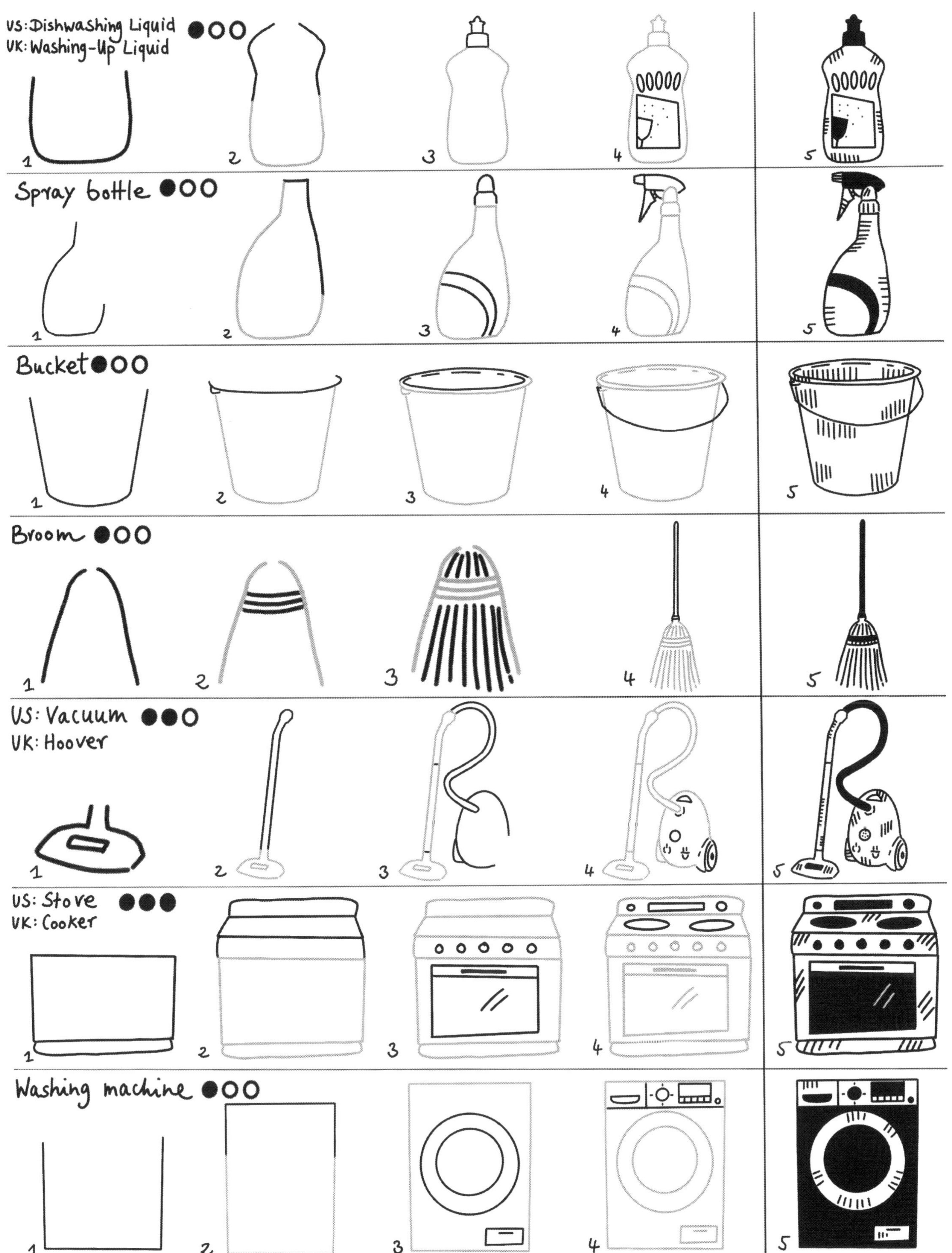
US: Dishwashing Liquid
UK: Washing-Up Liquid
1
2
3
4
5
Spray bottle
1
2
3
4
5
Bucket
1
2
3
4
5
Broom
1
2
3
4
5
US: Vacuum
UK: Hoover
1
2
3
4
5
US: Stove
UK: Cooker
1
2
3
4
5
Washing machine
1
2
3
4
5

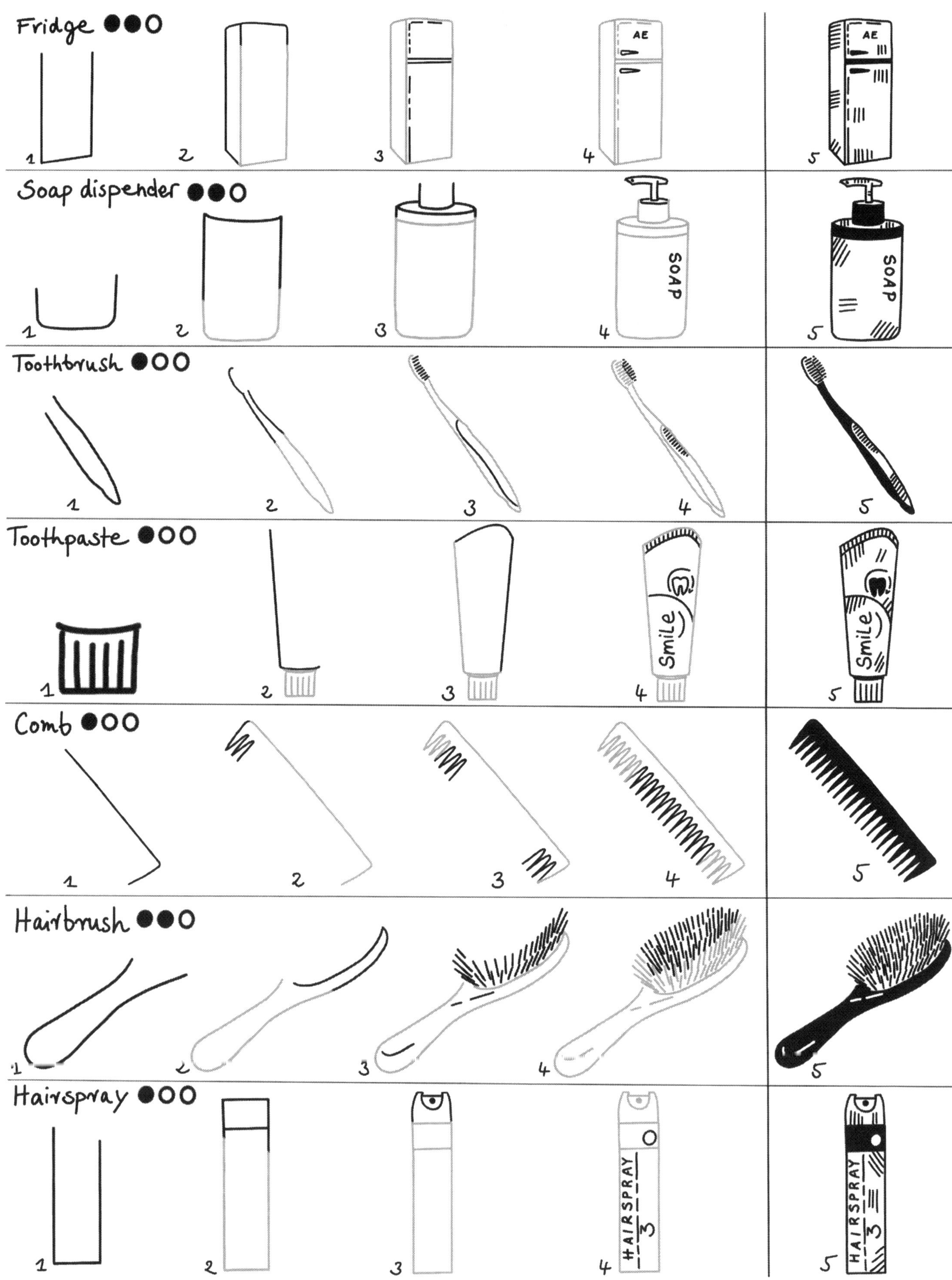

Fridge
1
2
3
4
AE
5
AE
Soap dispender
1
2
3
4
SOAP
5
SOAP
Toothbrush
1
2
3
4
5
Toothpaste
1
2
3
4
Smile
5
Smile
Comb
1
2
3
4
5
Hairbrush
1
2
3
4
5
Hairspray
1
2
3
4
HAIRSPRAY
3
5
HAIRSPRAY
3

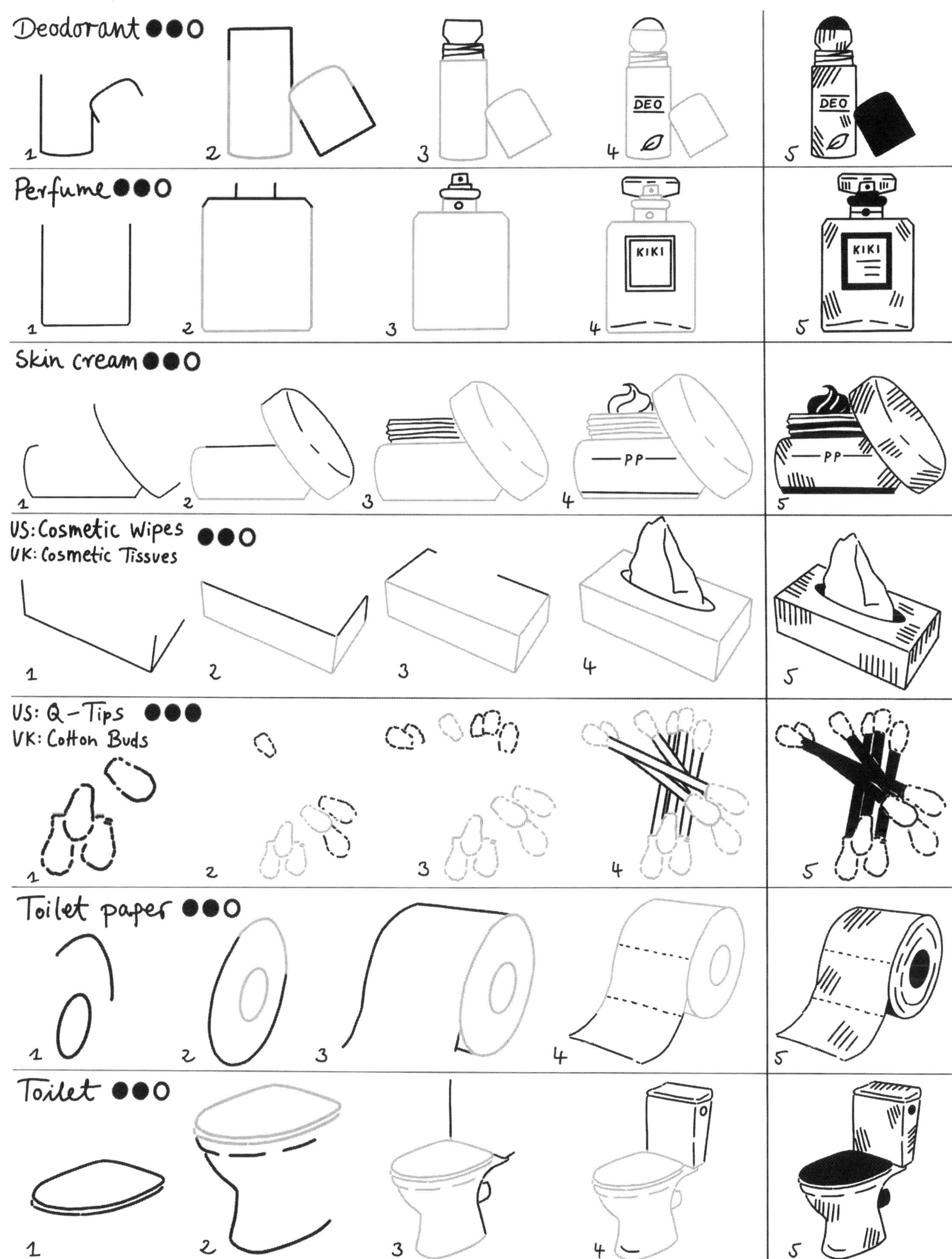
Deodorant
DEO
Perfume
KIKI
Skin cream
PP
US: Cosmetic Wipes
UK: Cosmetic Tissues
US: Q-Tips
UK: Cotton Buds
Toilet paper
Toilet

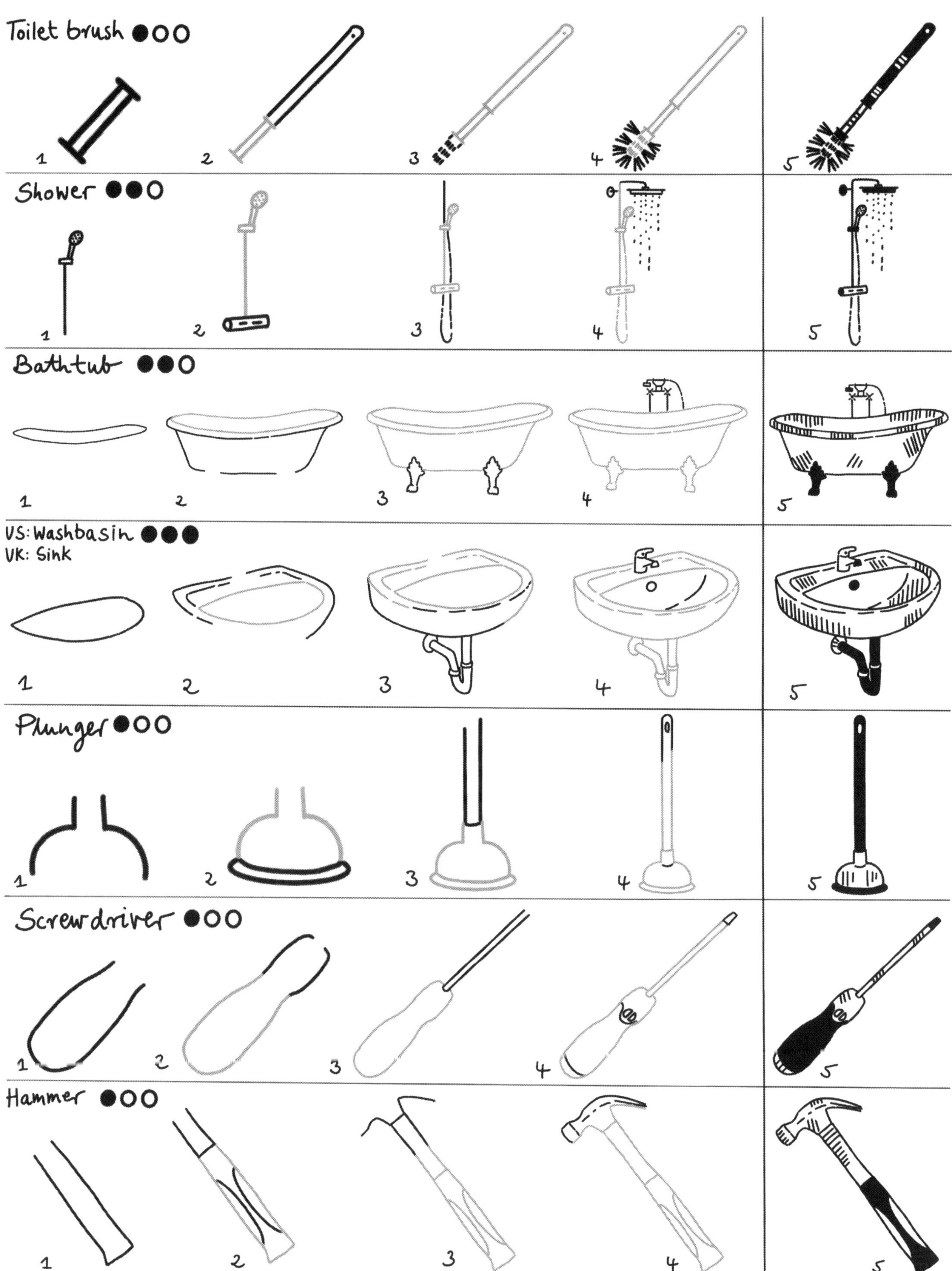
Toilet brush
1
2
3
4
5
Shower
1
2
3
4
5
Bathtub
1
2
3
4
5
US: Washbasin
UK: Sink
1
2
3
4
5
Plunger
1
2
3
4
5
Screwdriver
1
2
3
4
5
Hammer
1
2
3
4
5

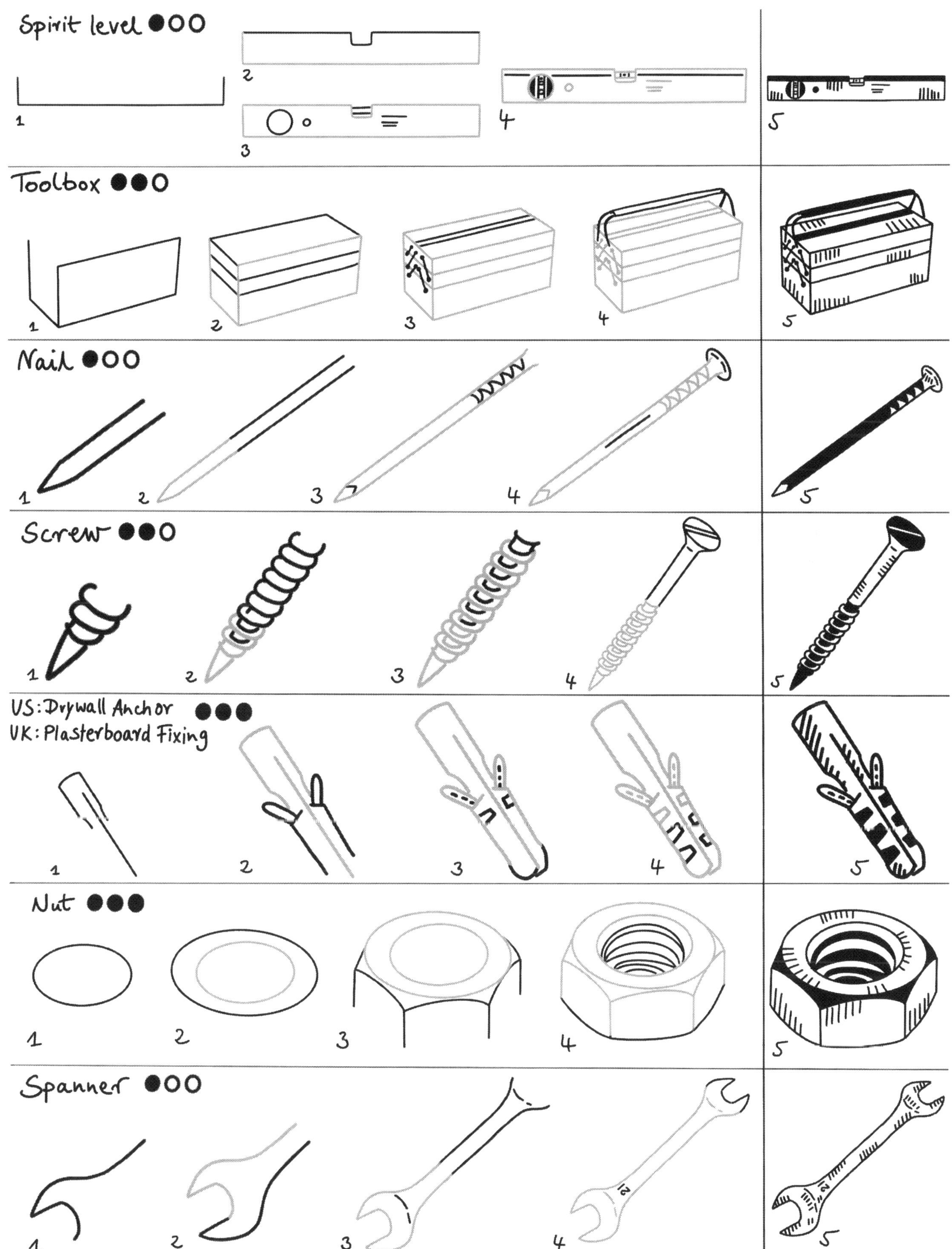
Spirit level
Toolbox
Nail
Screw
US: Drywall Anchor
UK: Plasterboard Fixing
Nut
Spanner

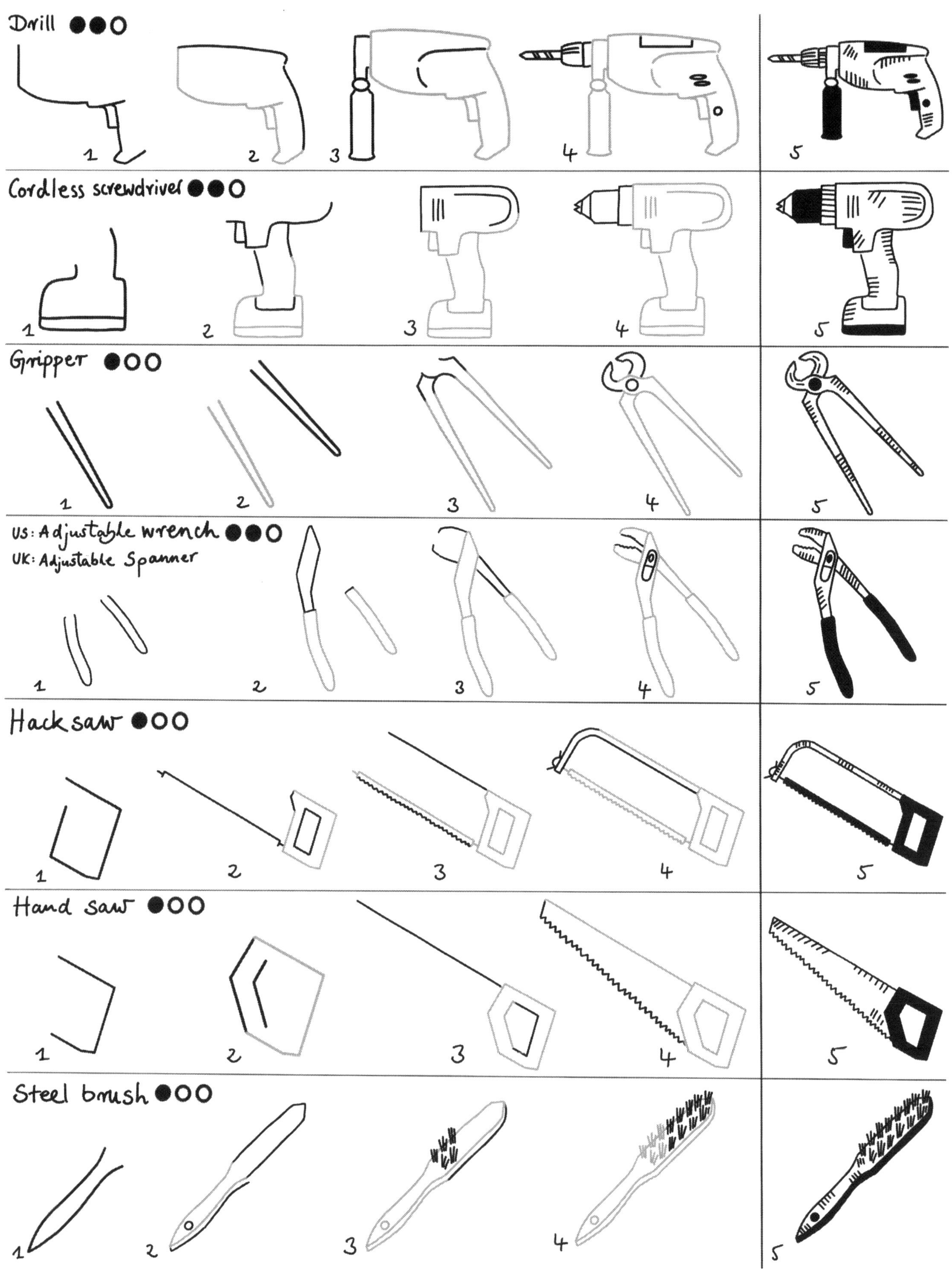
Drill
1
2
3
4
5
Cordless screwdriver
1
2
3
4
5
Gripper
1
2
3
4
5
US: Adjustable wrench
UK: Adjustable Spanner
1
2
3
4
5
Hacksaw
1
2
3
4
5
Hand saw
1
2
3
4
5
Steel brush
1
2
3
4
5

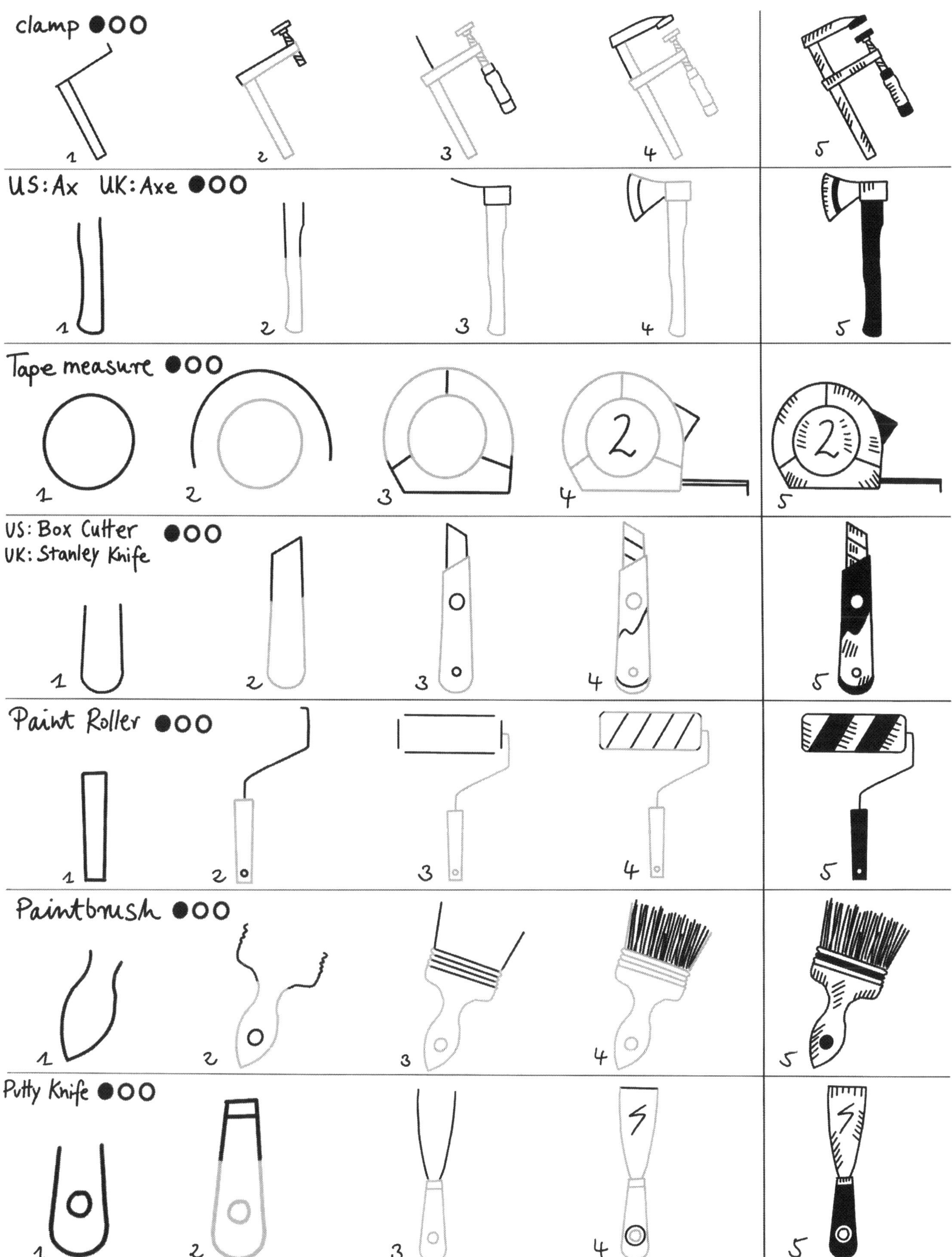
clamp
1
2
3
4
5
US: Ax UK: Axe
1
2
3
4
5
Tape measure
1
2
3
4
5
US: Box Cutter
UK: Stanley Knife
1
2
3
4
5
Paint Roller
1
2
3
4
5
Paintbrush
1
2
3
4
5
Putty Knife
1
2
3
4
5

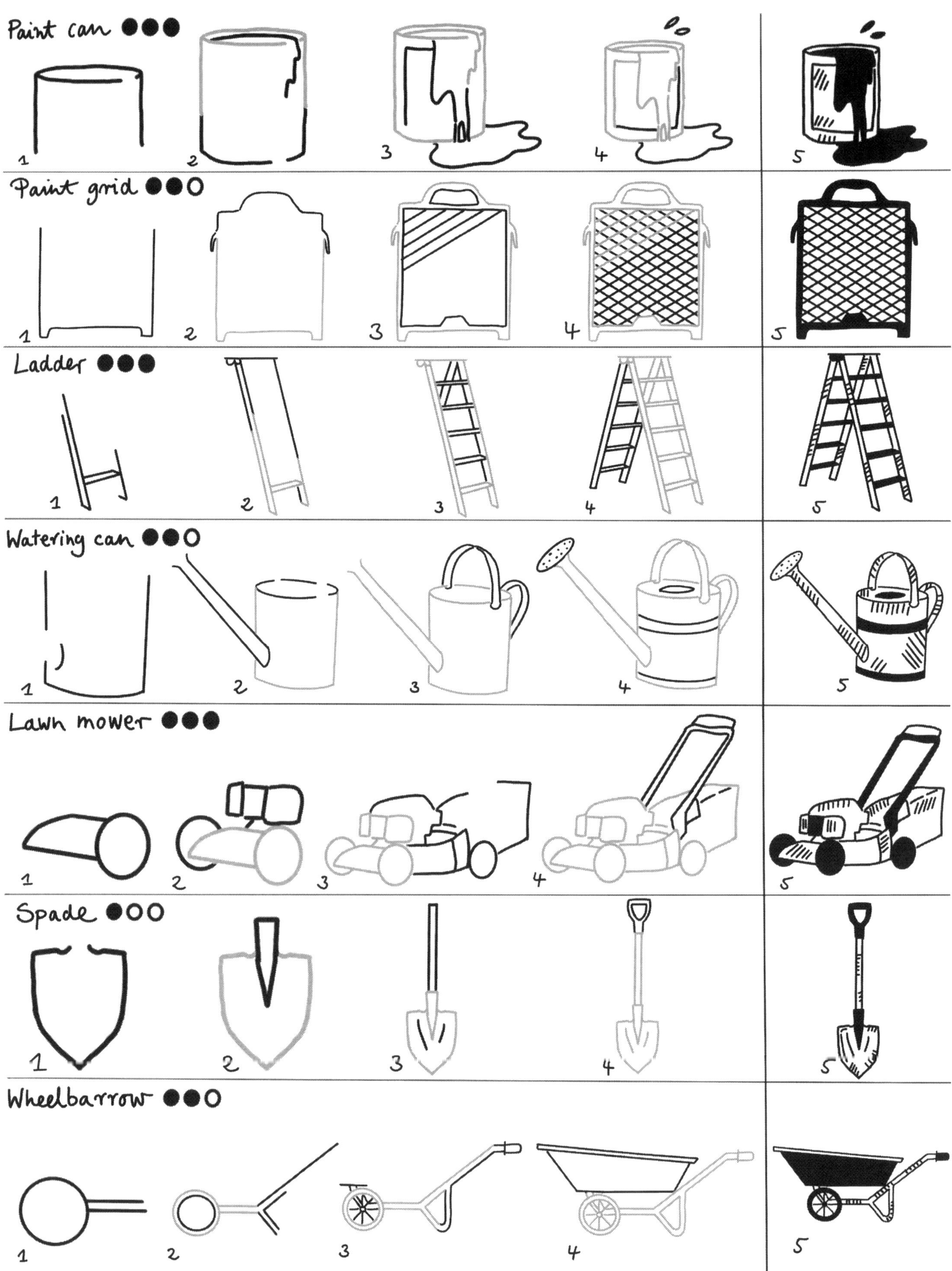
Paint can
1
2
3
4
5
Paint grid
1
2
3
4
5
Ladder
1
2
3
4
5
Watering can
1
2
3
4
5
Lawn mower
1
2
3
4
5
Spade
1
2
3
4
5
Wheelbarrow
1
2
3
4
5

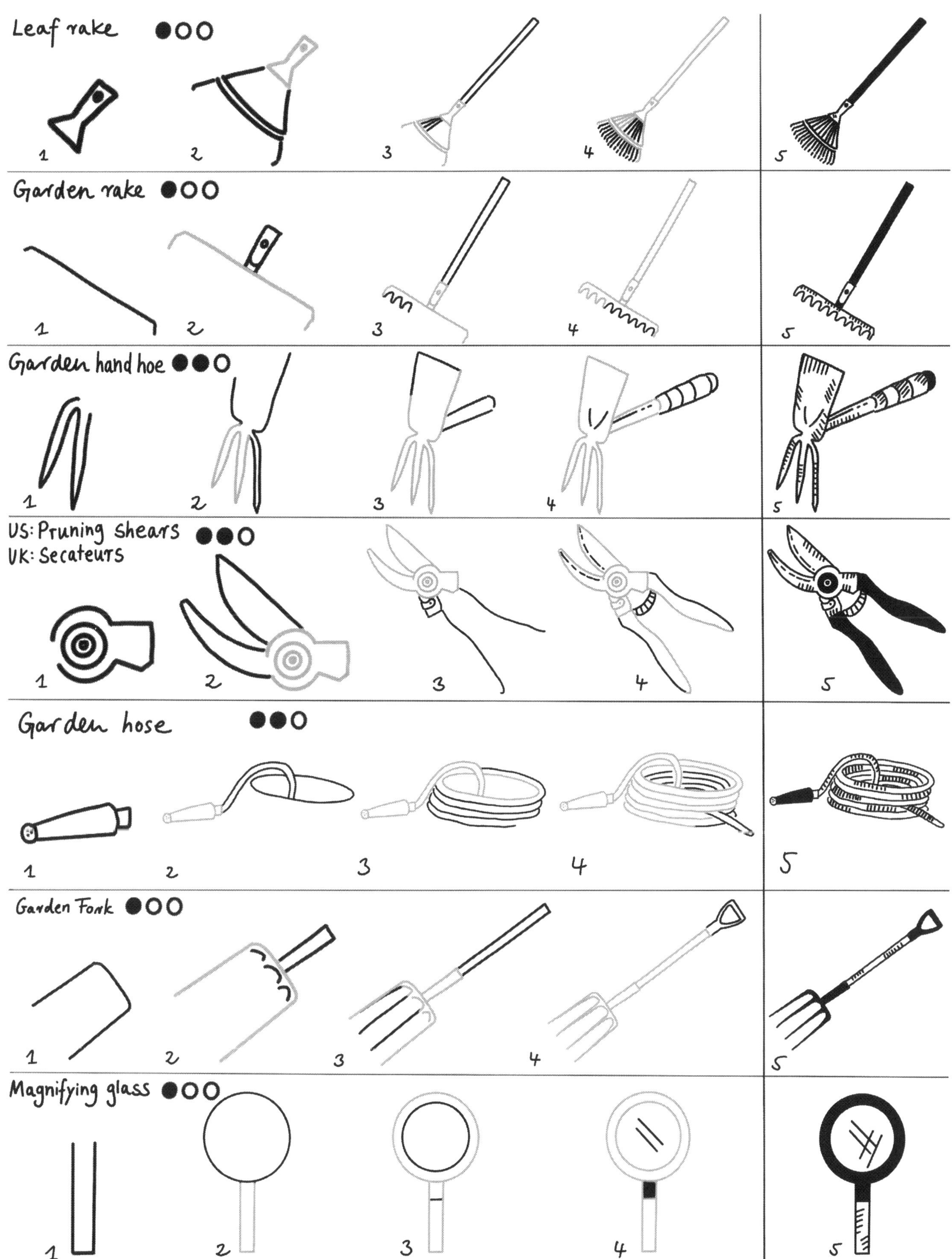
Leaf rake
1
2
3
4
5
Garden rake
1
2
3
4
5
Garden hand hoe
1
2
3
4
5
US: Pruning shears
UK: Secateurs
1
2
3
4
5
Garden hose
1
2
3
4
5
Garden Fork
1
2
3
4
5
Magnifying glass
1
2
3
4
5

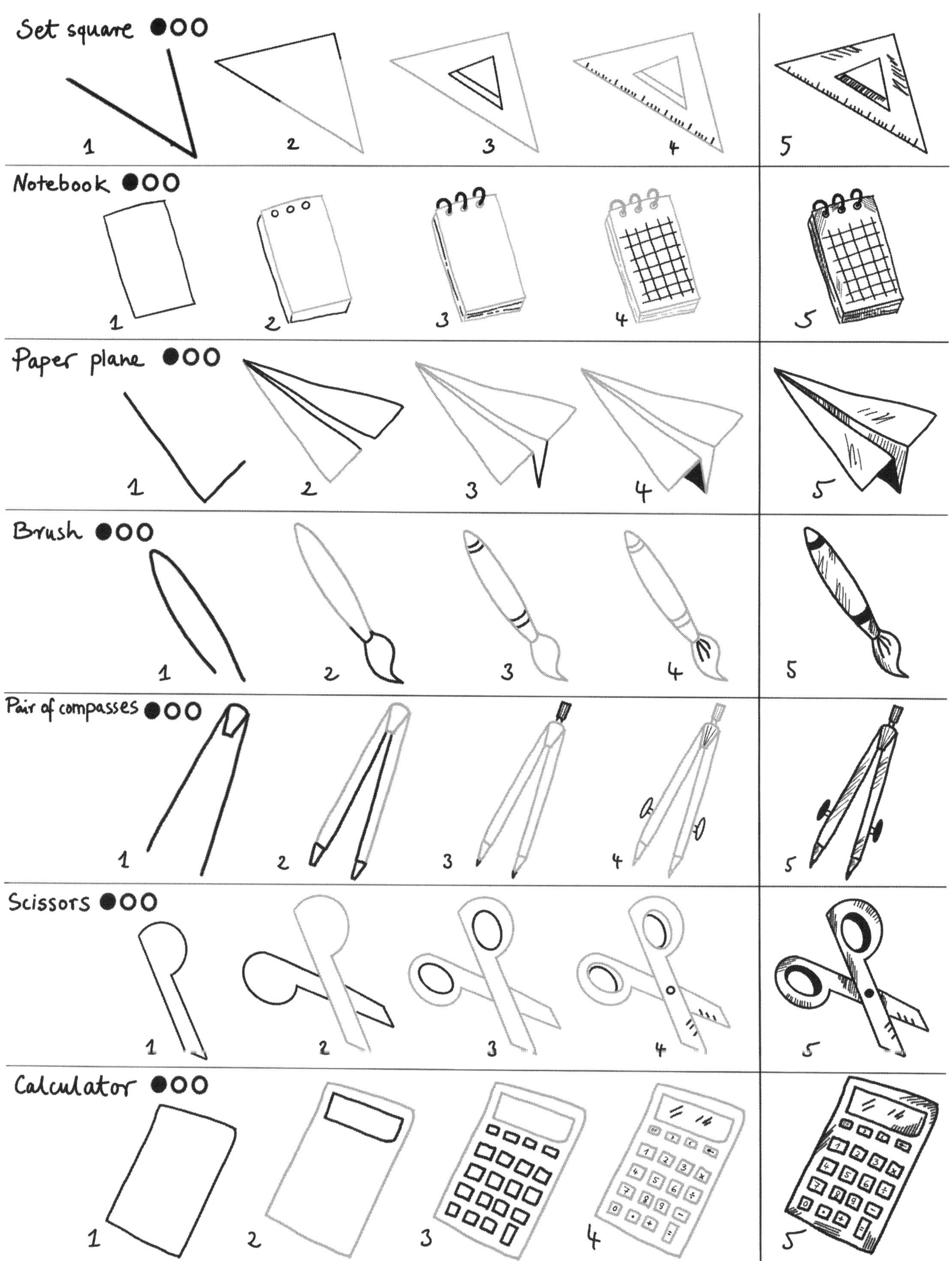
Set square
1
2
3
4
5
Notebook
1
2
3
4
5
Paper plane
1
2
3
4
5
Brush
1
2
3
4
5
Pair of compasses
1
2
3
4
5
Scissors
1
2
3
4
5
Calculator
1
2
3
4
5

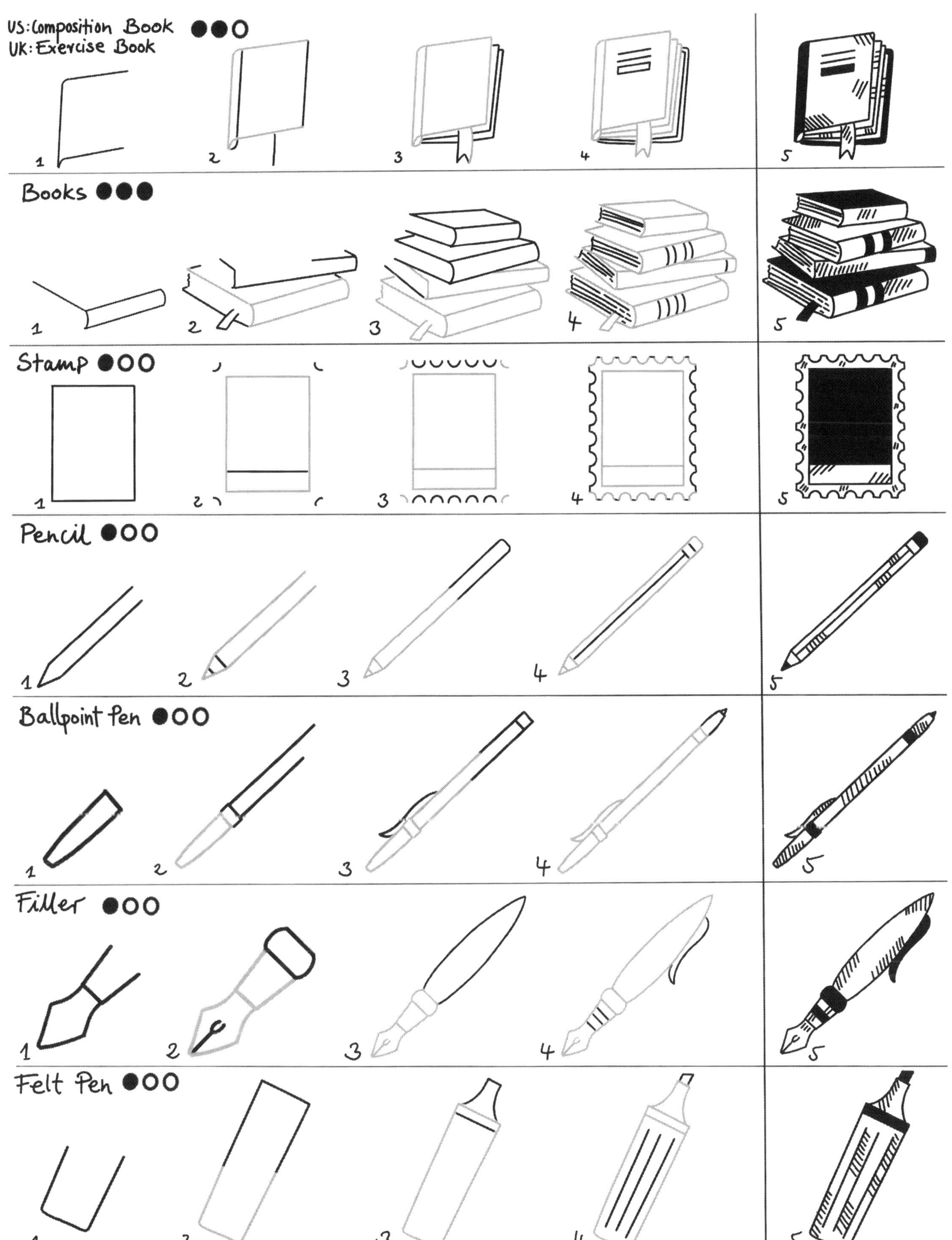
US: Composition Book
UK: Exercise Book
1
2
3
4
5
Books
1
2
3
4
5
Stamp
1
2
3
4
5
Pencil
1
2
3
4
5
Ballpoint Pen
1
2
3
4
5
Filler
1
2
3
4
5
Felt Pen
1
2
3
4
5

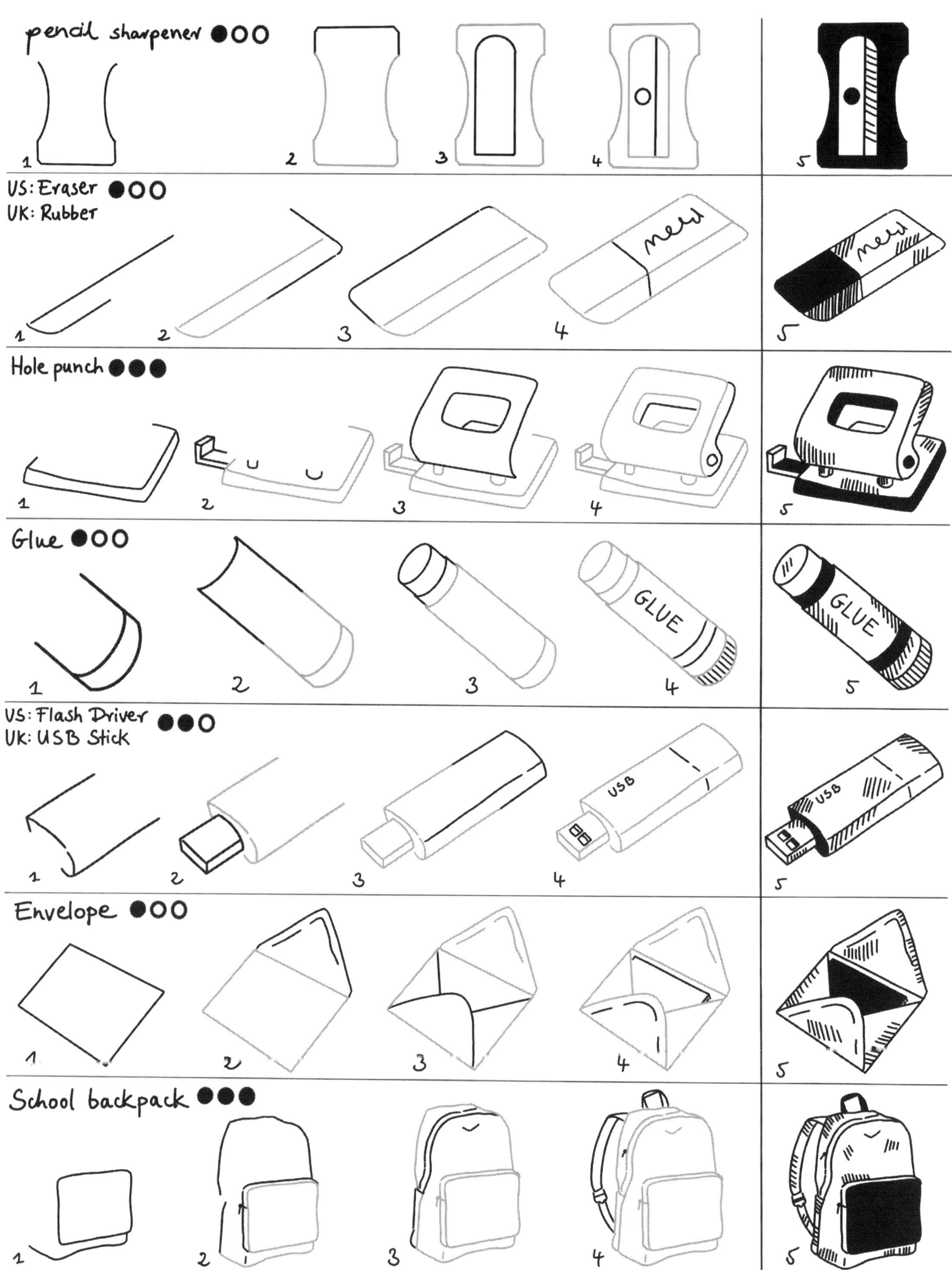
pencil sharpener
1
2
3
4
5
US: Eraser
UK: Rubber
1
2
3
4
5
Hole punch
1
2
3
4
5
Glue
GLUE
1
2
3
4
5
US: Flash Driver
UK: USB Stick
USB
1
2
3
4
5
Envelope
1
2
3
4
5
School backpack
1
2
3
4
5

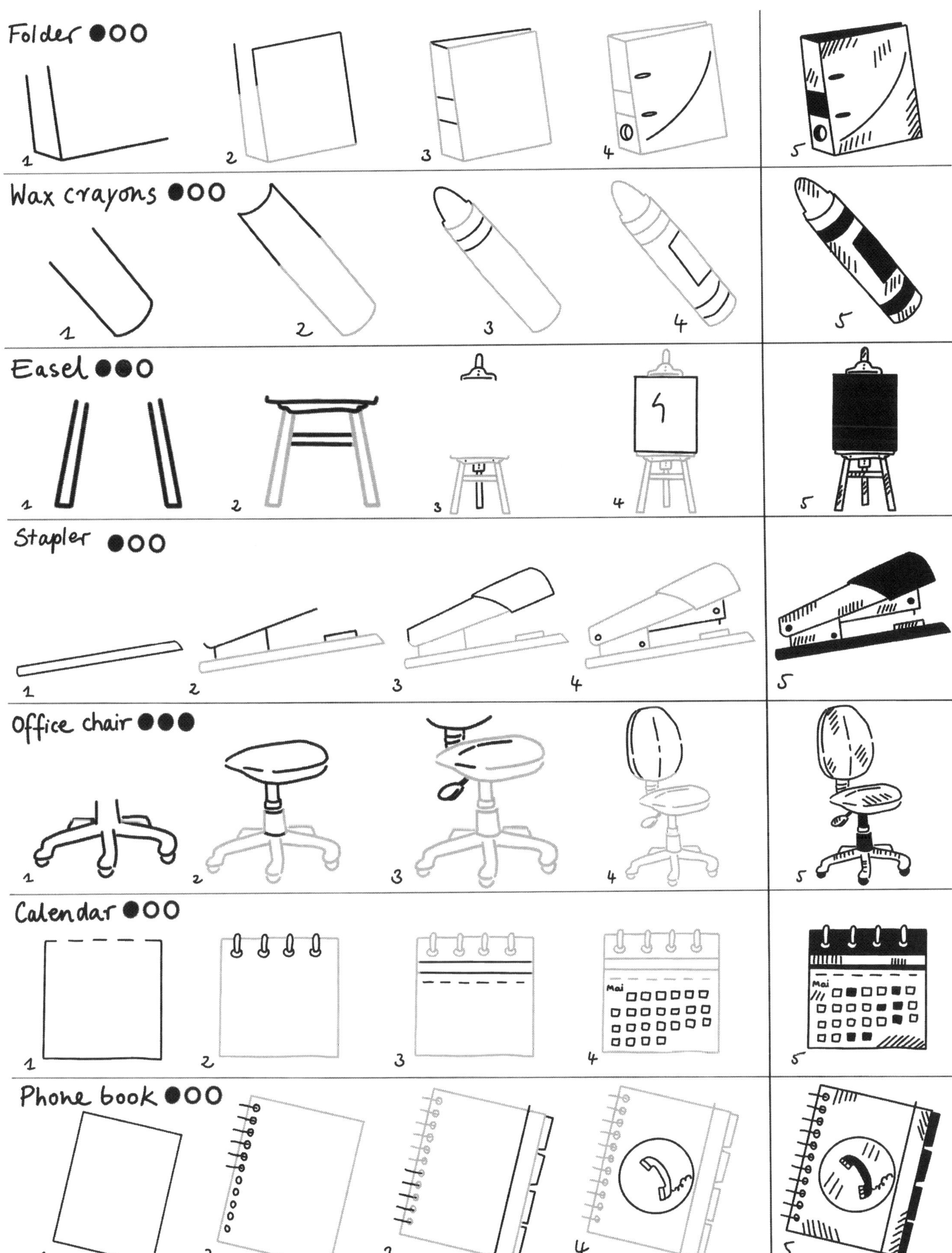
Folder
Wax crayons
Easel
Stapler
Office chair
Calendar
Mai
Mai
Phone book

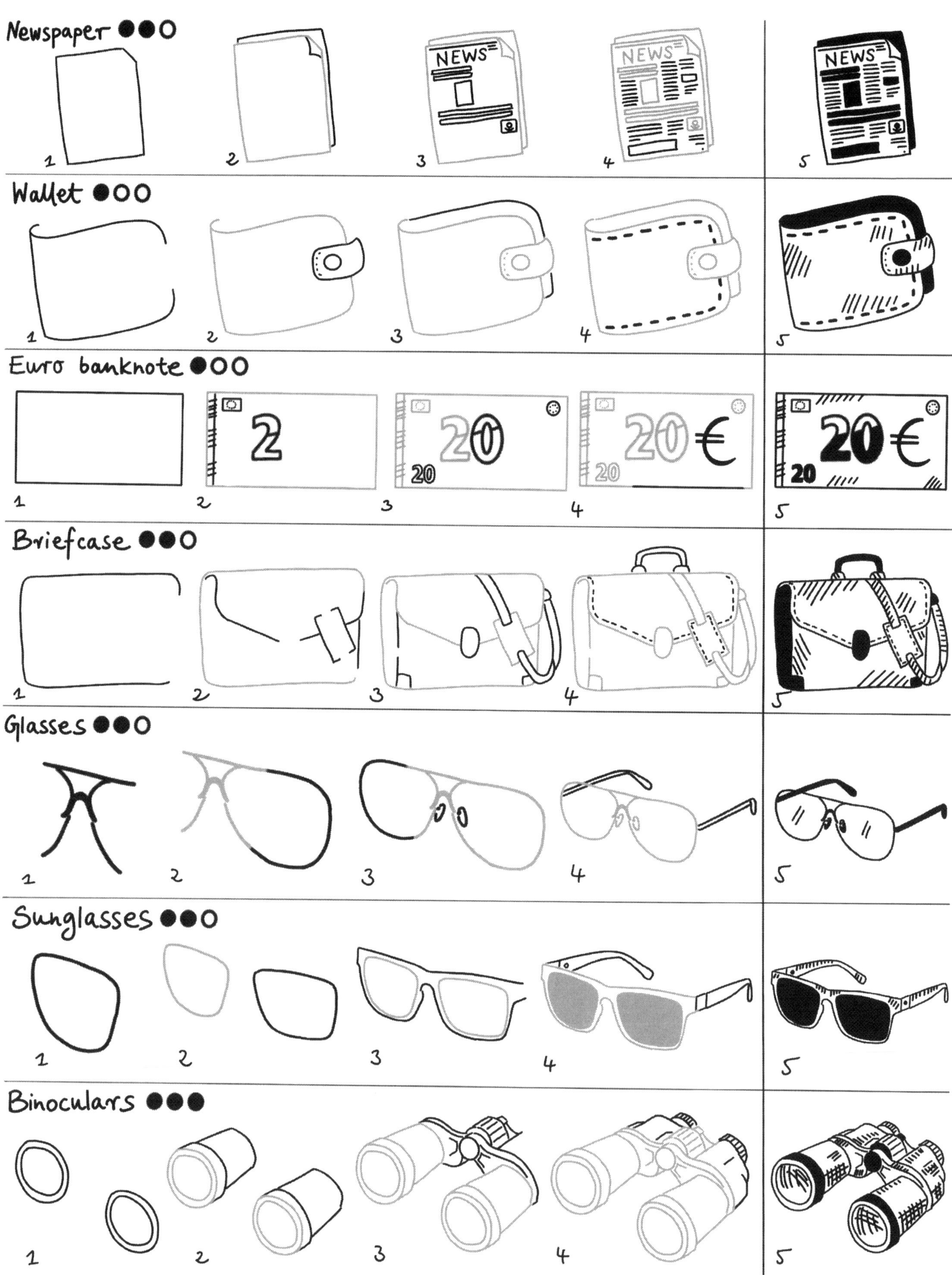
Newspaper
NEWS
1 2 3 4 5
Wallet
1 2 3 4 5
Euro banknote
2
20
20€
1 2 3 4 5
Briefcase
1 2 3 4 5
Glasses
1 2 3 4 5
Sunglasses
1 2 3 4 5
Binoculars
1 2 3 4 5

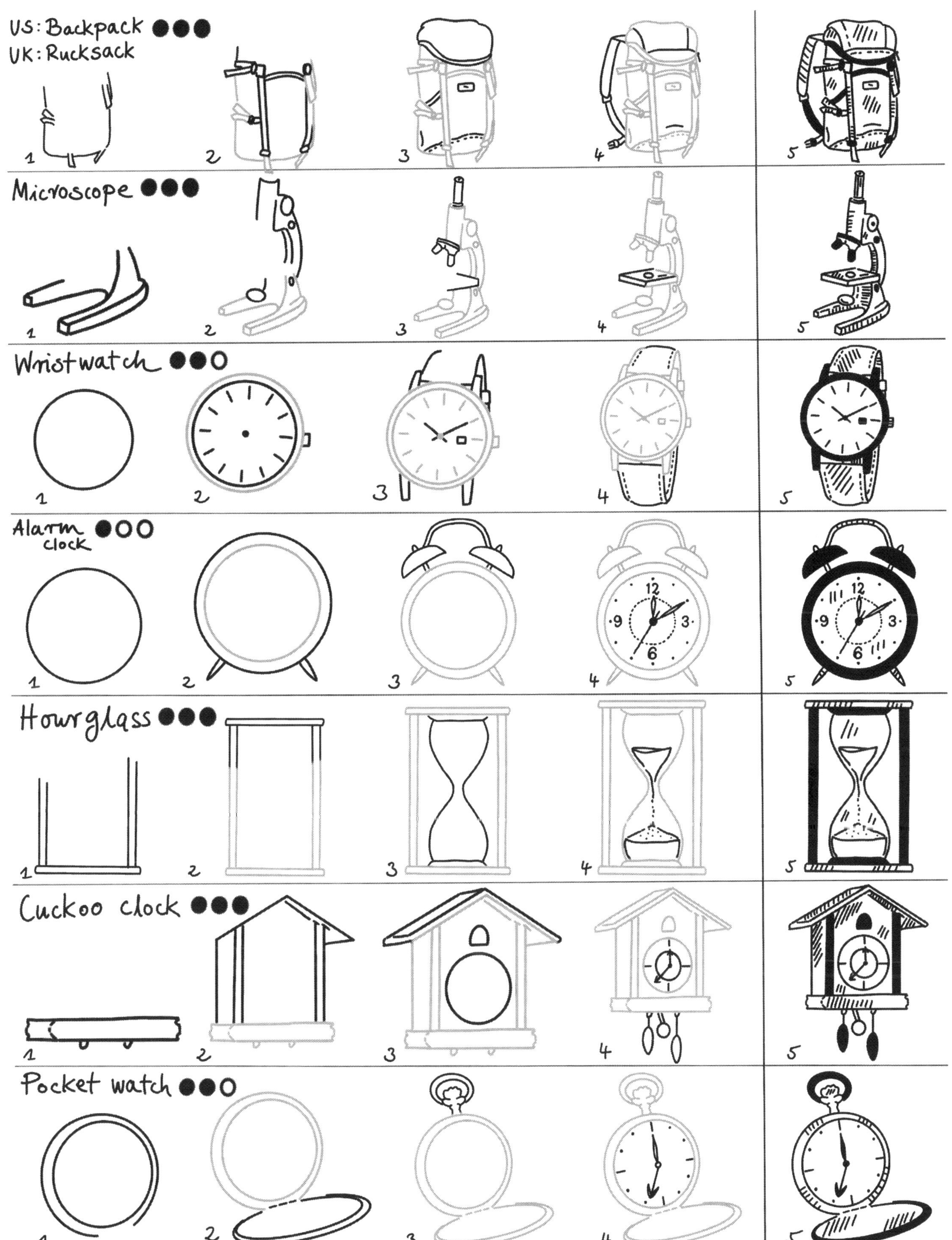
US: Backpack
UK: Rucksack
Microscope
Wristwatch
Alarm clock
12
3
6
9
Hourglass
Cuckoo clock
Pocket watch

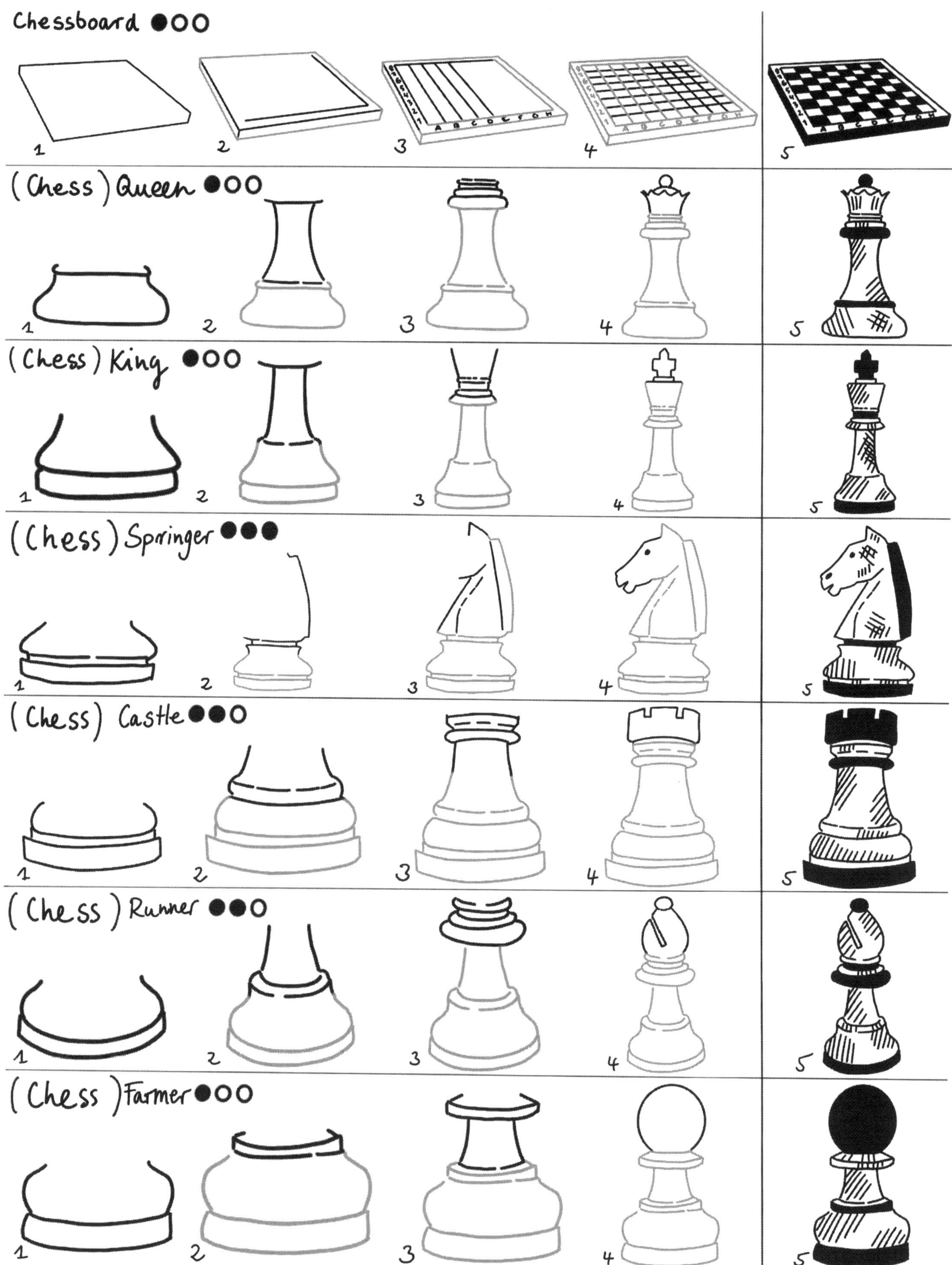
Chessboard
1
2
3
4
5
(Chess) Queen
1
2
3
4
5
(Chess) King
1
2
3
4
5
(Chess) Springer
1
2
3
4
5
(Chess) Castle
1
2
3
4
5
(Chess) Runner
1
2
3
4
5
(Chess) Farmer
1
2
3
4
5

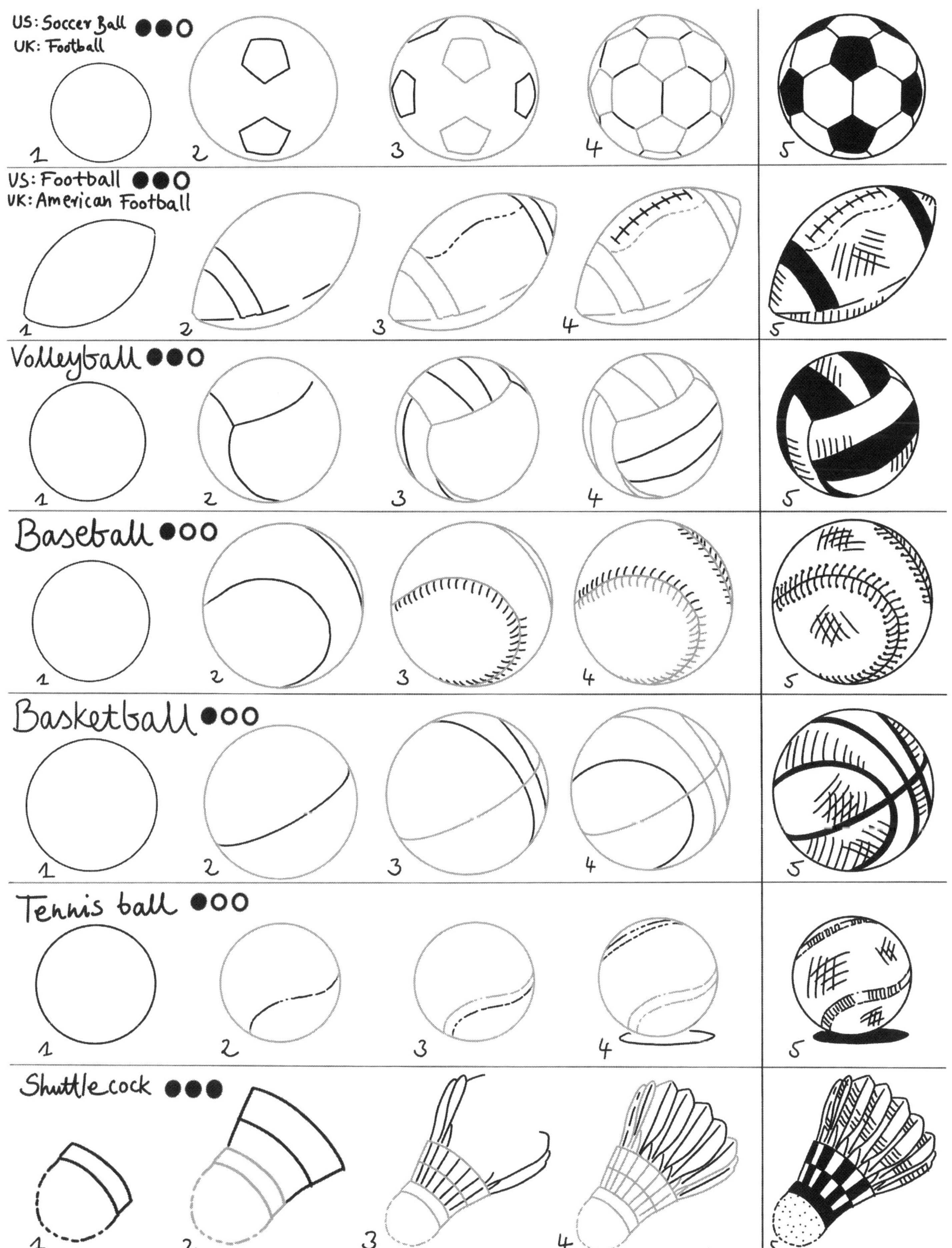
US: Soccer Ball
UK: Football
1
2
3
4
5
US: Football
UK: American Football
1
2
3
4
5
Volleyball
1
2
3
4
5
Baseball
1
2
3
4
5
Basketball
1
2
3
4
5
Tennis ball
1
2
3
4
5
Shuttlecock
1
2
3
4
5

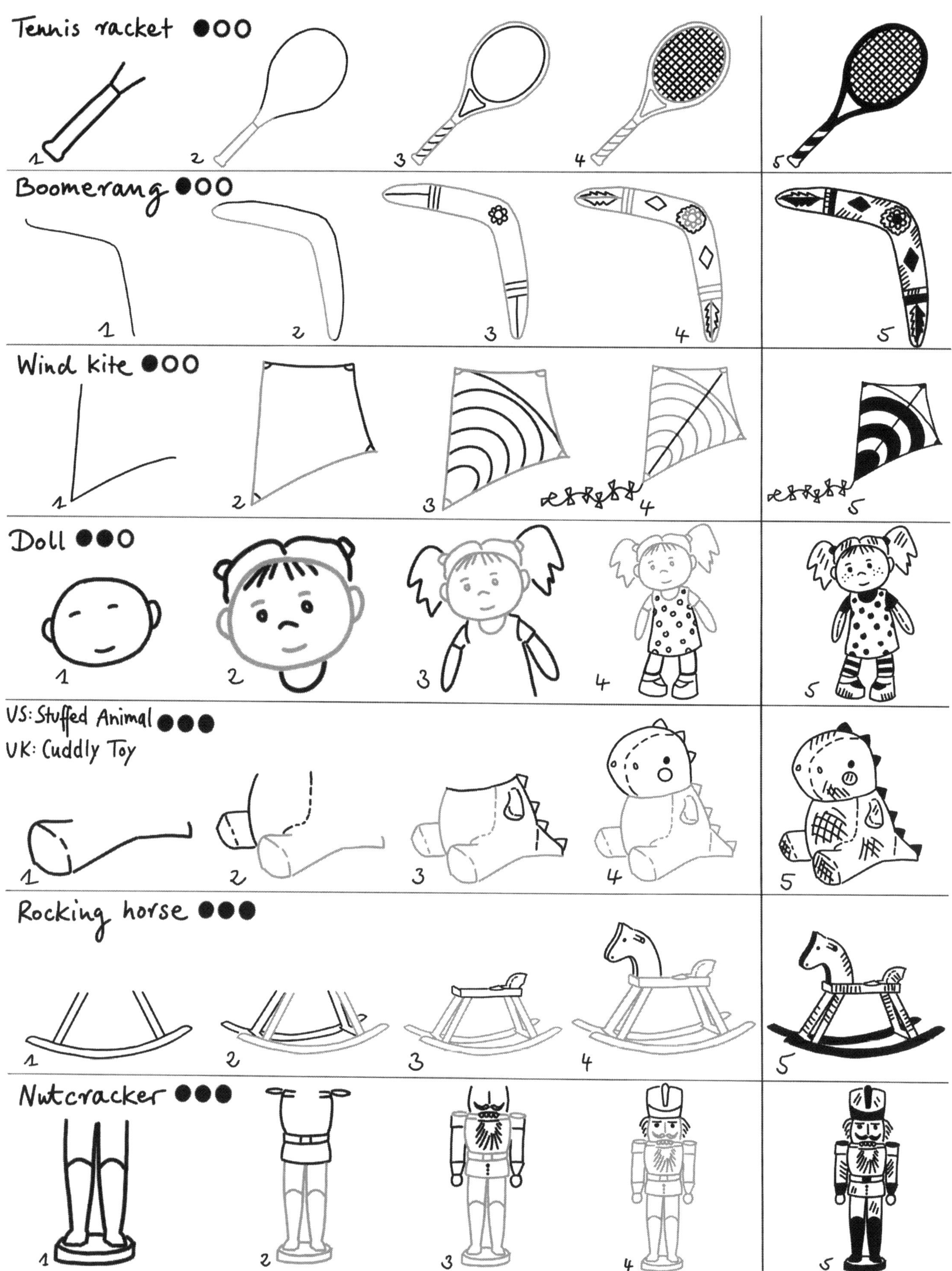
Tennis racket
1
2
3
4
5
Boomerang
1
2
3
4
5
Wind kite
1
2
3
4
5
Doll
1
2
3
4
5
US: Stuffed Animal
UK: Cuddly Toy
1
2
3
4
5
Rocking horse
1
2
3
4
5
Nutcracker
1
2
3
4
5

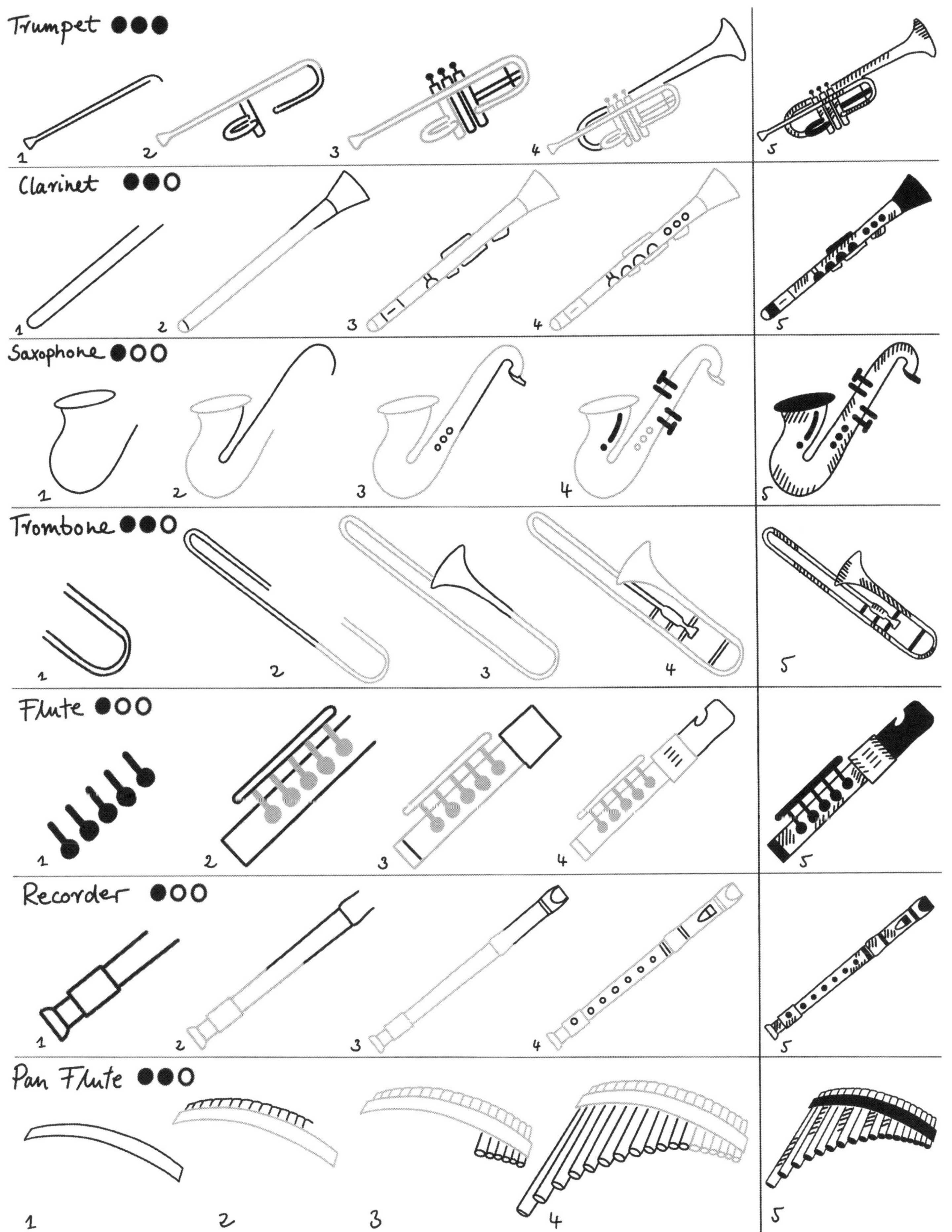
Trumpet ●●●
1
2
3
4
5
Clarinet ●●○
1
2
3
4
5
Saxophone ●○○
1
2
3
4
5
Trombone ●●○
1
2
3
4
5
Flute ●○○
1
2
3
4
5
Recorder ●○○
1
2
3
4
5
Pan Flute ●●○
1
2
3
4
5

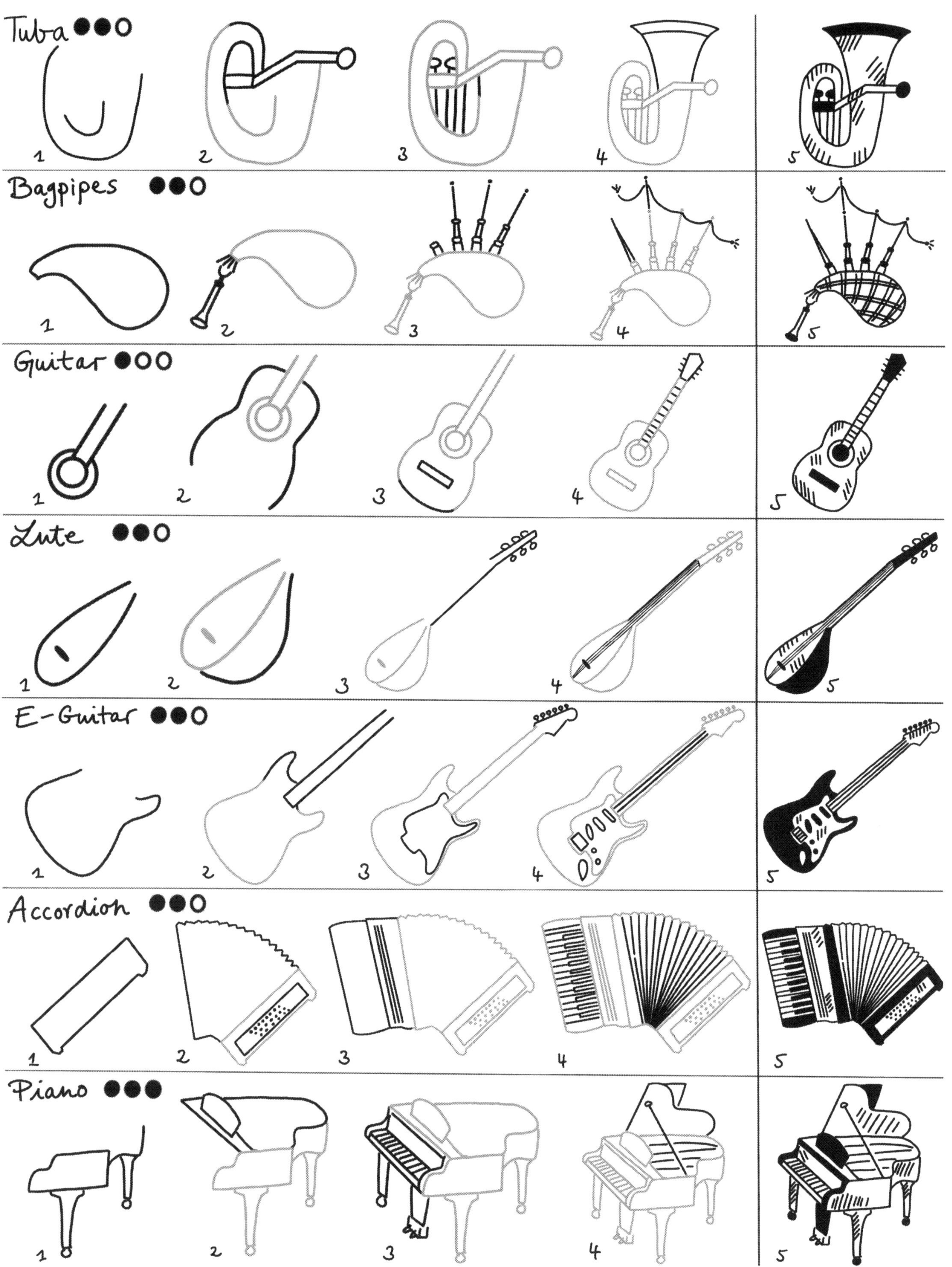
Tuba
1
2
3
4
5
Bagpipes
1
2
3
4
5
Guitar
1
2
3
4
5
Lute
1
2
3
4
5
E-Guitar
1
2
3
4
5
Accordion
1
2
3
4
5
Piano
1
2
3
4
5

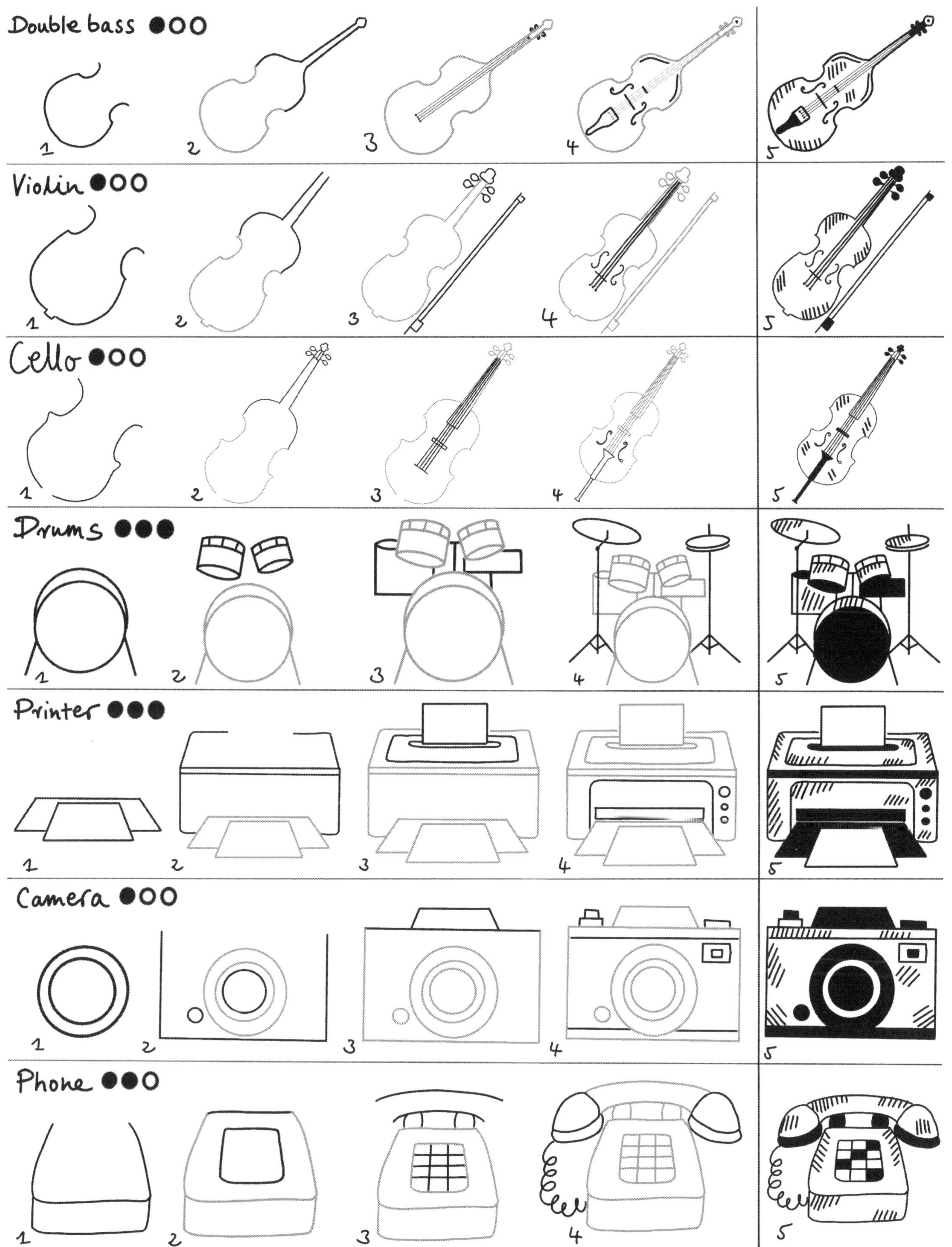
Double bass
1
2
3
4
5
Violin
1
2
3
4
5
Cello
1
2
3
4
5
Drums
1
2
3
4
5
Printer
1
2
3
4
5
Camera
1
2
3
4
5
Phone
1
2
3
4
5

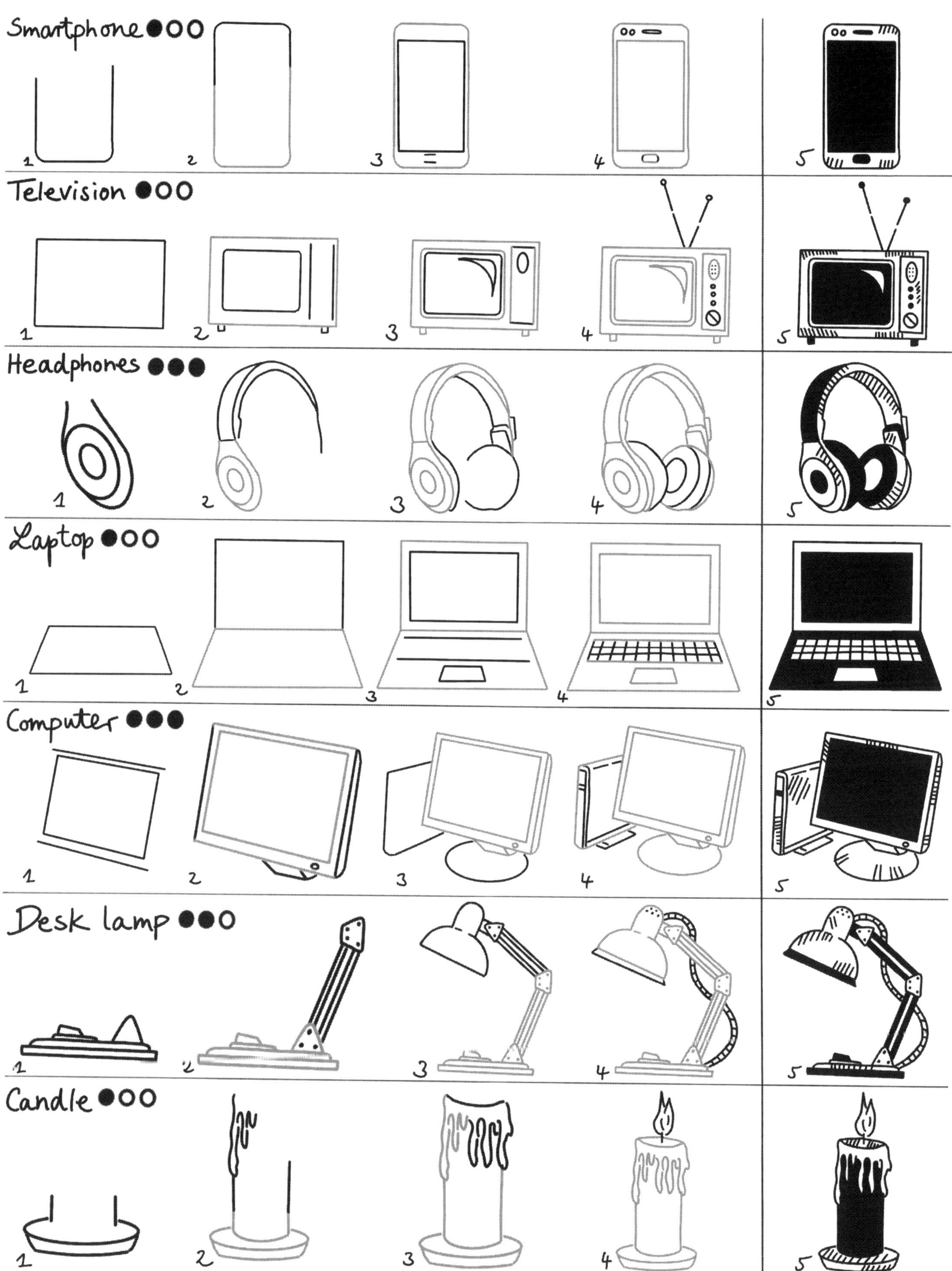

Smartphone
1
2
3
4
5
Television
1
2
3
4
5
Headphones
1
2
3
4
5
Laptop
1
2
3
4
5
Computer
1
2
3
4
5
Desk lamp
1
2
3
4
5
Candle
1
2
3
4
5

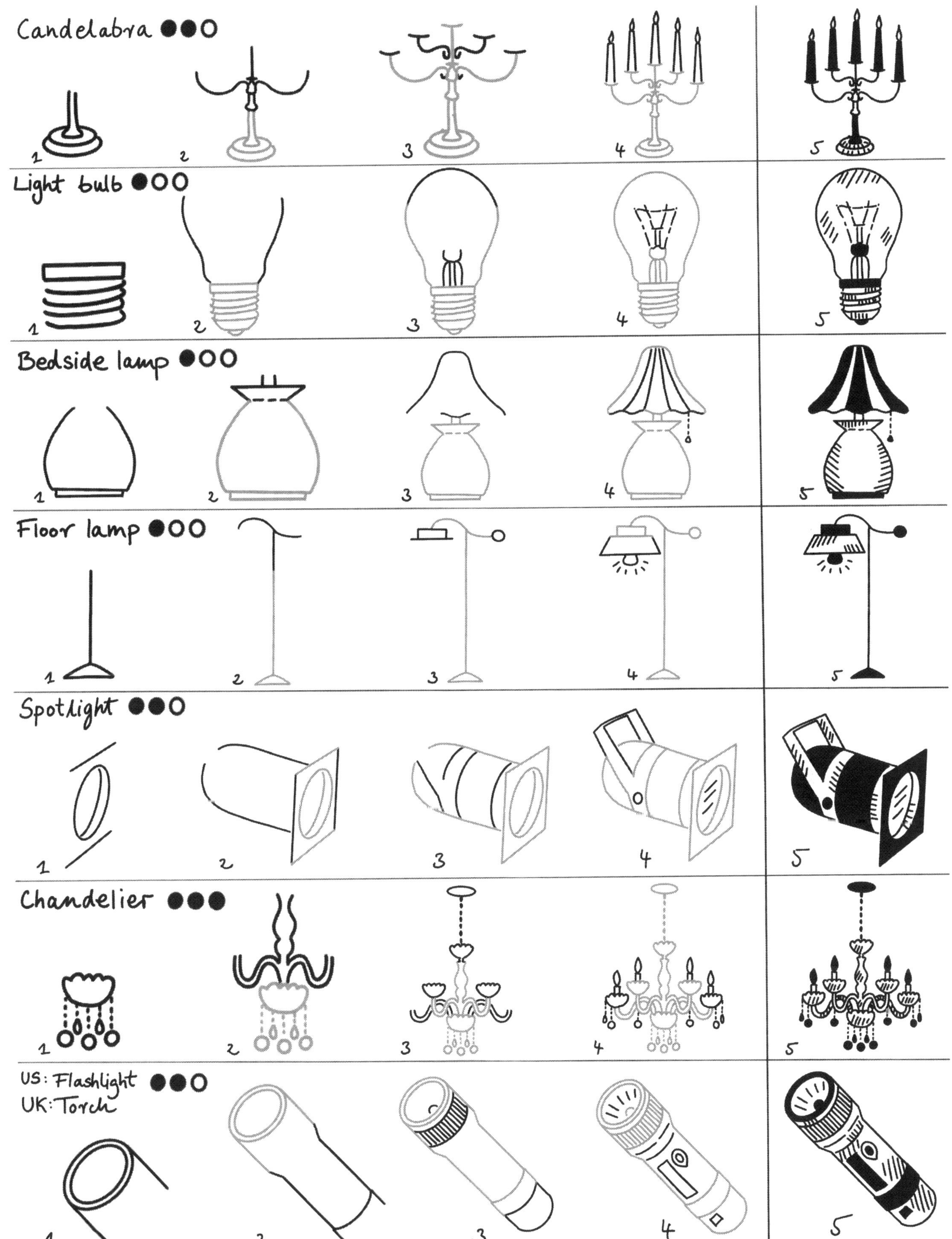
Candelabra ●●○
1
2
3
4
5
Light bulb ●○○
1
2
3
4
5
Bedside lamp ●○○
1
2
3
4
5
Floor lamp ●○○
1
2
3
4
5
Spotlight ●●○
1
2
3
4
5
Chandelier ●●●
1
2
3
4
5
US: Flashlight ●●○
UK: Torch
1
2
3
4
5

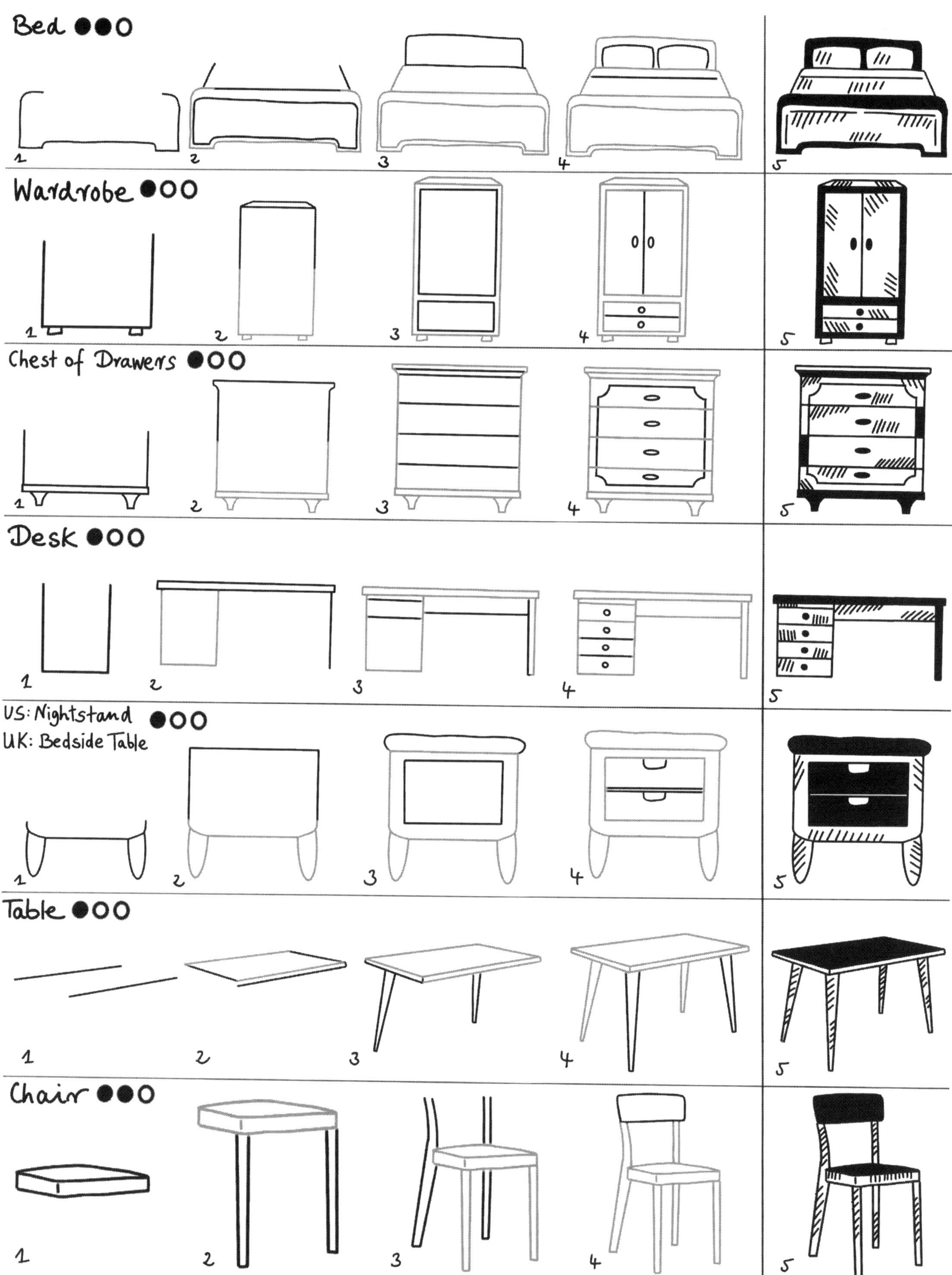
Bed
1
2
3
4
5
Wardrobe
1
2
3
4
5
Chest of Drawers
1
2
3
4
5
Desk
1
2
3
4
5
US: Nightstand
UK: Bedside Table
1
2
3
4
5
Table
1
2
3
4
5
Chair
1
2
3
4
5

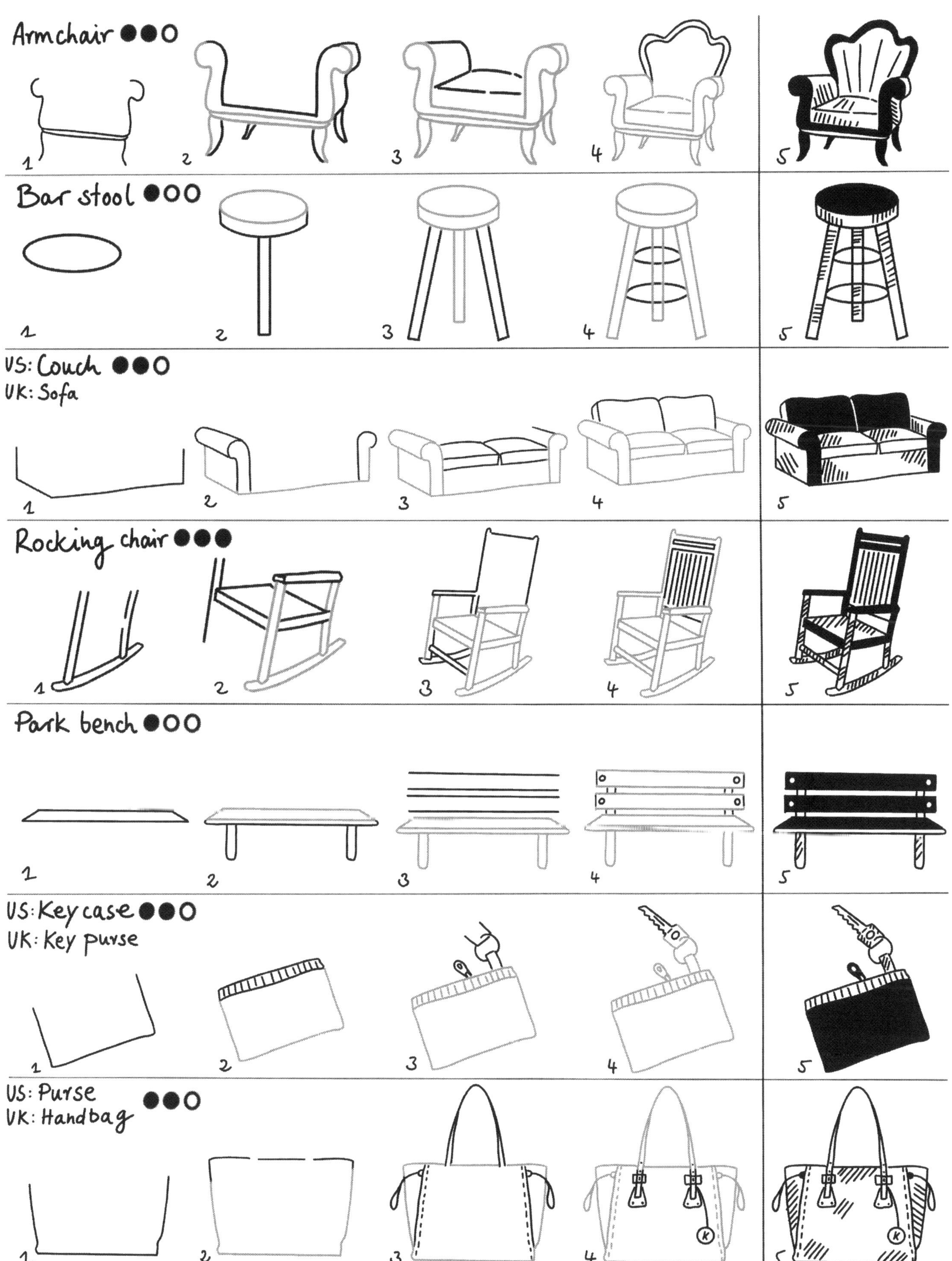

Armchair
1
2
3
4
5
Bar stool
1
2
3
4
5
US: Couch
UK: Sofa
1
2
3
4
5
Rocking chair
1
2
3
4
5
Park bench
1
2
3
4
5
US: Key case
UK: Key purse
1
2
3
4
5
US: Purse
UK: Handbag
1
2
3
4
5

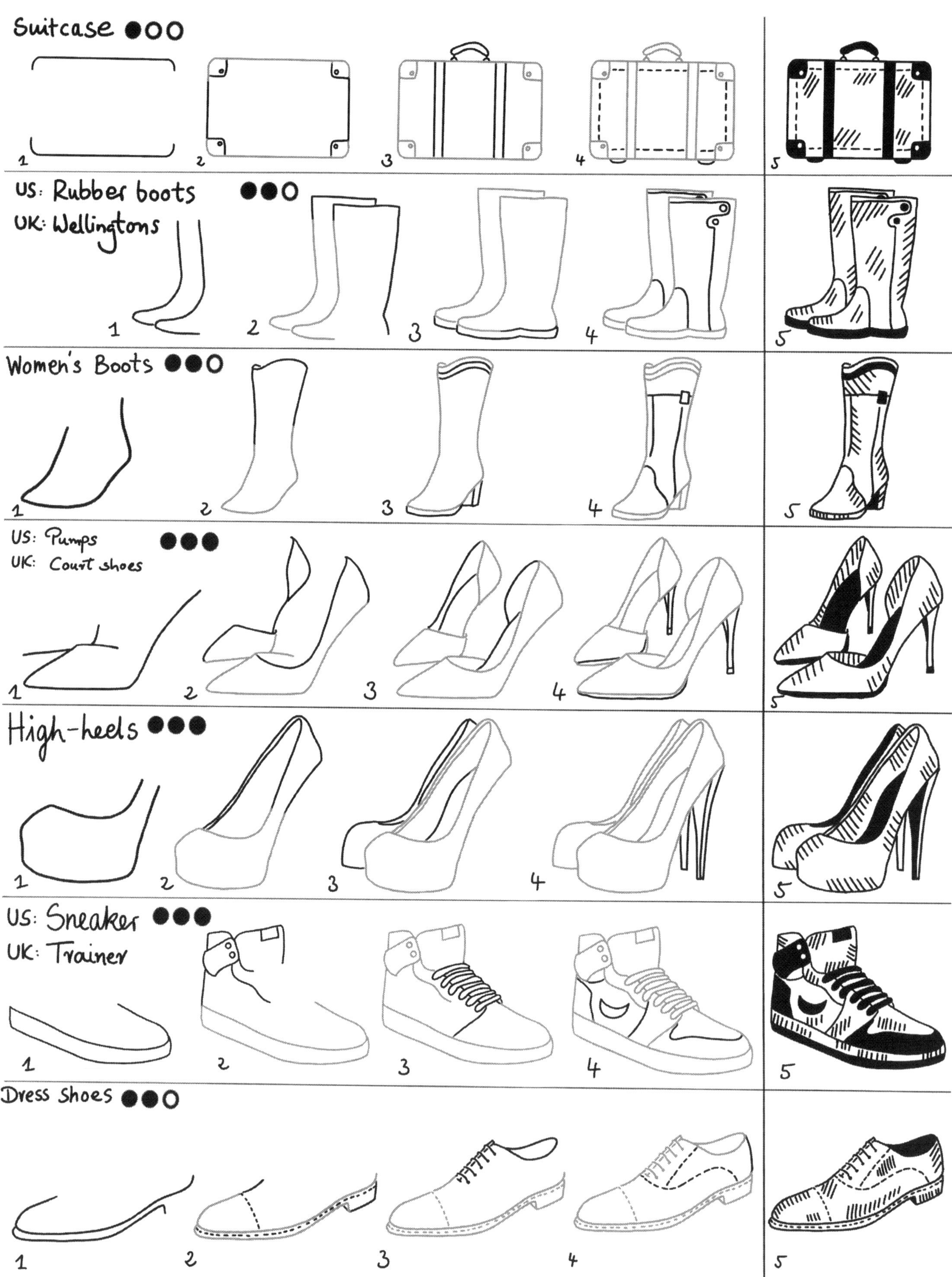
Suitcase
US: Rubber boots
UK: Wellingtons
Women's Boots
US: Pumps
UK: Court shoes
High-heels
US: Sneaker
UK: Trainer
Dress shoes

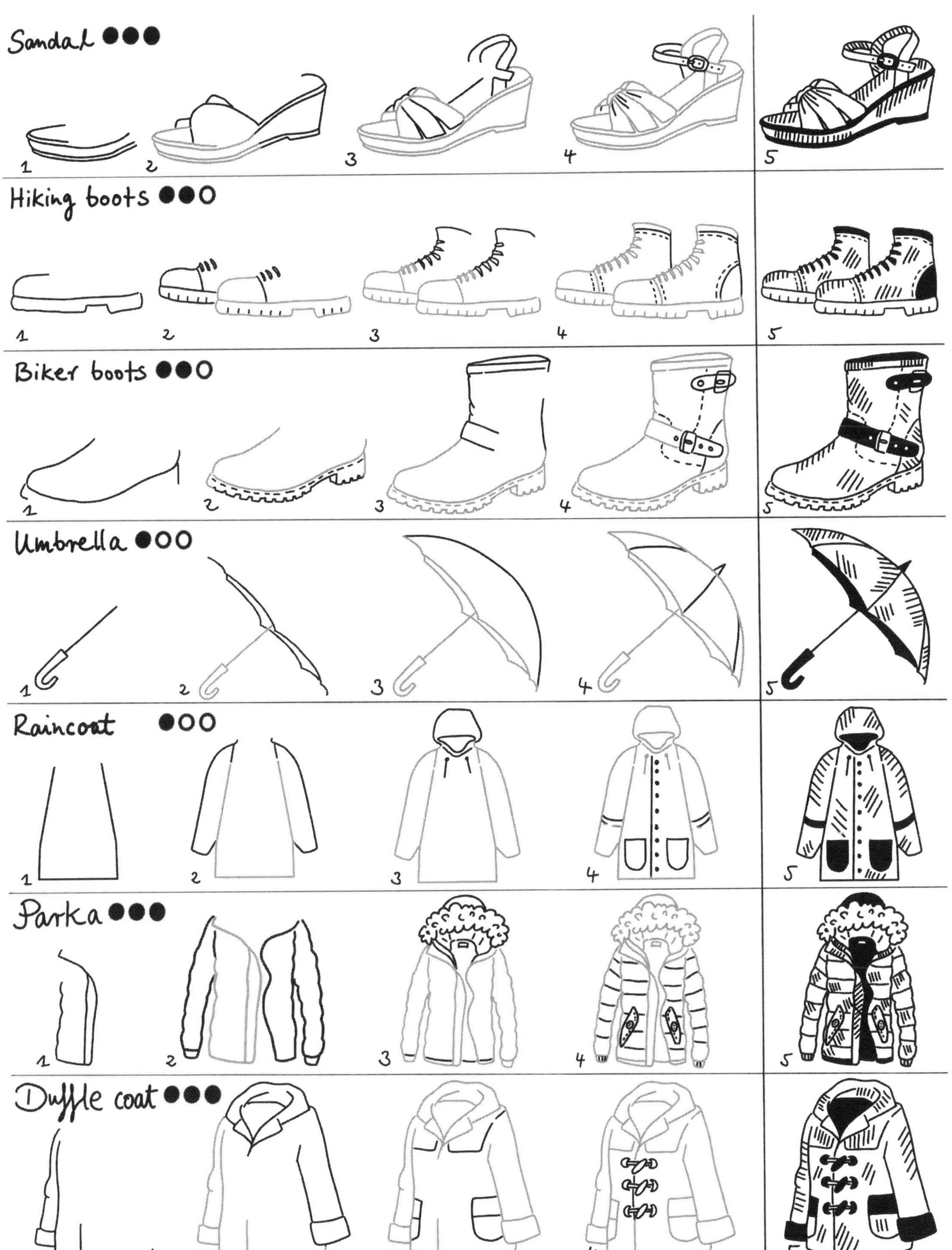
Sandal
1
2
3
4
5
Hiking boots
1
2
3
4
5
Biker boots
1
2
3
4
5
Umbrella
1
2
3
4
5
Raincoat
1
2
3
4
5
Parka
1
2
3
4
5
Duffle coat
1
2
3
4
5

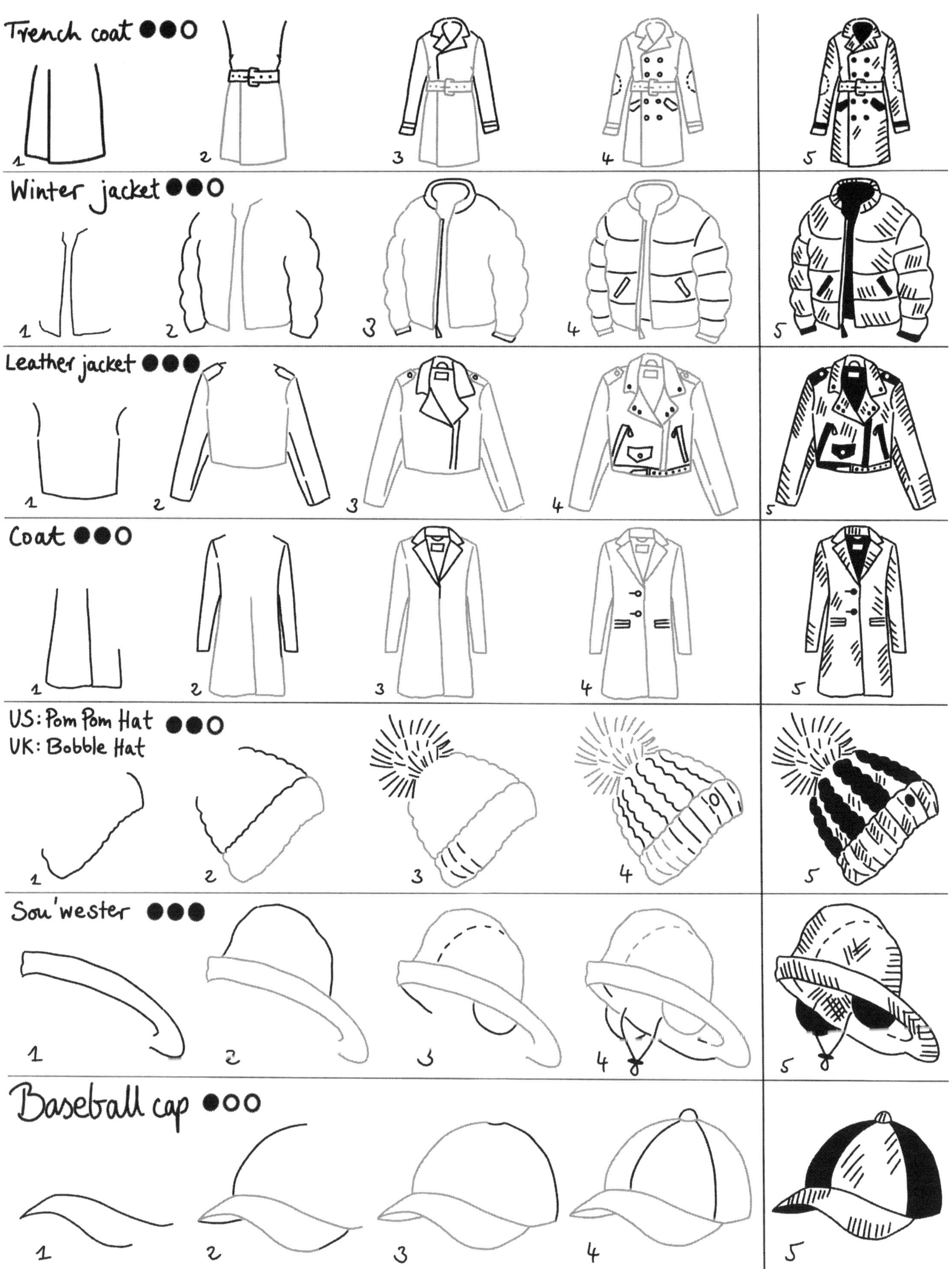
Trench coat ●●○
1
2
3
4
5
Winter jacket ●●○
1
2
3
4
5
Leather jacket ●●●
1
2
3
4
5
Coat ●●○
1
2
3
4
5
US: Pom Pom Hat ●●○
UK: Bobble Hat
1
2
3
4
5
Sou'wester ●●●
1
2
3
4
5
Baseball cap ●○○
1
2
3
4
5

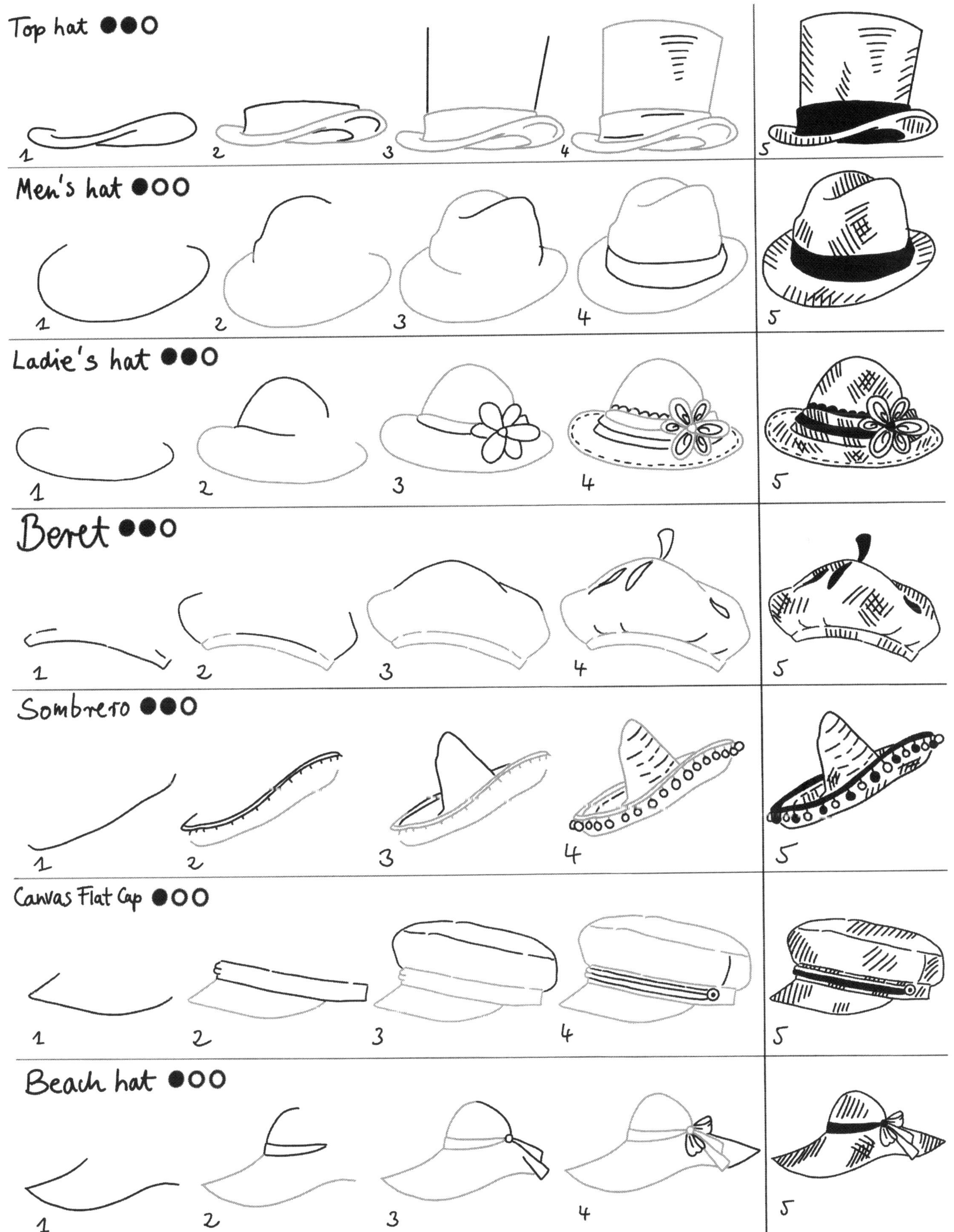
Top hat
1
2
3
4
5
Men's hat
1
2
3
4
5
Ladie's hat
1
2
3
4
5
Beret
1
2
3
4
5
Sombrero
1
2
3
4
5
Canvas Flat Cap
1
2
3
4
5
Beach hat
1
2
3
4
5

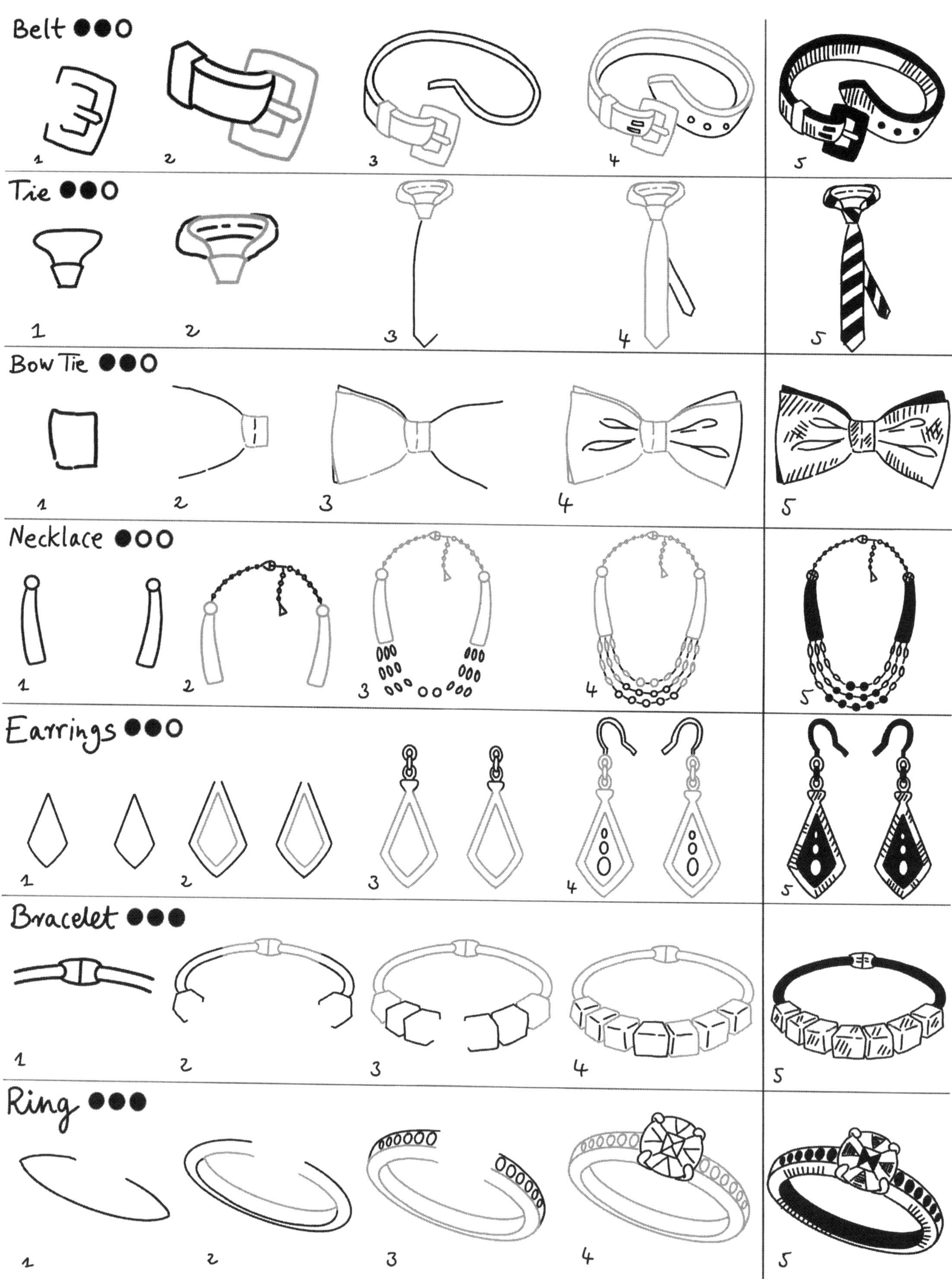
Belt
1
2
3
4
5
Tie
1
2
3
4
5
Bow Tie
1
2
3
4
5
Necklace
1
2
3
4
5
Earrings
1
2
3
4
5
Bracelet
1
2
3
4
5
Ring
1
2
3
4
5

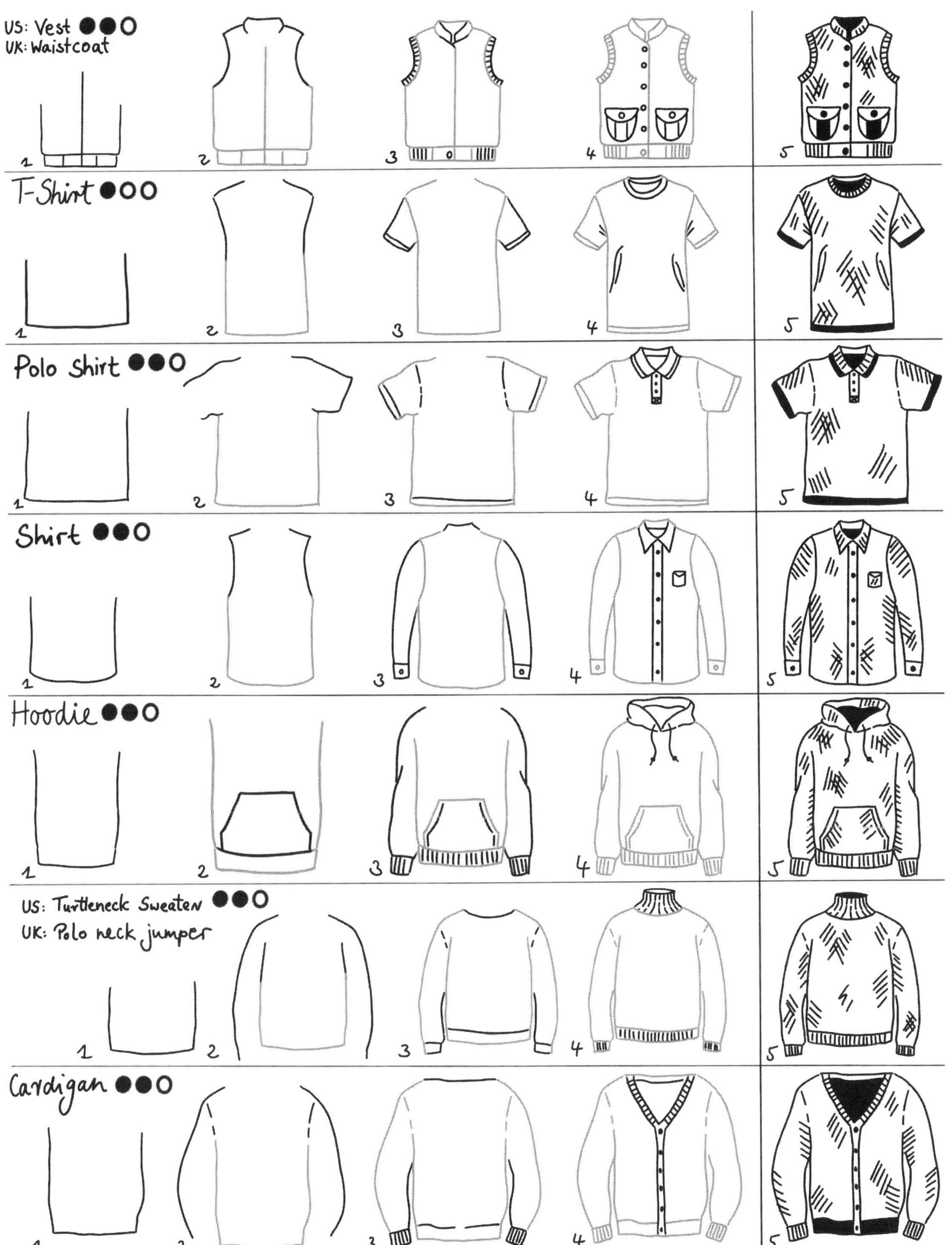

US: Vest
UK: Waistcoat
T-Shirt
Polo Shirt
Shirt
Hoodie
US: Turtleneck Sweater
UK: Polo neck jumper
Cardigan

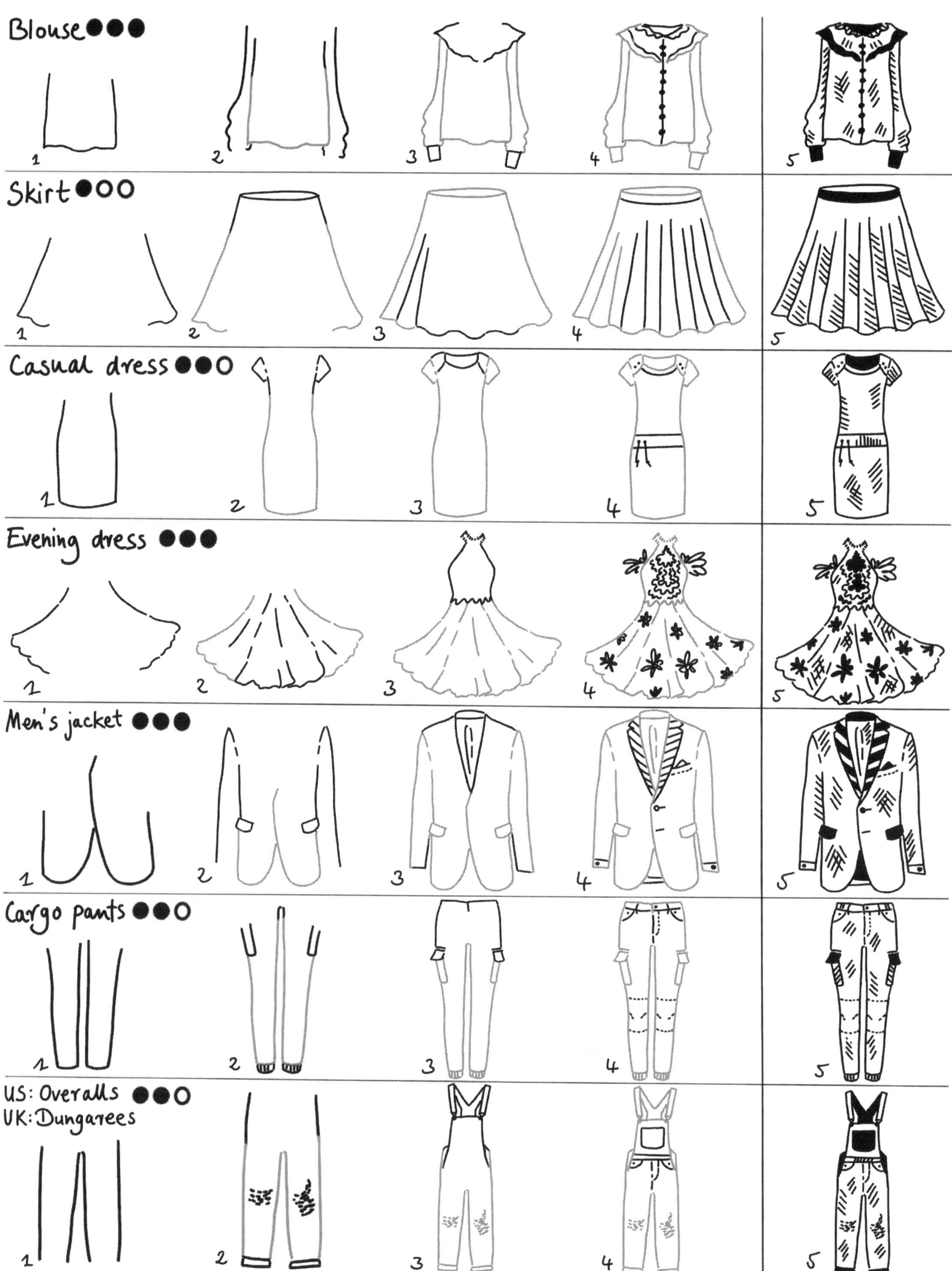
Blouse
1
2
3
4
5
Skirt
1
2
3
4
5
Casual dress
1
2
3
4
5
Evening dress
1
2
3
4
5
Men's jacket
1
2
3
4
5
Cargo pants
1
2
3
4
5
US: Overalls
UK: Dungarees
1
2
3
4
5

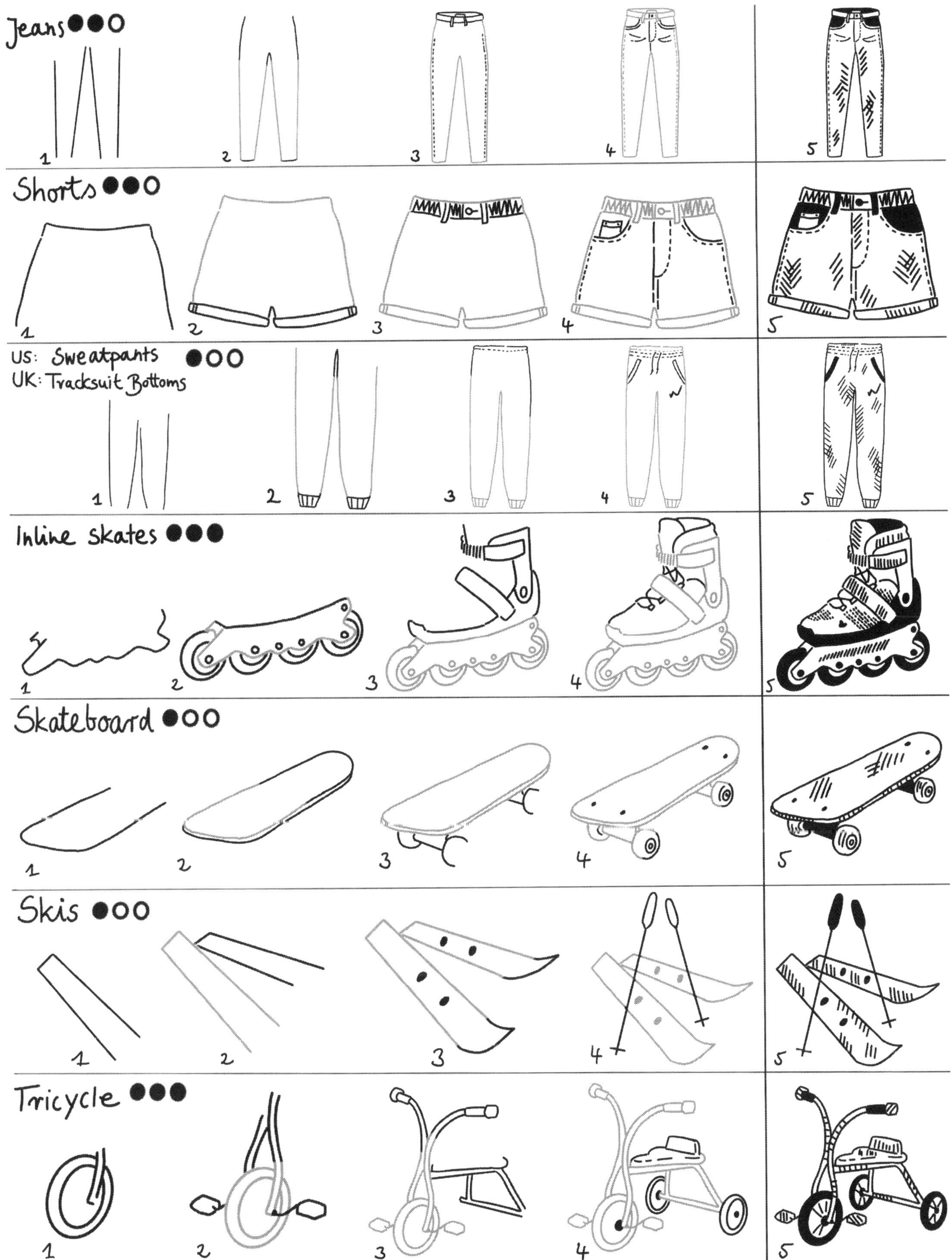
Jeans
1
2
3
4
5
Shorts
1
2
3
4
5
US: Sweatpants
UK: Tracksuit Bottoms
1
2
3
4
5
Inline skates
1
2
3
4
5
Skateboard
1
2
3
4
5
Skis
1
2
3
4
5
Tricycle
1
2
3
4
5

# PEOPLE

Stick figure
1
2
3
4
5
Walking
1
2
3
4
5
Sitting
1
2
3
4
5
Lying down
1
2
3
4
5
Running
1
2
3
4
5
US: playing soccer
UK: Playing football
1
2
3
4
5
Doing yoga
1
2
3
4
5

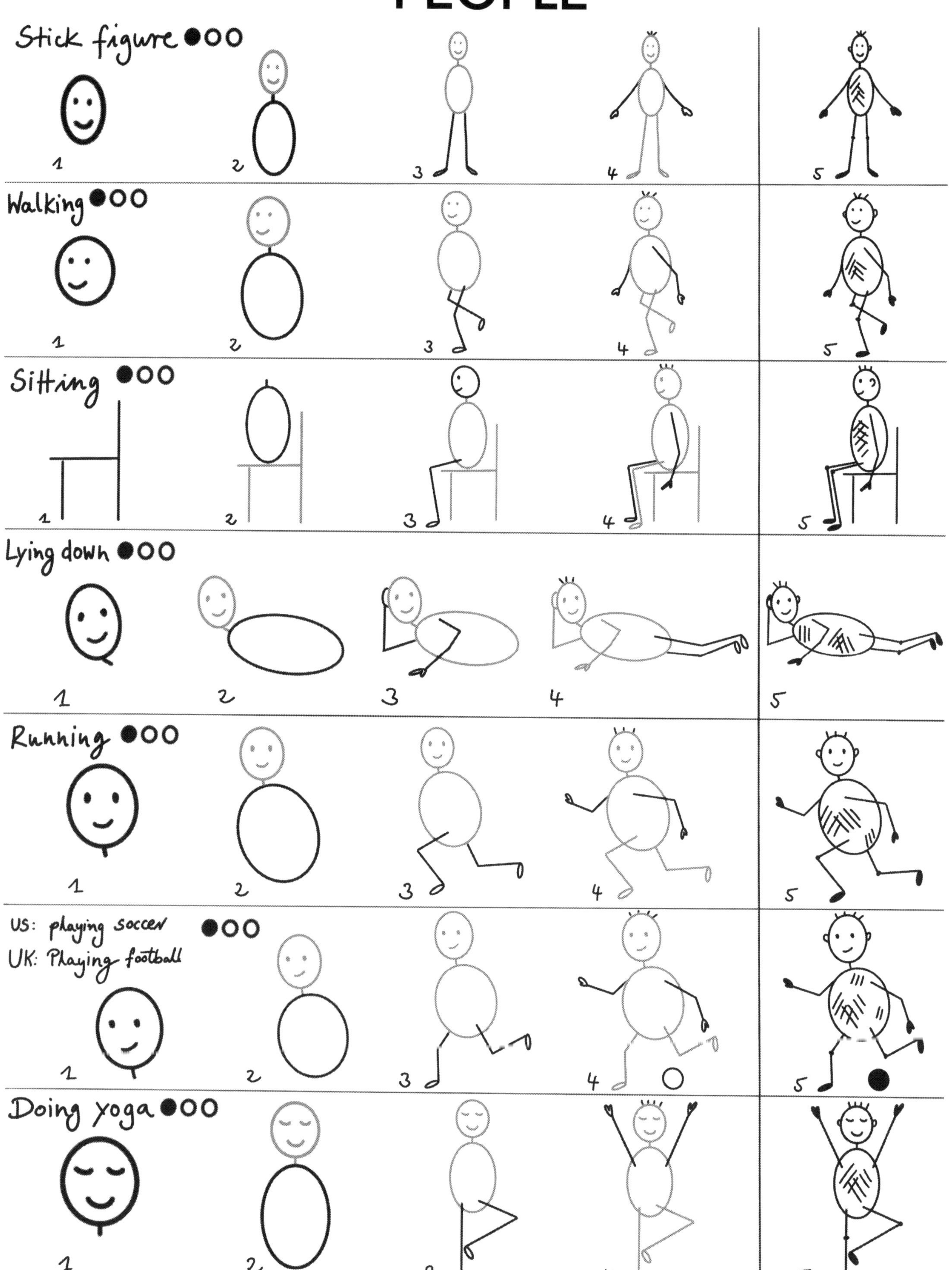

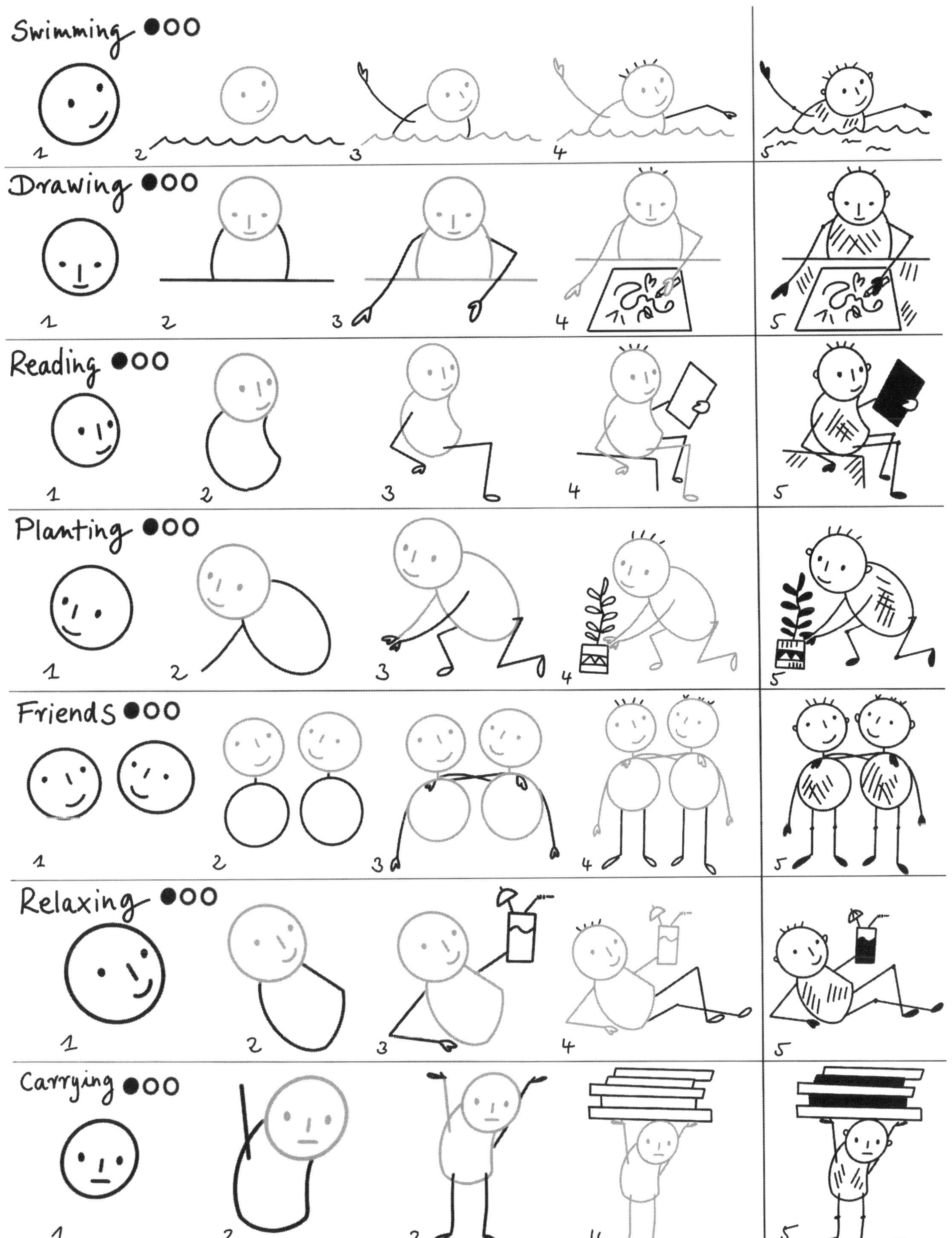
Swimming
1
2
3
4
5
Drawing
1
2
3
4
5
Reading
1
2
3
4
5
Planting
1
2
3
4
5
Friends
1
2
3
4
5
Relaxing
1
2
3
4
5
Carrying
1
2
3
4
5

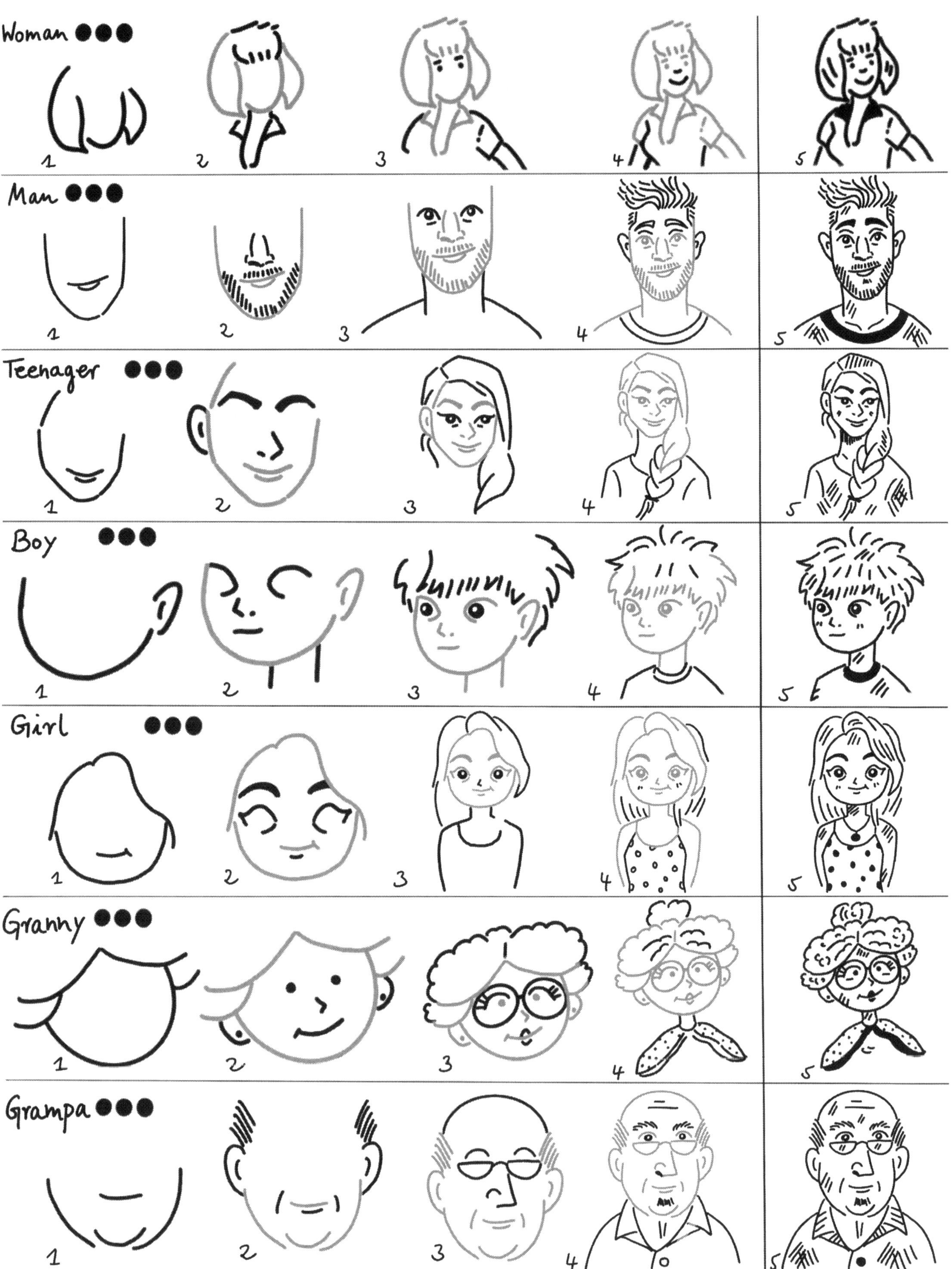
Woman
1
2
3
4
5
Man
1
2
3
4
5
Teenager
1
2
3
4
5
Boy
1
2
3
4
5
Girl
1
2
3
4
5
Granny
1
2
3
4
5
Grampa
1
2
3
4
5

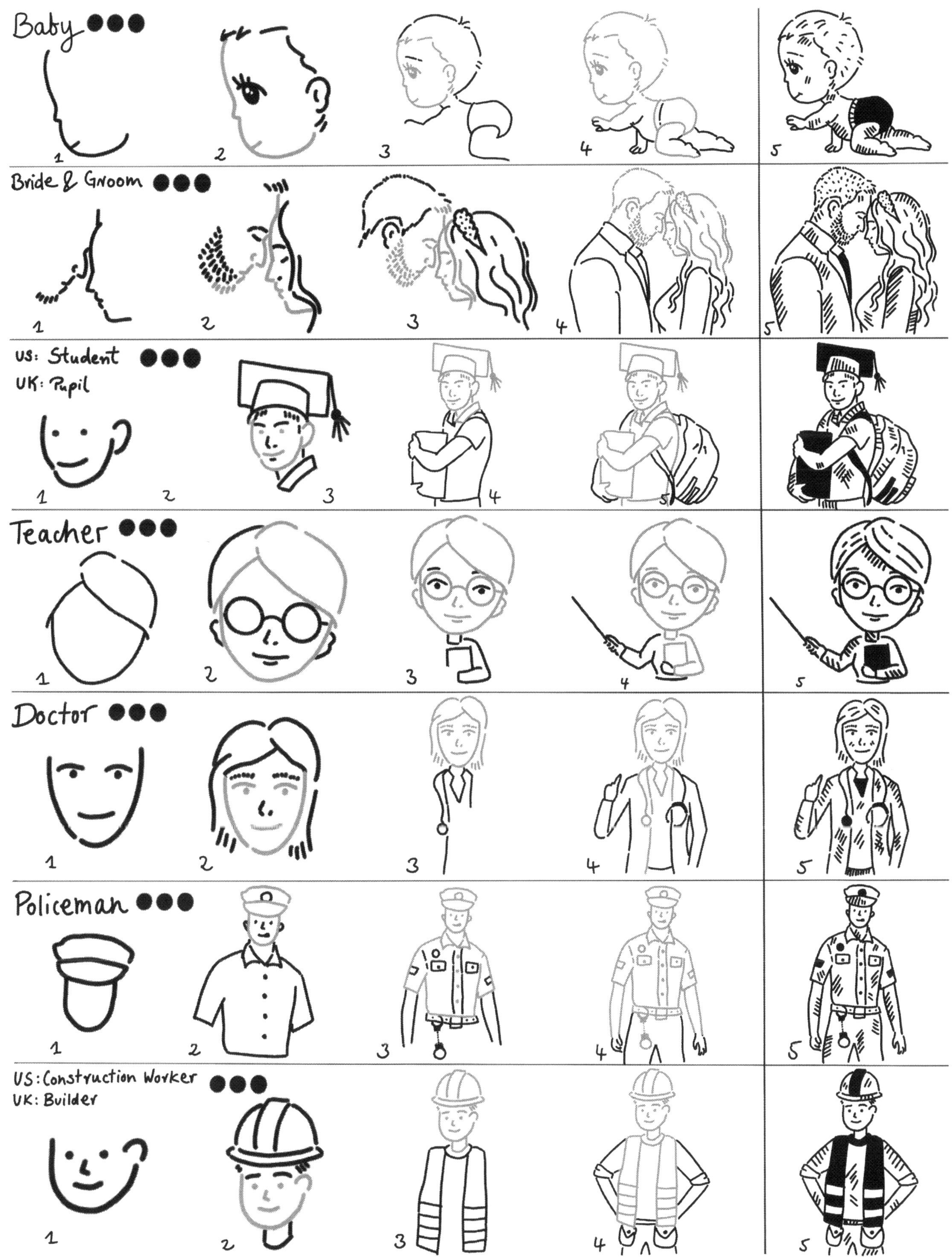
Baby
1
2
3
4
5
Bride & Groom
1
2
3
4
5
US: Student
UK: Pupil
1
2
3
4
5
Teacher
1
2
3
4
5
Doctor
1
2
3
4
5
Policeman
1
2
3
4
5
US: Construction Worker
UK: Builder
1
2
3
4
5

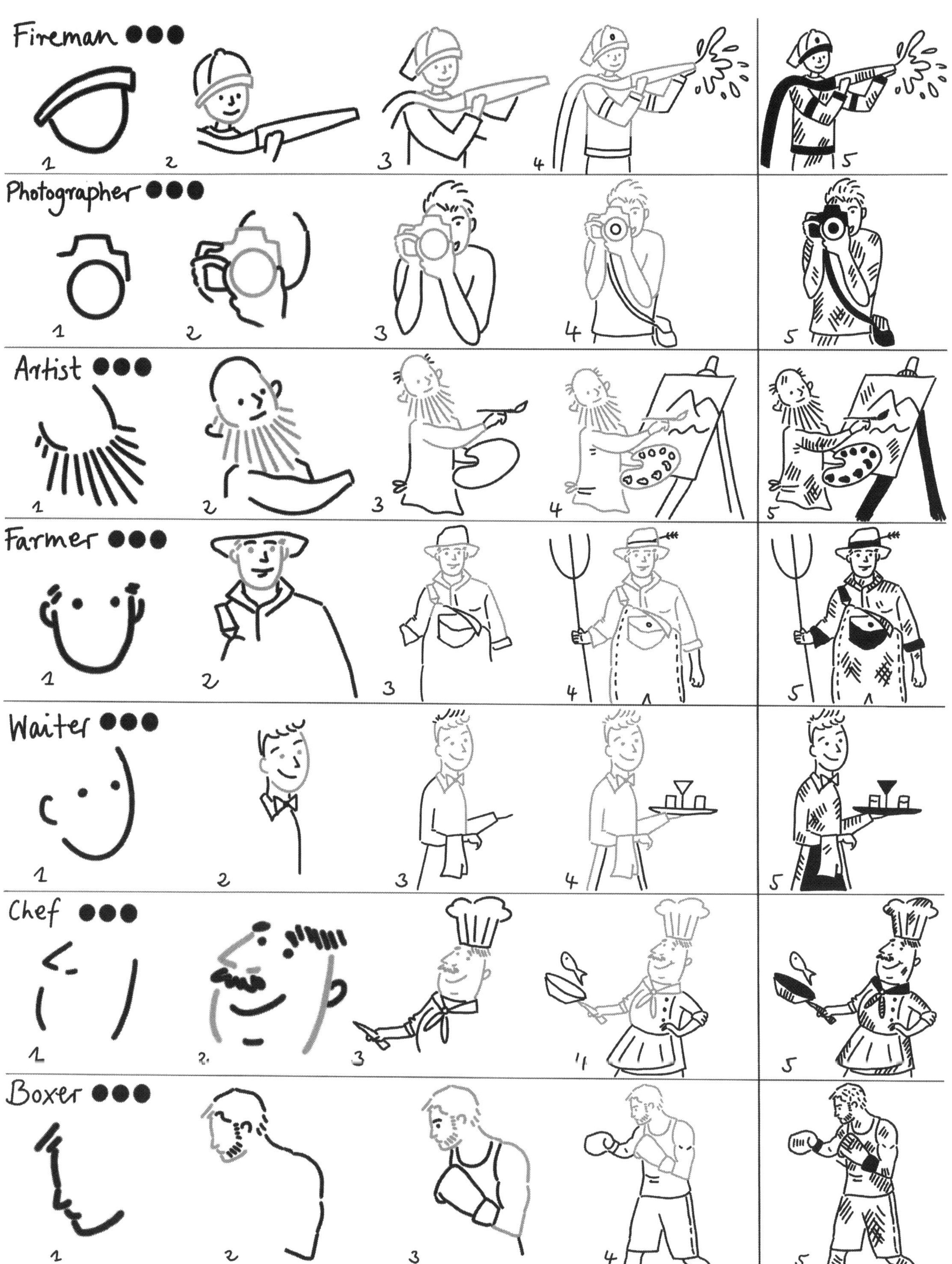
Fireman
1
2
3
4
5
Photographer
1
2
3
4
5
Artist
1
2
3
4
5
Farmer
1
2
3
4
5
Waiter
1
2
3
4
5
Chef
1
2
3
4
5
Boxer
1
2
3
4
5

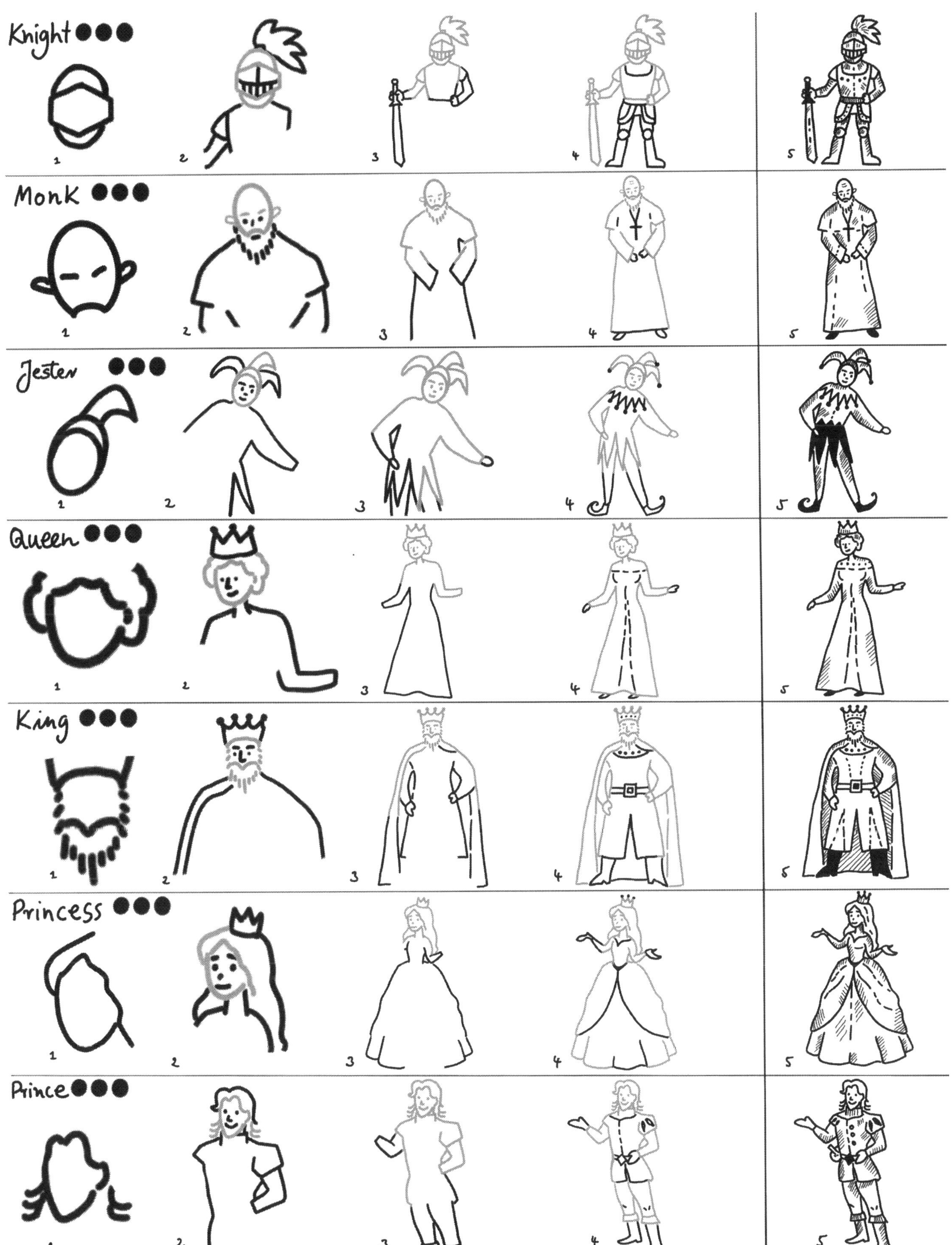
Knight
1
2
3
4
5
Monk
1
2
3
4
5
Jester
1
2
3
4
5
Queen
1
2
3
4
5
King
1
2
3
4
5
Princess
1
2
3
4
5
Prince
1
2
3
4
5

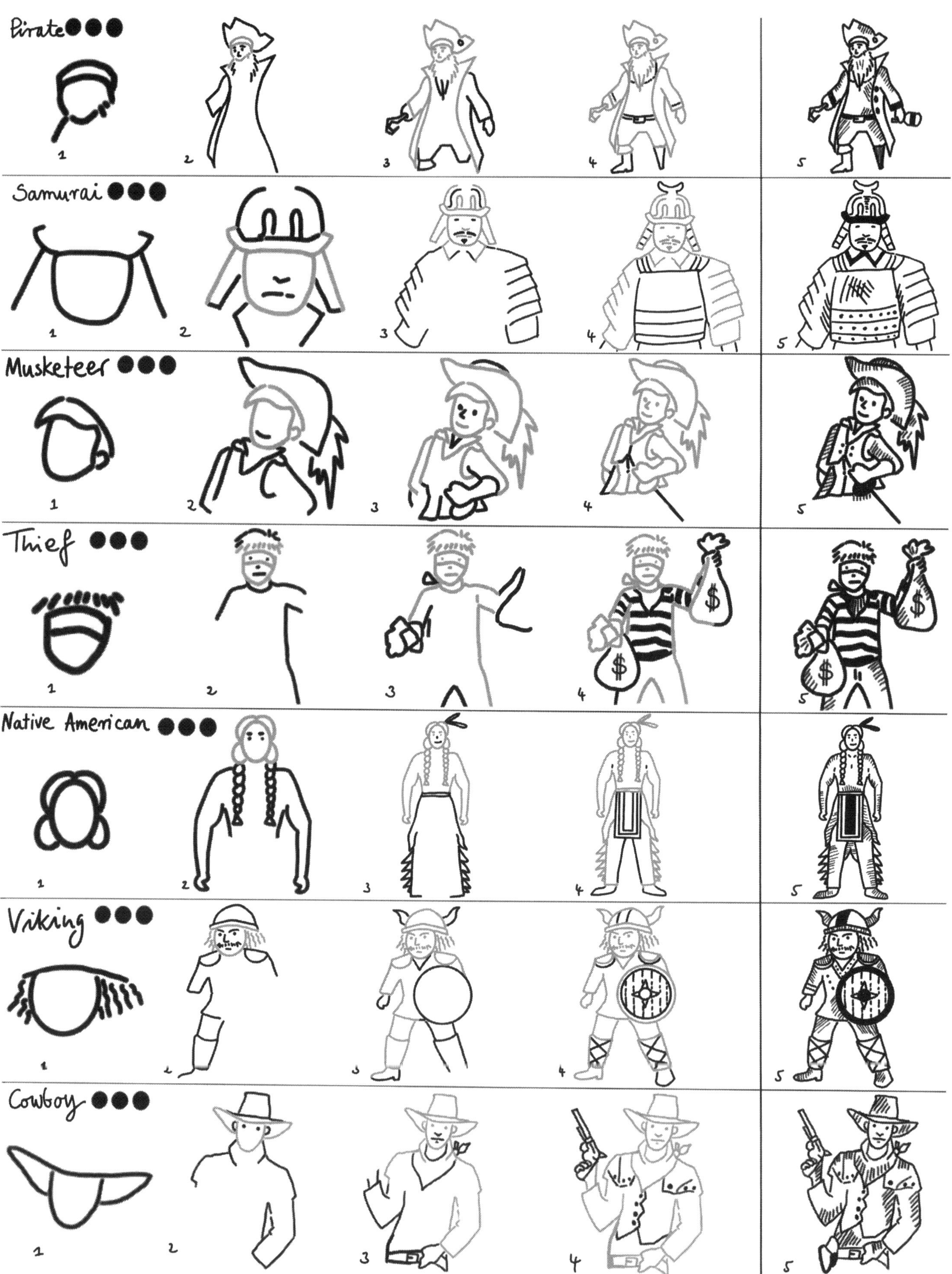
Pirate
1
2
3
4
5
Samurai
1
2
3
4
5
Musketeer
1
2
3
4
5
Thief
1
2
3
4
5
Native American
1
2
3
4
5
Viking
1
2
3
4
5
Cowboy
1
2
3
4
5

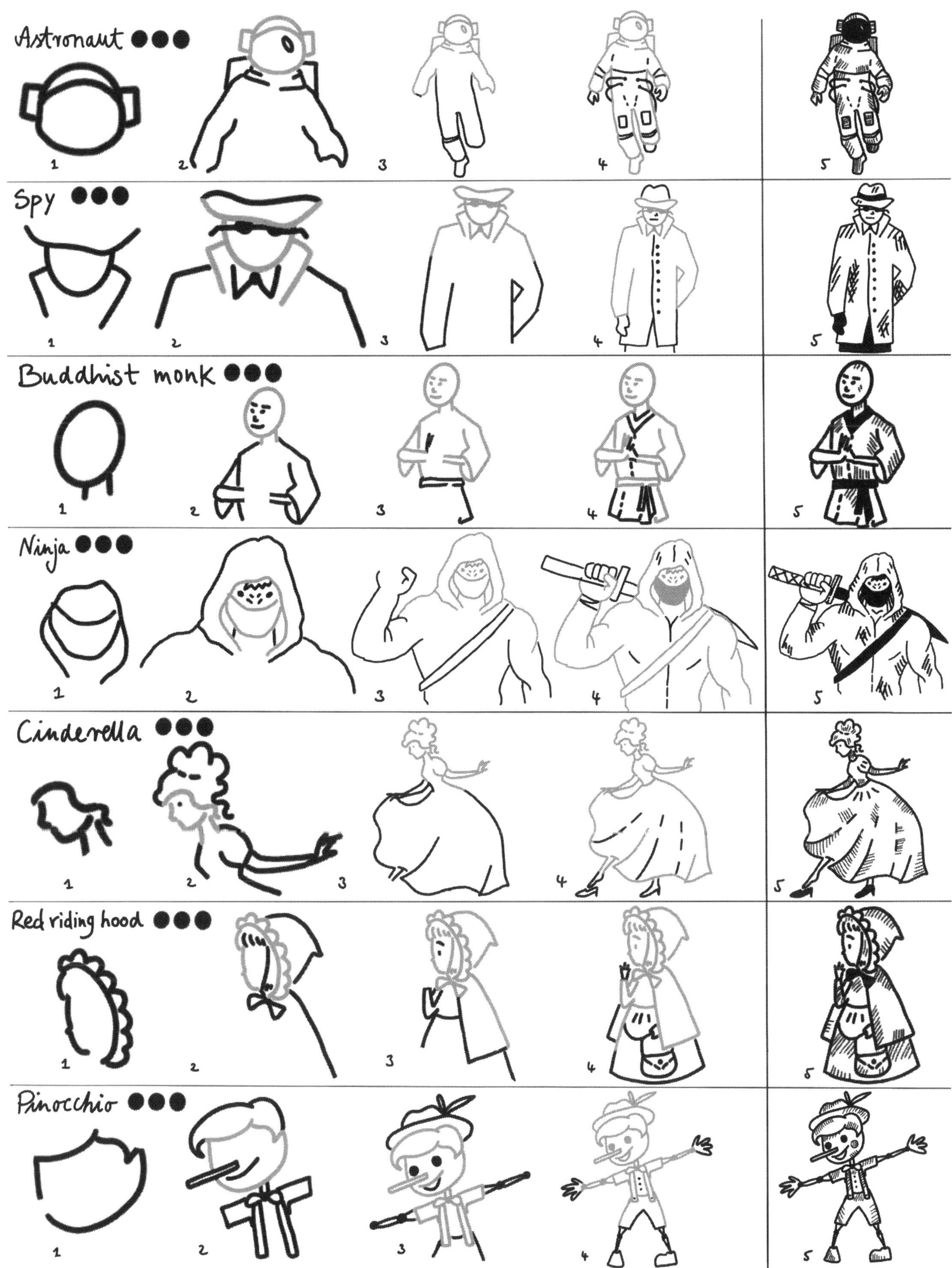
Astronaut
1
2
3
4
5
Spy
1
2
3
4
5
Buddhist monk
1
2
3
4
5
Ninja
1
2
3
4
5
Cinderella
1
2
3
4
5
Red riding hood
1
2
3
4
5
Pinocchio
1
2
3
4
5

# MYTHICAL CREATURES

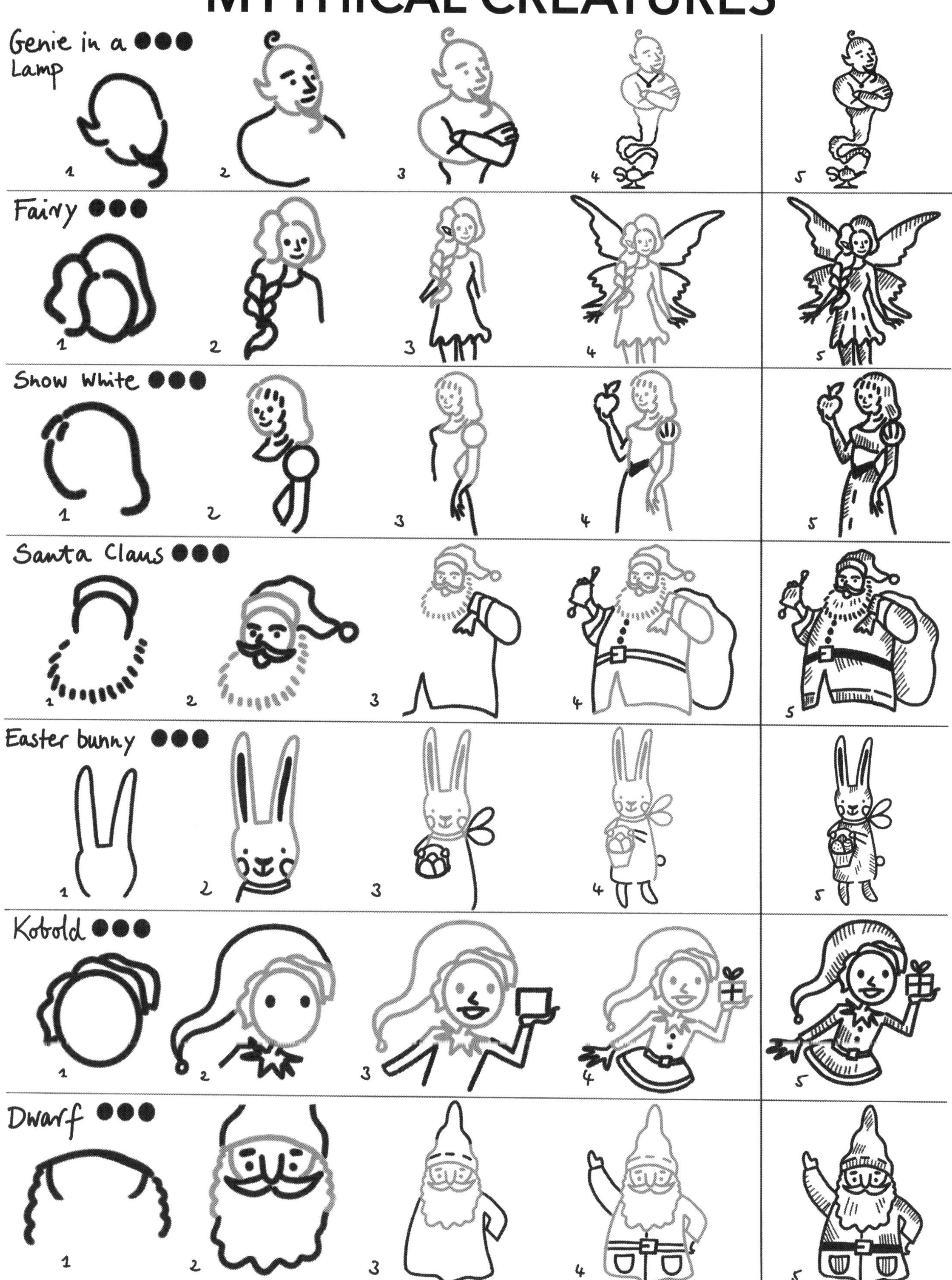

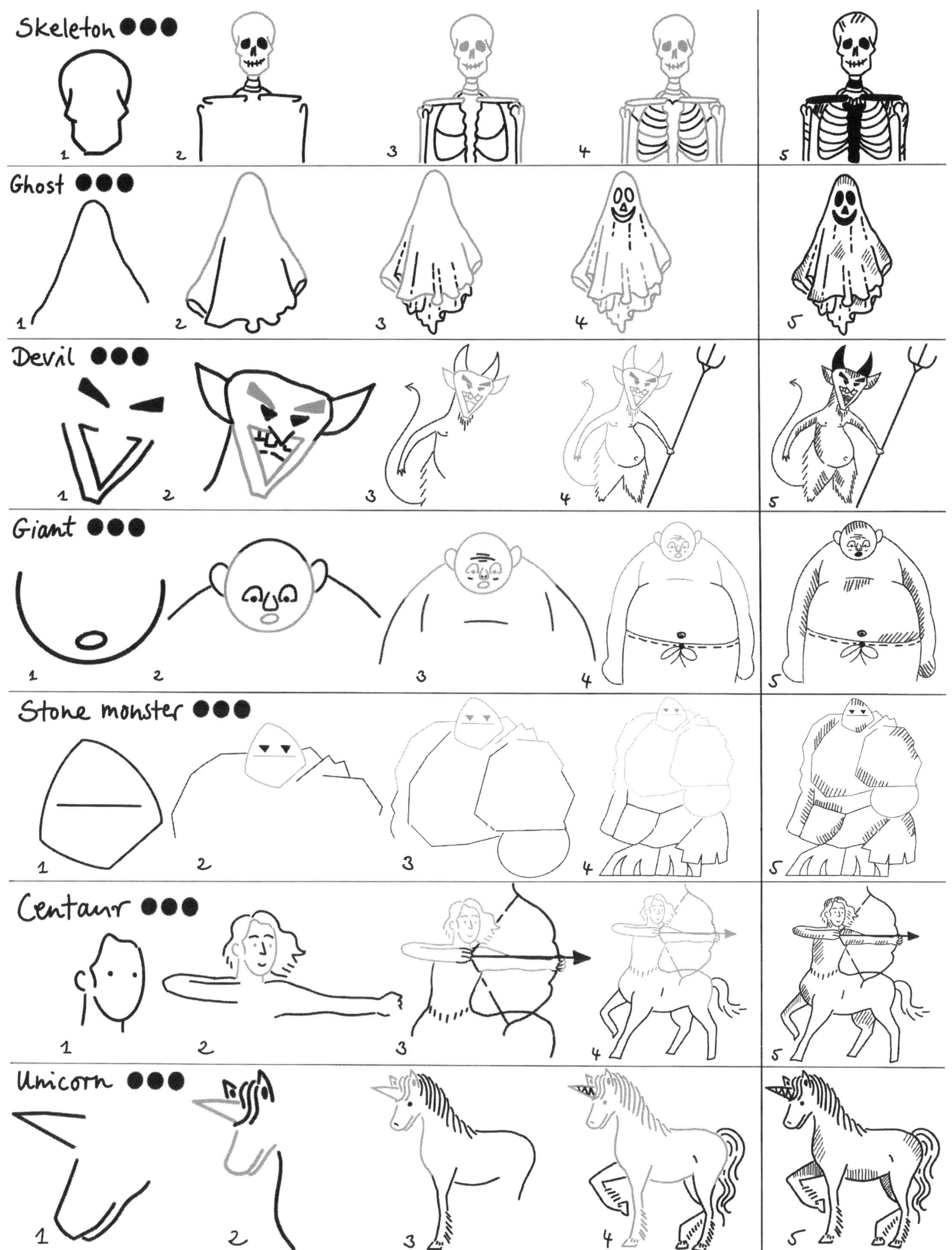
Skeleton
1
2
3
4
5
Ghost
1
2
3
4
5
Devil
1
2
3
4
5
Giant
1
2
3
4
5
Stone monster
1
2
3
4
5
Centaur
1
2
3
4
5
Unicorn
1
2
3
4
5

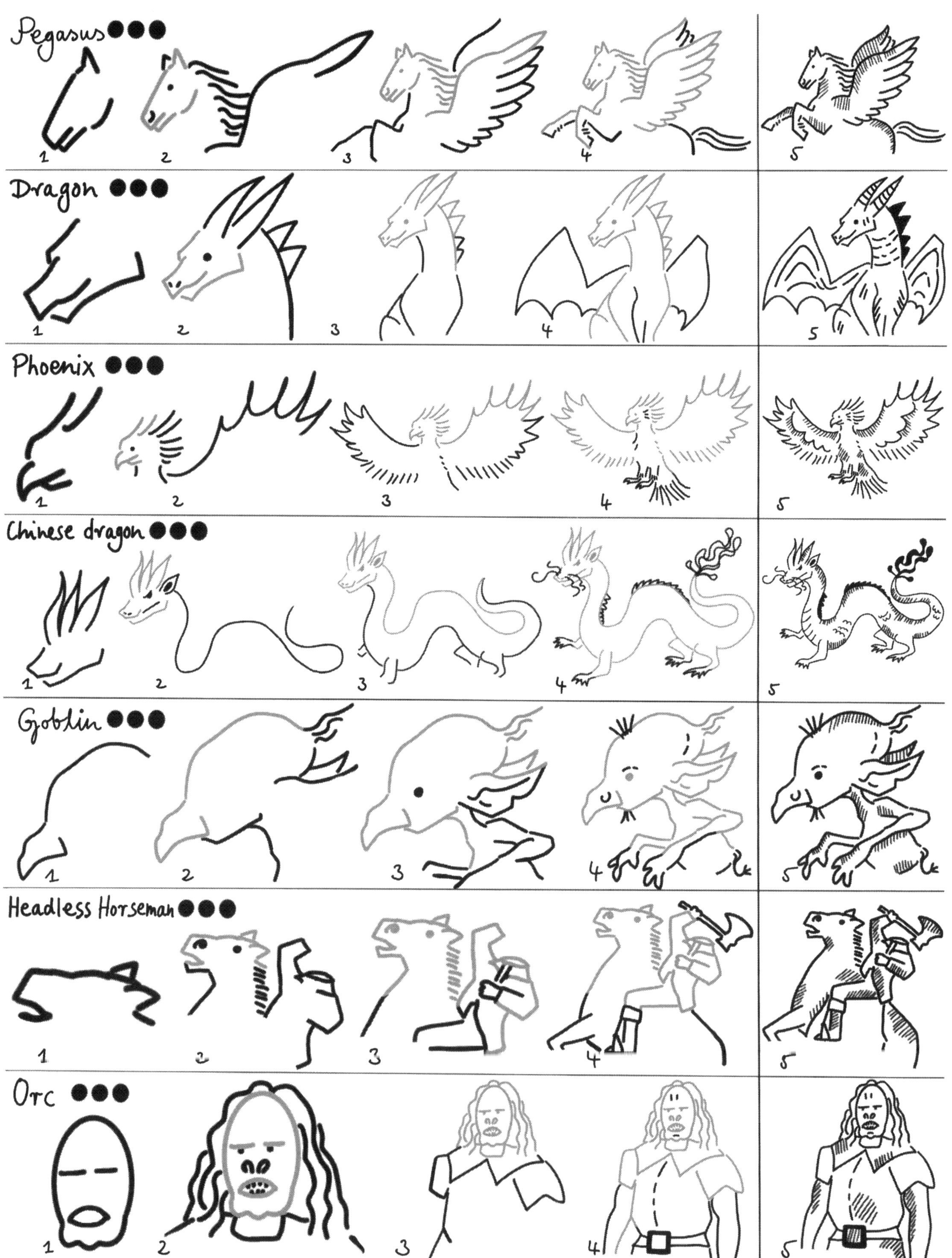
Pegasus ●●●
1
2
3
4
5
Dragon ●●●
1
2
3
4
5
Phoenix ●●●
1
2
3
4
5
Chinese dragon ●●●
1
2
3
4
5
Goblin ●●●
1
2
3
4
5
Headless Horseman ●●●
1
2
3
4
5
Orc ●●●
1
2
3
4
5

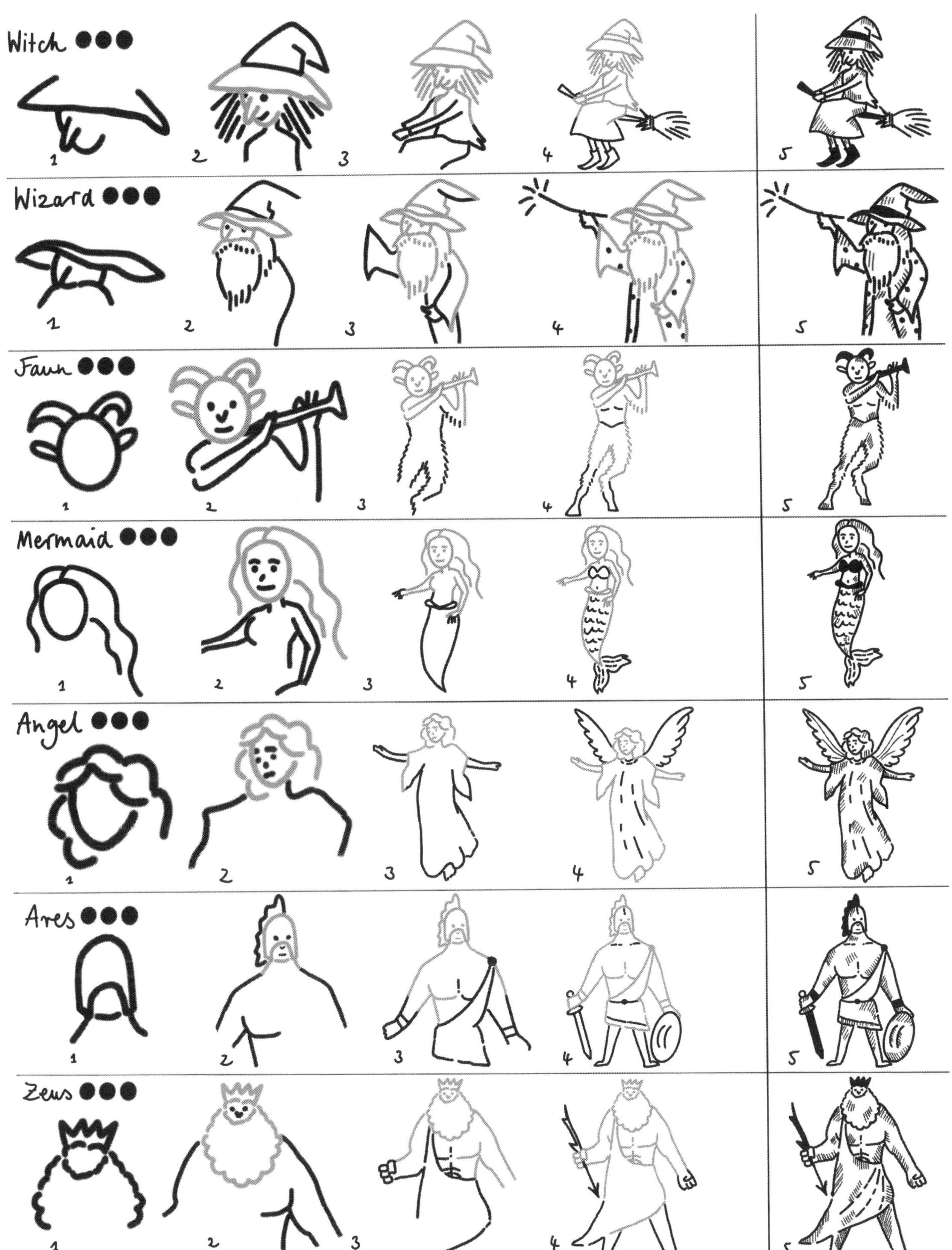
Witch ●●●
1
2
3
4
5
Wizard ●●●
1
2
3
4
5
Faun ●●●
1
2
3
4
5
Mermaid ●●●
1
2
3
4
5
Angel ●●●
1
2
3
4
5
Ares ●●●
1
2
3
4
5
Zeus ●●●
1
2
3
4
5

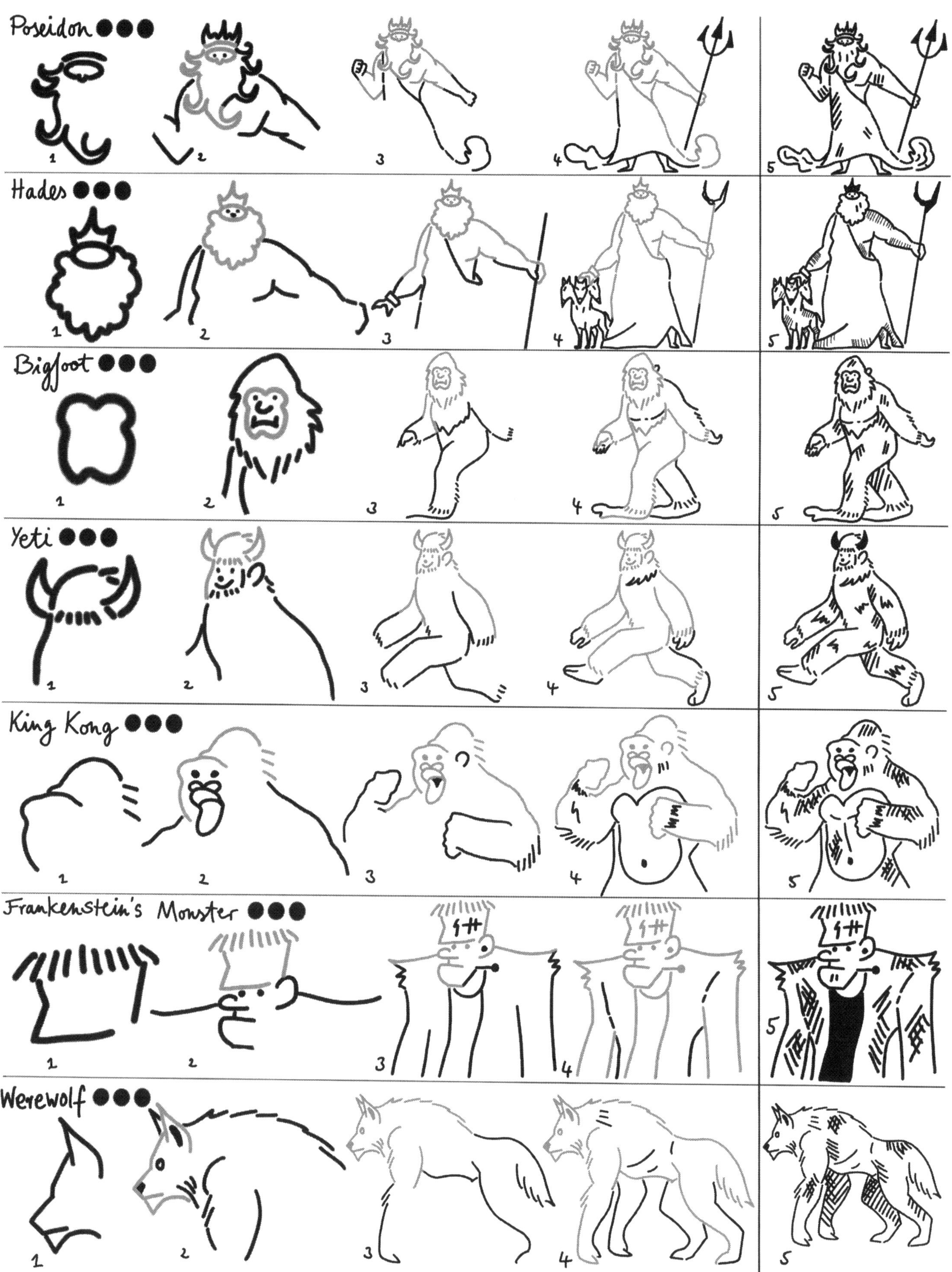
Poseidon ●●●
1
2
3
4
5
Hades ●●●
1
2
3
4
5
Bigfoot ●●●
1
2
3
4
5
Yeti ●●●
1
2
3
4
5
King Kong ●●●
1
2
3
4
5
Frankenstein's Monster ●●●
1
2
3
4
5
Werewolf ●●●
1
2
3
4
5

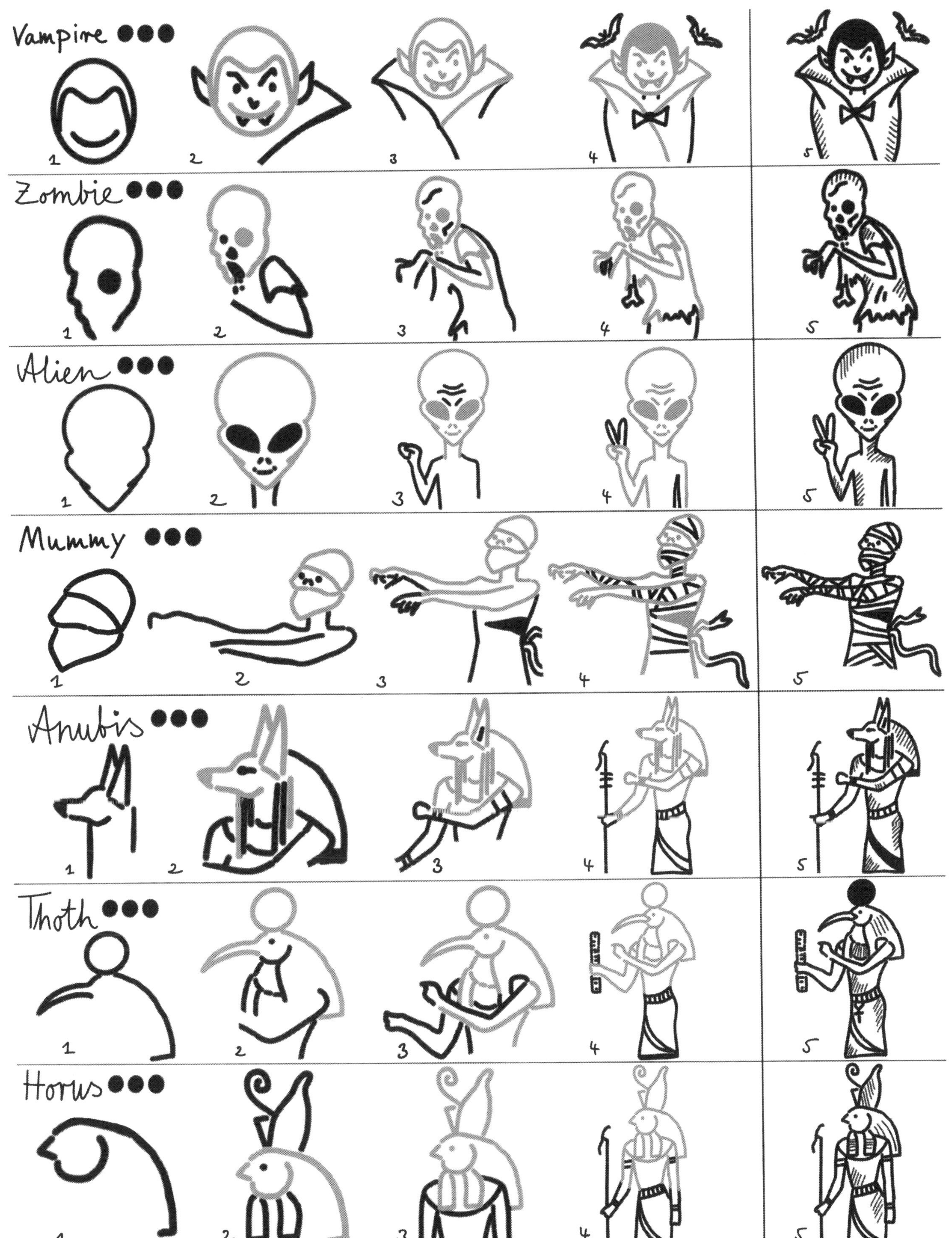
Vampire
1
2
3
4
5
Zombie
1
2
3
4
5
Alien
1
2
3
4
5
Mummy
1
2
3
4
5
Anubis
1
2
3
4
5
Thoth
1
2
3
4
5
Horus
1
2
3
4
5

# ANIMALS

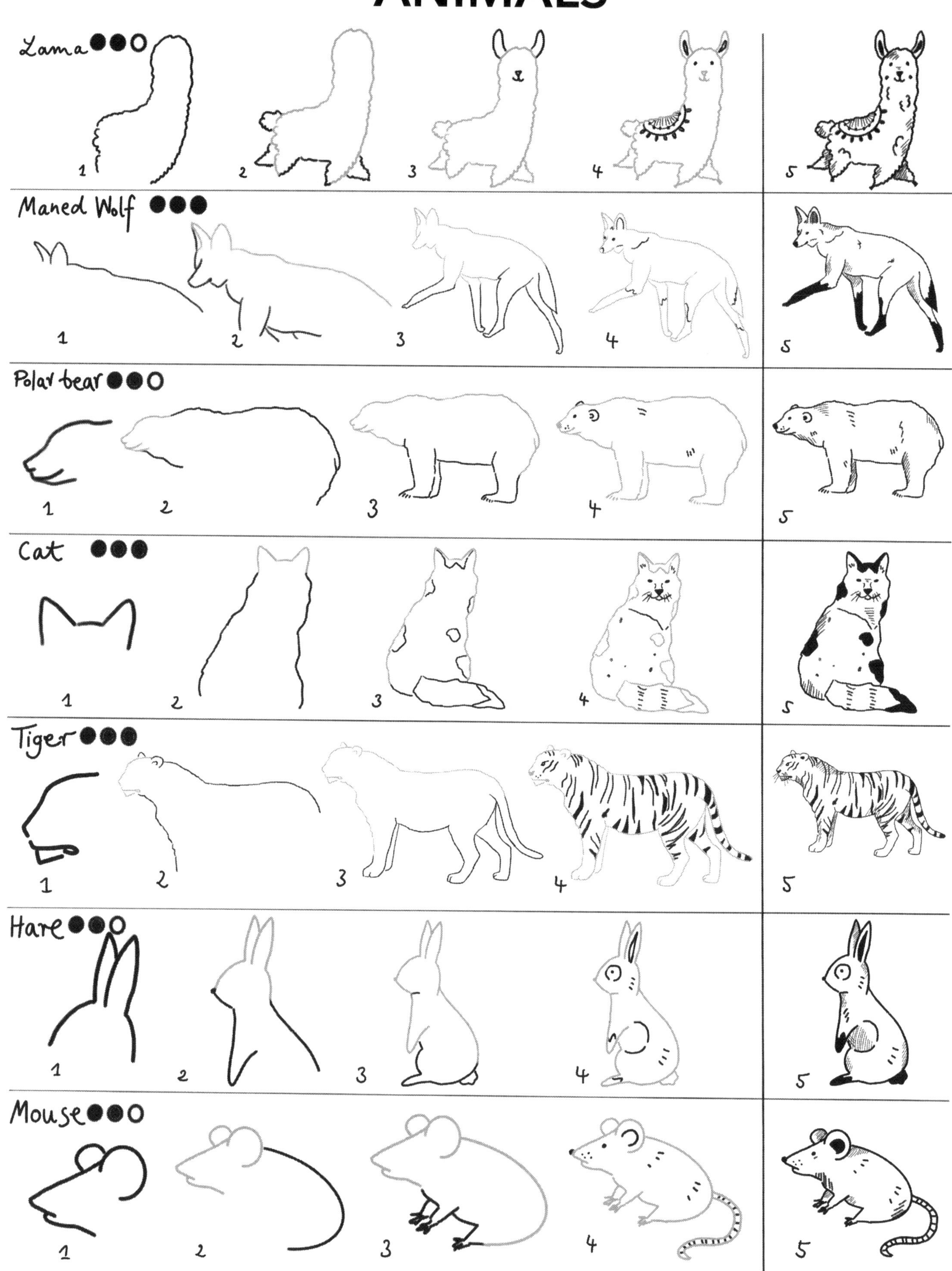

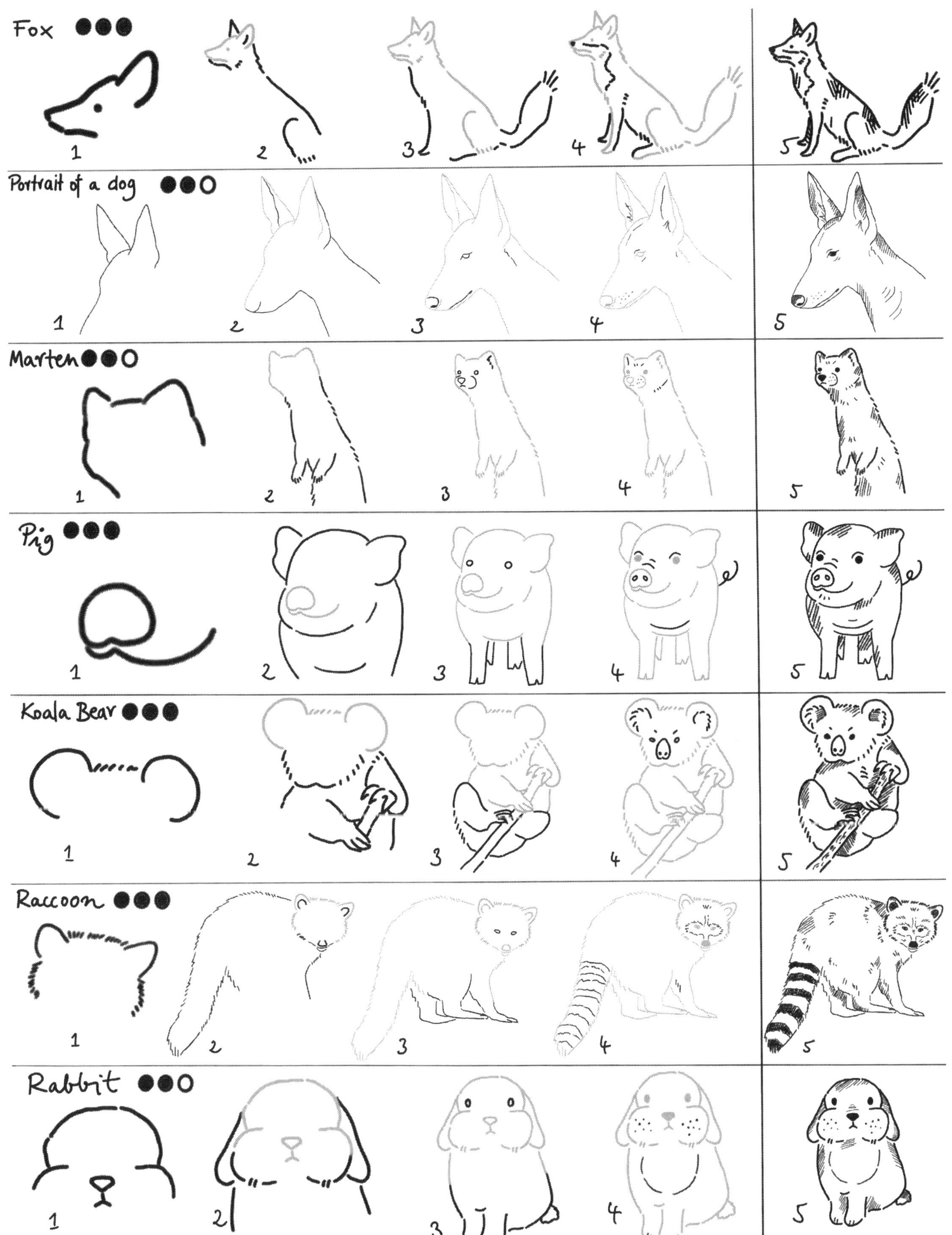
Fox
1
2
3
4
5
Portrait of a dog
1
2
3
4
5
Marten
1
2
3
4
5
Pig
1
2
3
4
5
Koala Bear
1
2
3
4
5
Raccoon
1
2
3
4
5
Rabbit
1
2
3
4
5

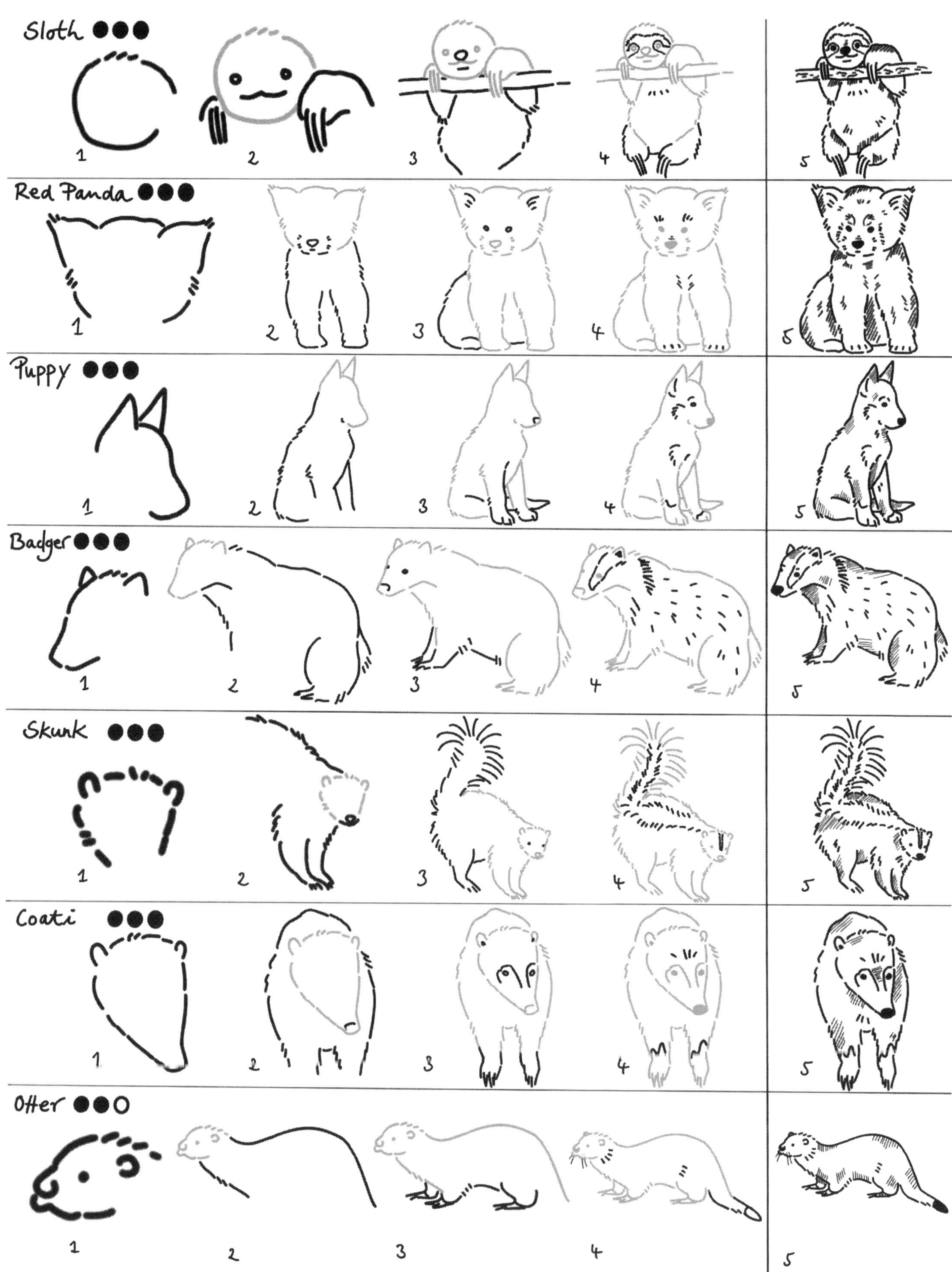
Sloth
1
2
3
4
5
Red Panda
1
2
3
4
5
Puppy
1
2
3
4
5
Badger
1
2
3
4
5
Skunk
1
2
3
4
5
Coati
1
2
3
4
5
Otter
1
2
3
4
5

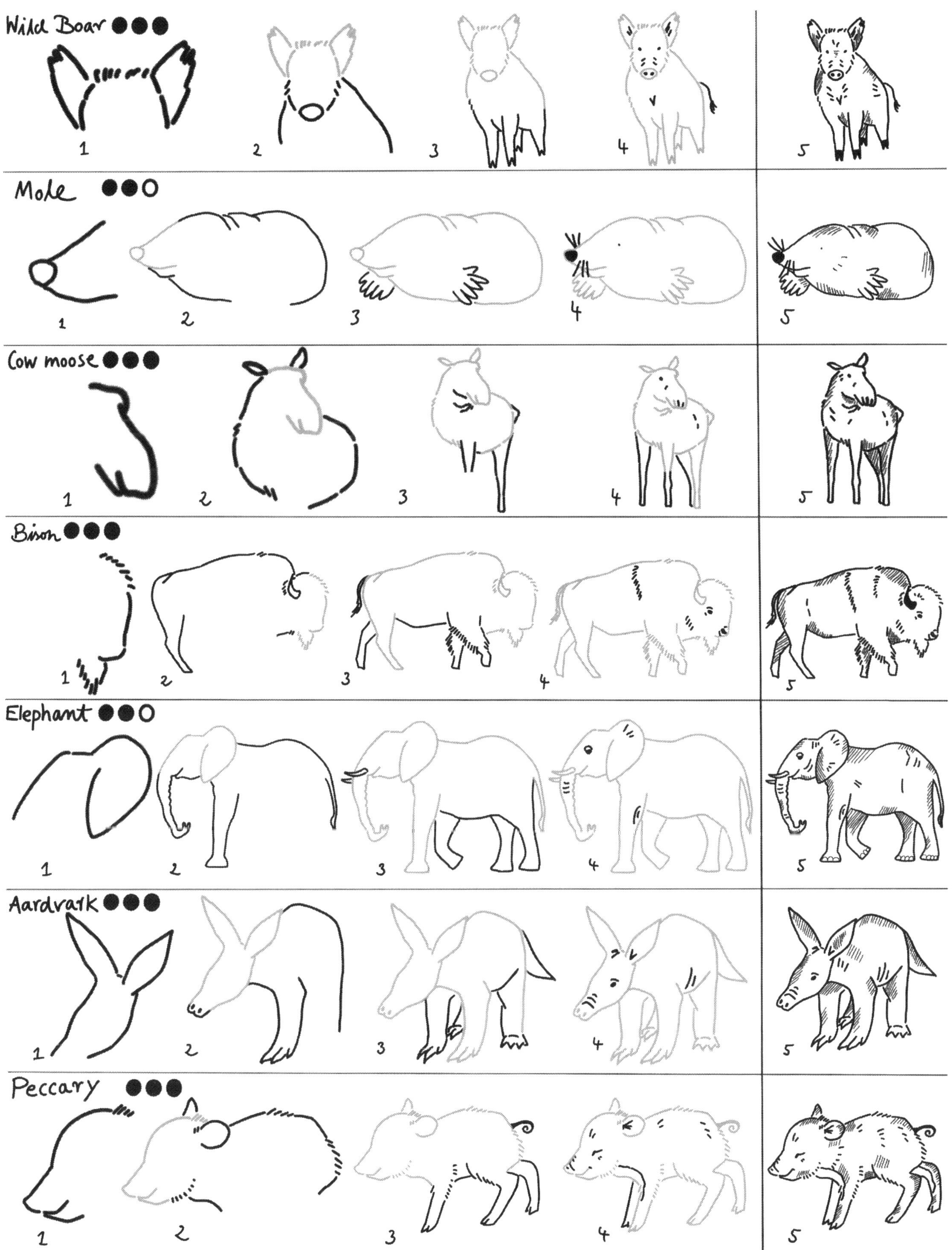
Wild Boar ●●●
1
2
3
4
5
Mole ●●○
1
2
3
4
5
Cow moose ●●●
1
2
3
4
5
Bison ●●●
1
2
3
4
5
Elephant ●●○
1
2
3
4
5
Aardvark ●●●
1
2
3
4
5
Peccary ●●●
1
2
3
4
5

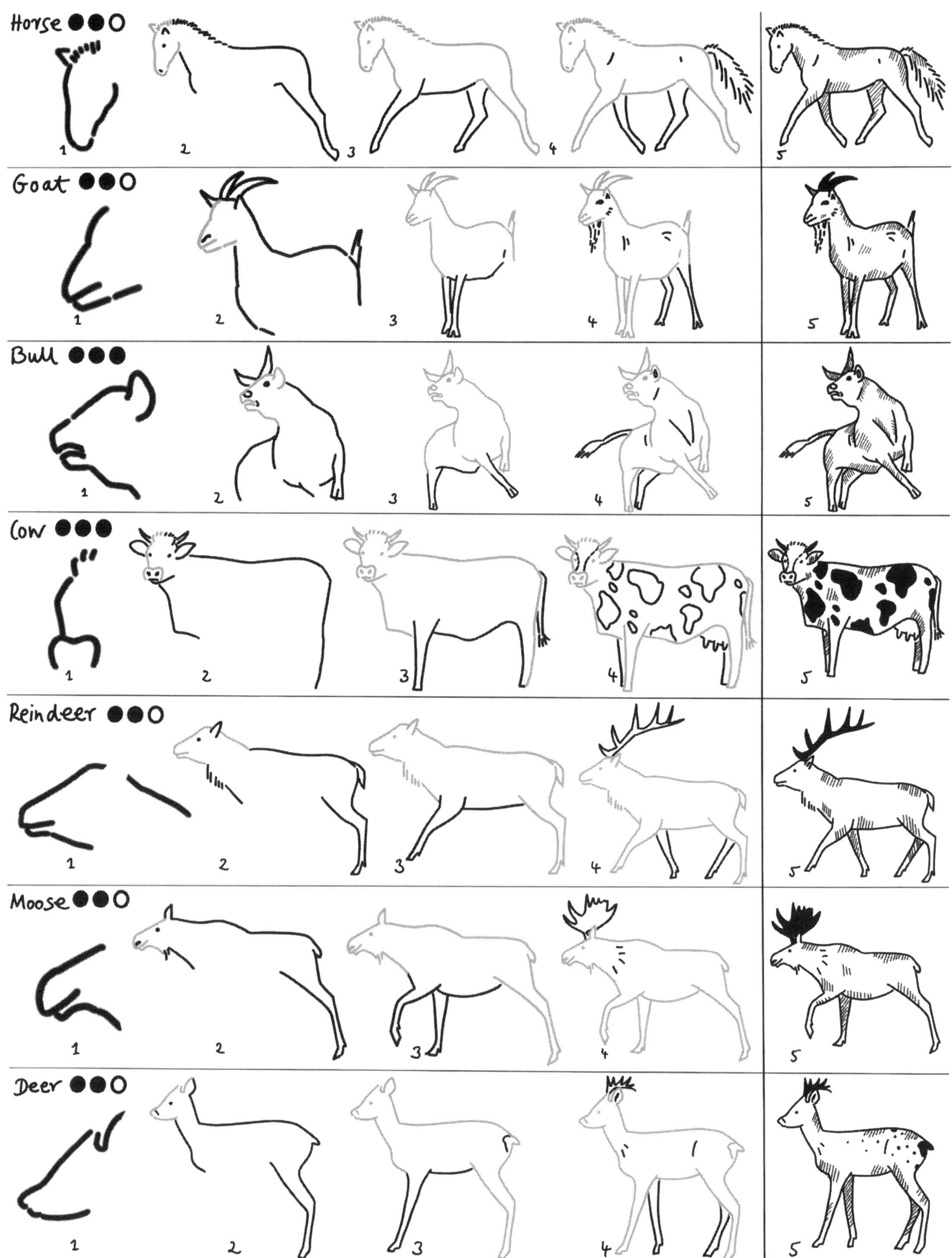
Horse
1
2
3
4
5
Goat
1
2
3
4
5
Bull
1
2
3
4
5
Cow
1
2
3
4
5
Reindeer
1
2
3
4
5
Moose
1
2
3
4
5
Deer
1
2
3
4
5

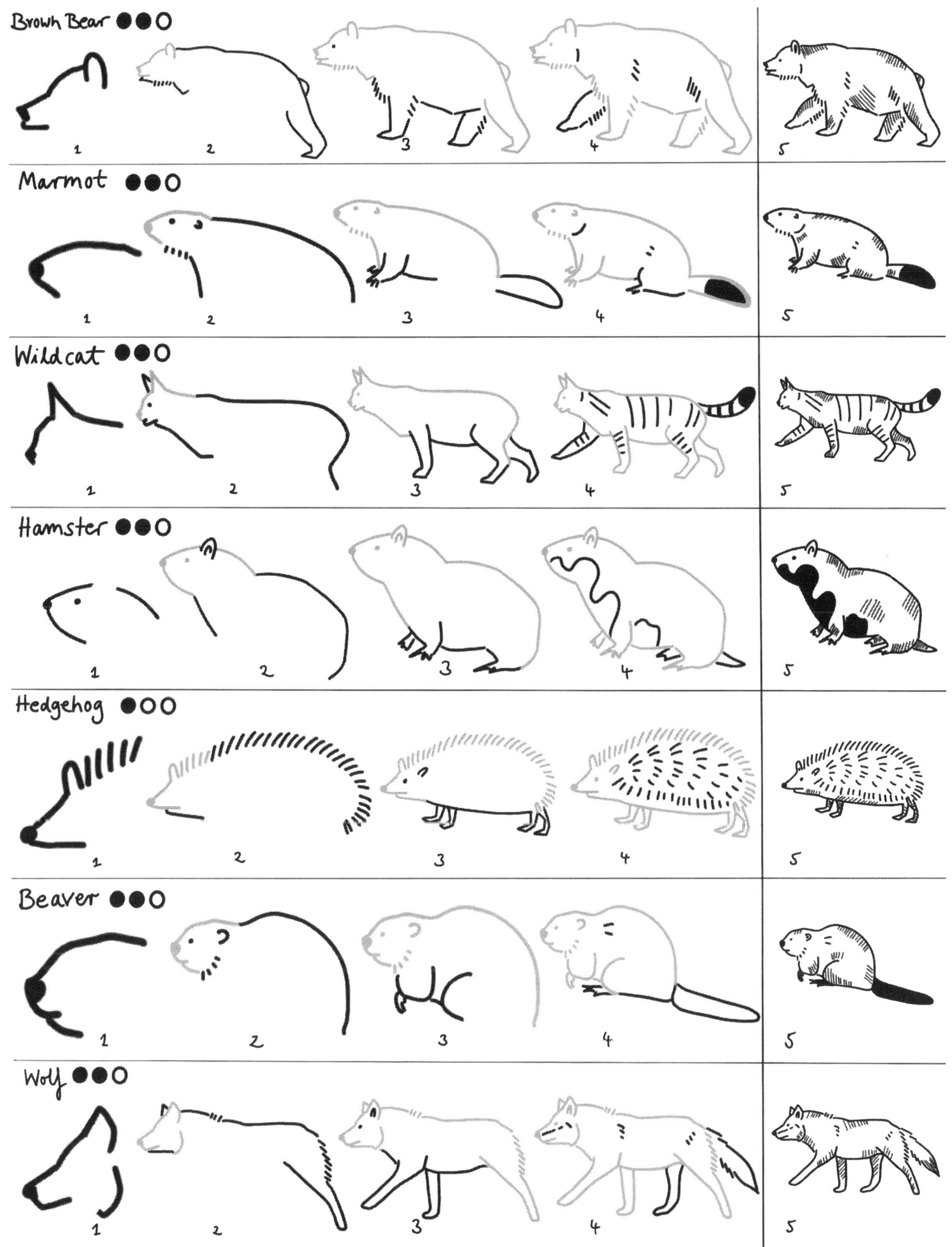
Brown Bear
1
2
3
4
5
Marmot
1
2
3
4
5
Wildcat
1
2
3
4
5
Hamster
1
2
3
4
5
Hedgehog
1
2
3
4
5
Beaver
1
2
3
4
5
Wolf
1
2
3
4
5

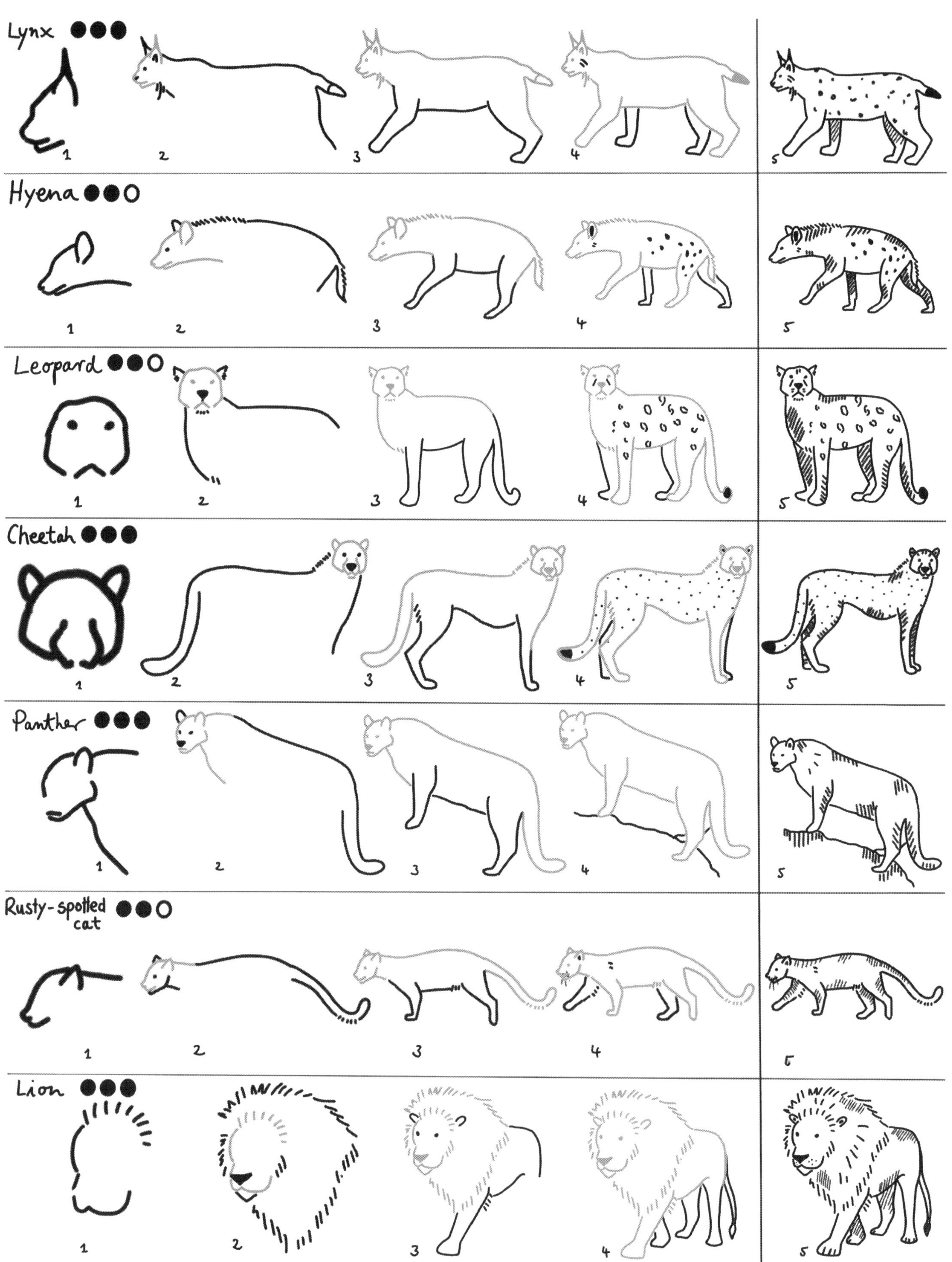
Lynx
1
2
3
4
5
Hyena
1
2
3
4
5
Leopard
1
2
3
4
5
Cheetah
1
2
3
4
5
Panther
1
2
3
4
5
Rusty-spotted cat
1
2
3
4
5
Lion
1
2
3
4
5

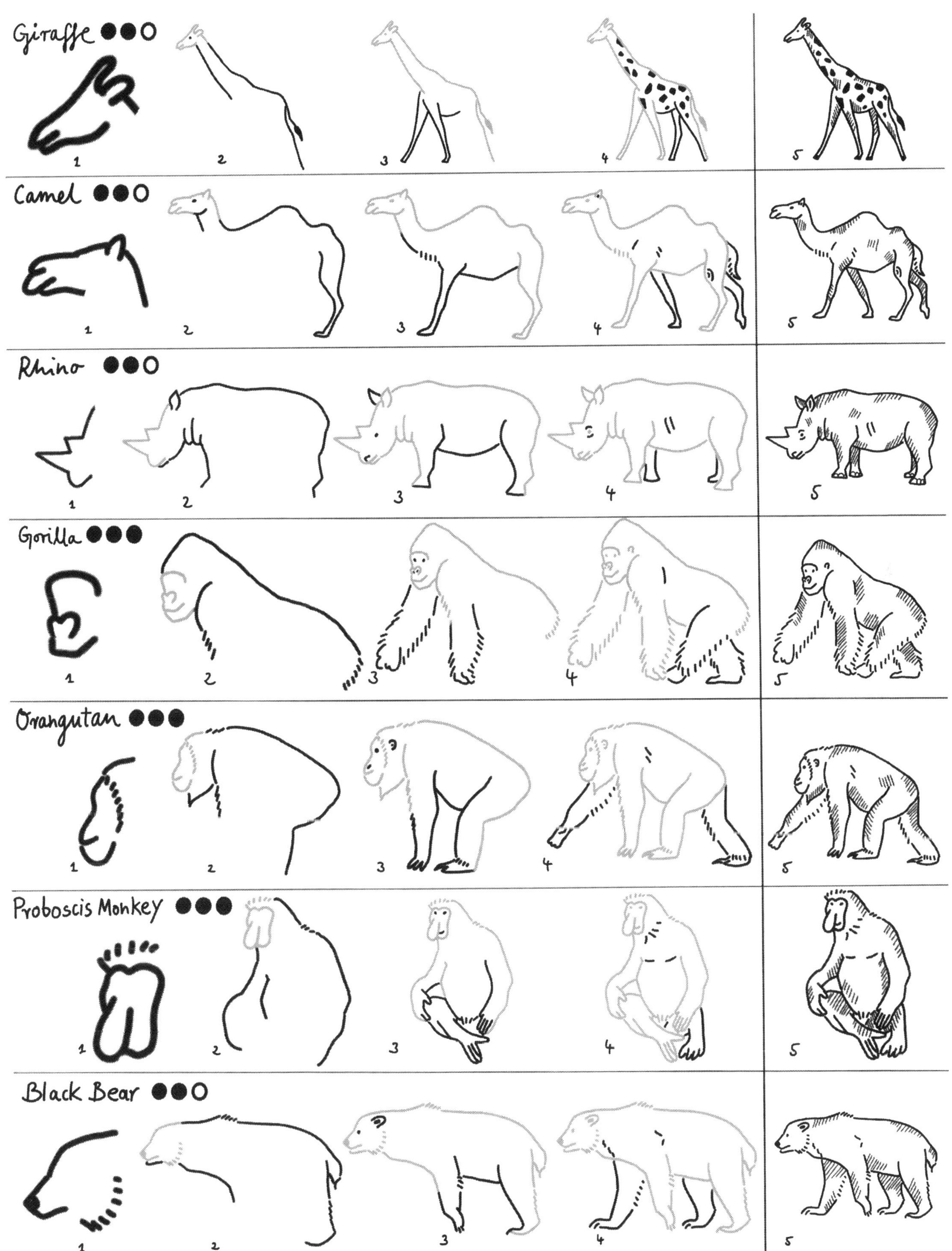

Giraffe
1
2
3
4
5
Camel
1
2
3
4
5
Rhino
1
2
3
4
5
Gorilla
1
2
3
4
5
Orangutan
1
2
3
4
5
Proboscis Monkey
1
2
3
4
5
Black Bear
1
2
3
4
5

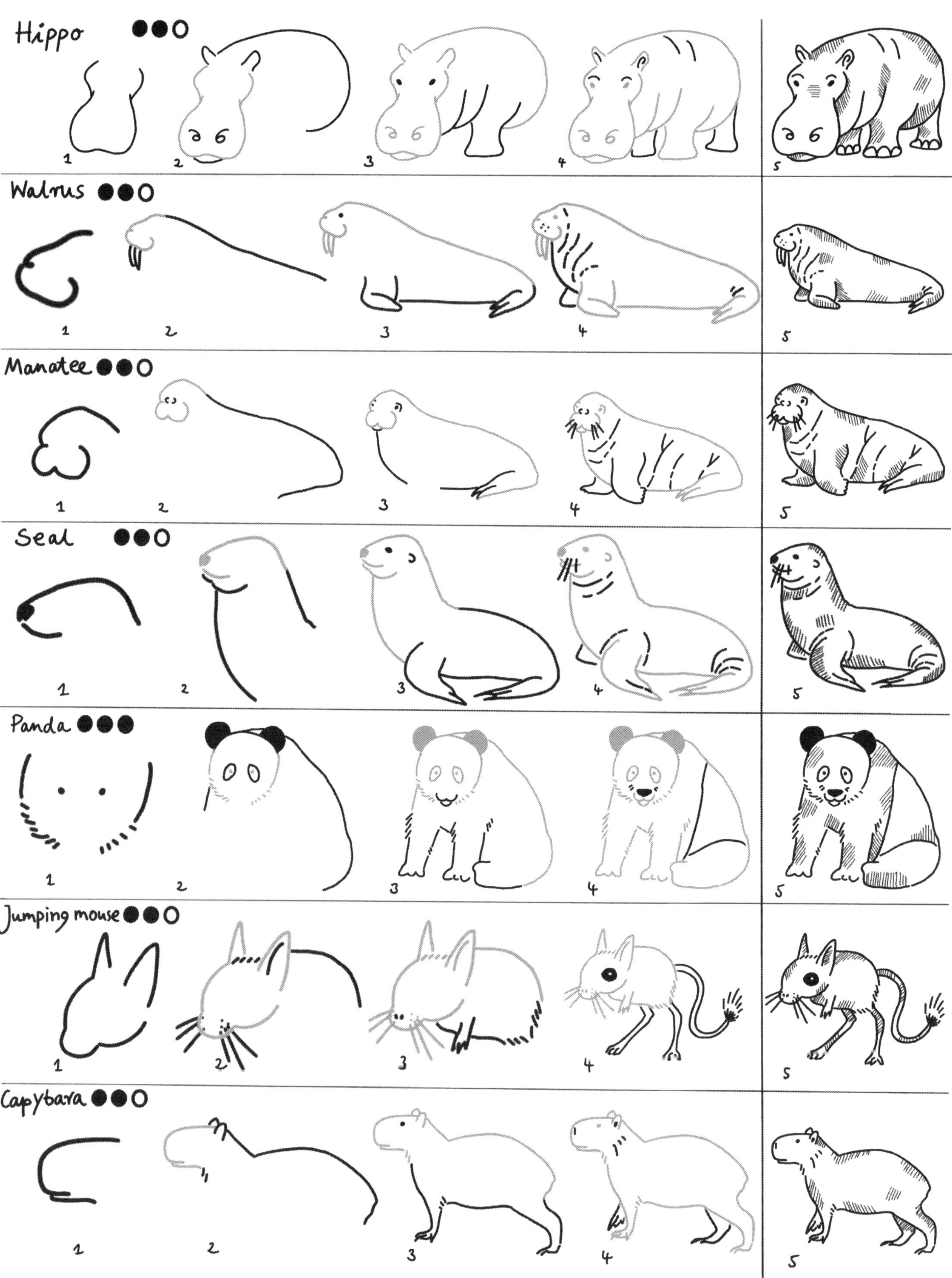
Hippo
1
2
3
4
5
Walrus
1
2
3
4
5
Manatee
1
2
3
4
5
Seal
1
2
3
4
5
Panda
1
2
3
4
5
Jumping mouse
1
2
3
4
5
Capybara
1
2
3
4
5

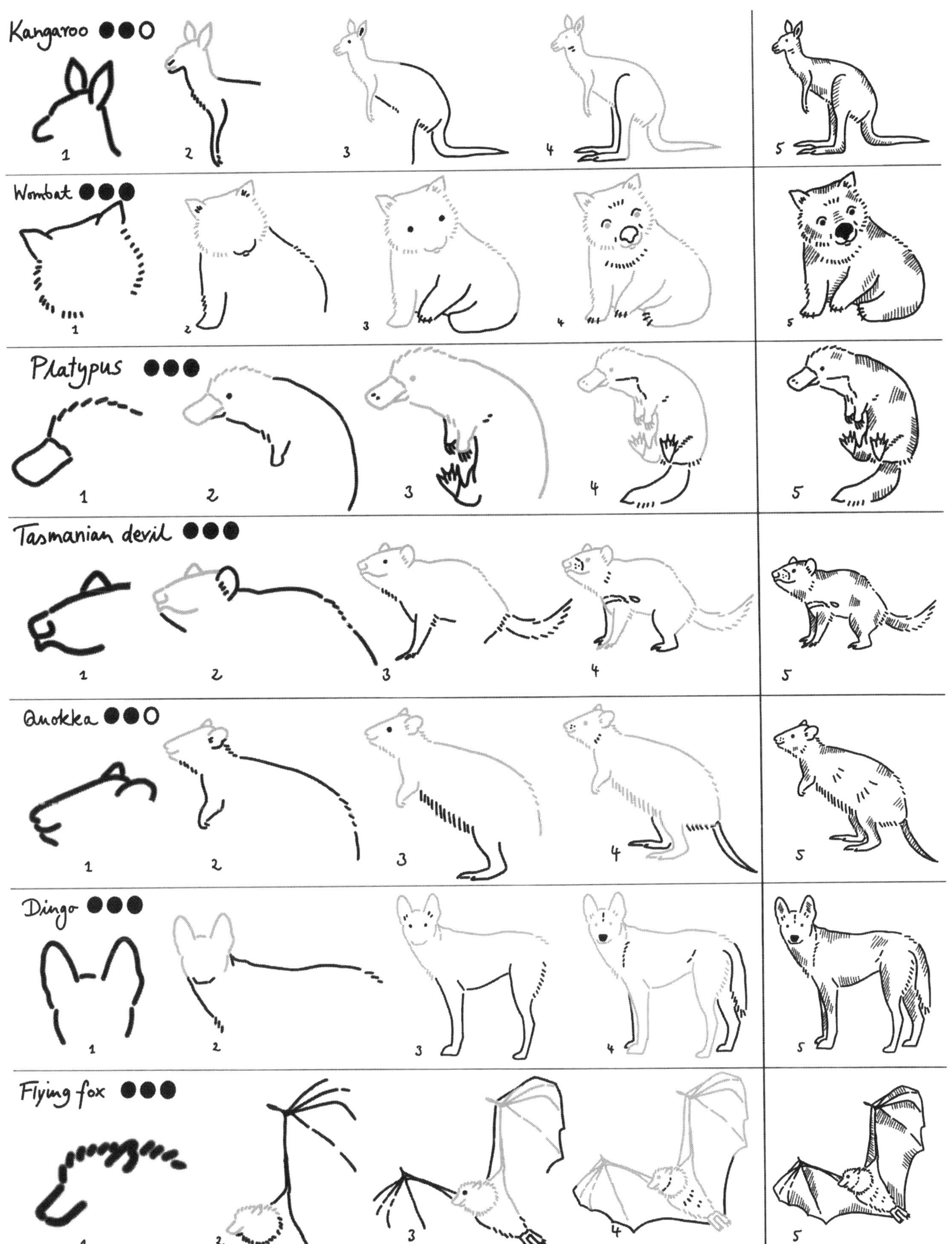

Kangaroo
1
2
3
4
5
Wombat
1
2
3
4
5
Platypus
1
2
3
4
5
Tasmanian devil
1
2
3
4
5
Quokka
1
2
3
4
5
Dingo
1
2
3
4
5
Flying fox
1
2
3
4
5

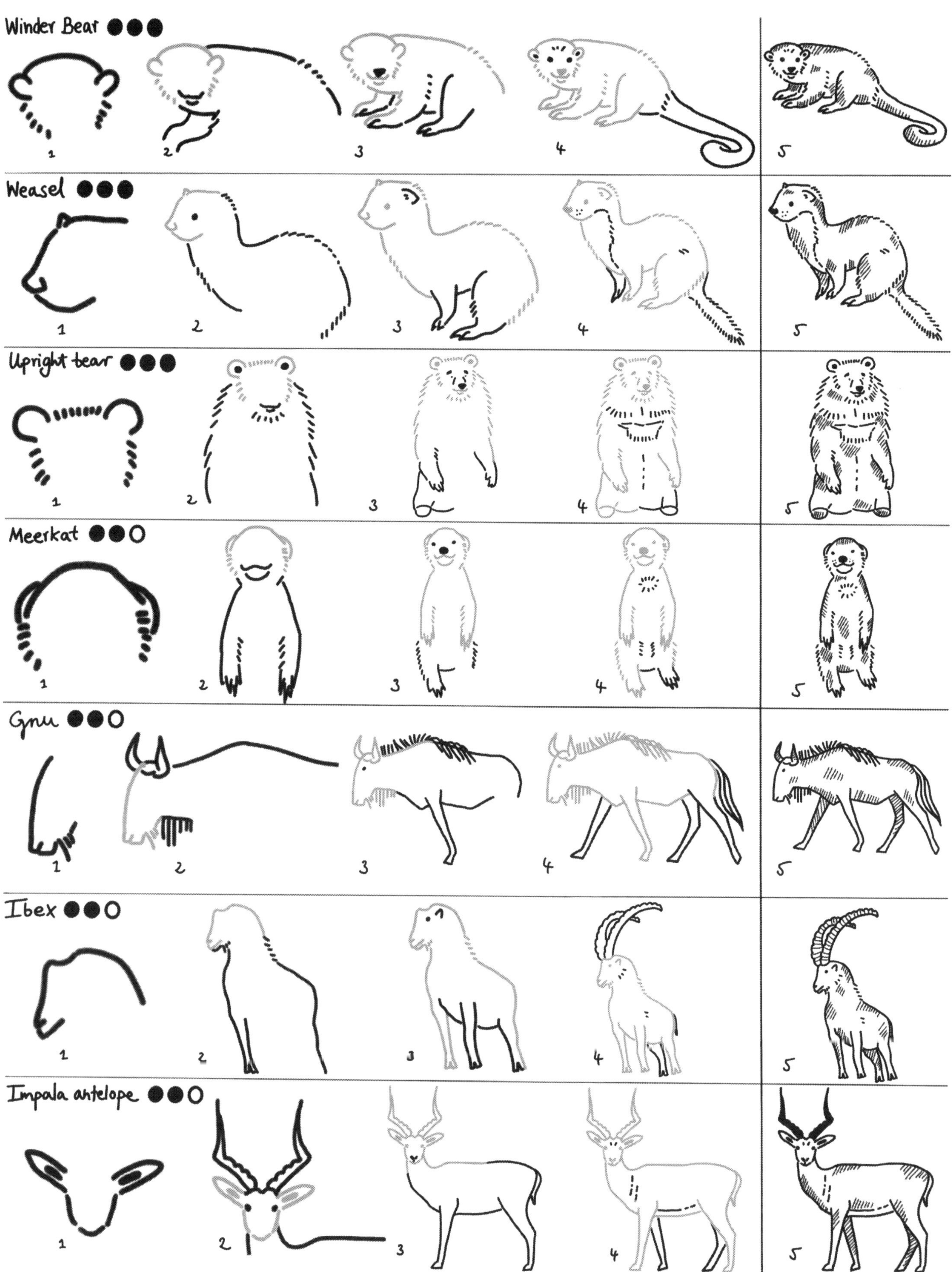
Winder Bear ●●●
1
2
3
4
5
Weasel ●●●
1
2
3
4
5
Upright bear ●●●
1
2
3
4
5
Meerkat ●●○
1
2
3
4
5
Gnu ●●○
1
2
3
4
5
Ibex ●●○
1
2
3
4
5
Impala antelope ●●○
1
2
3
4
5

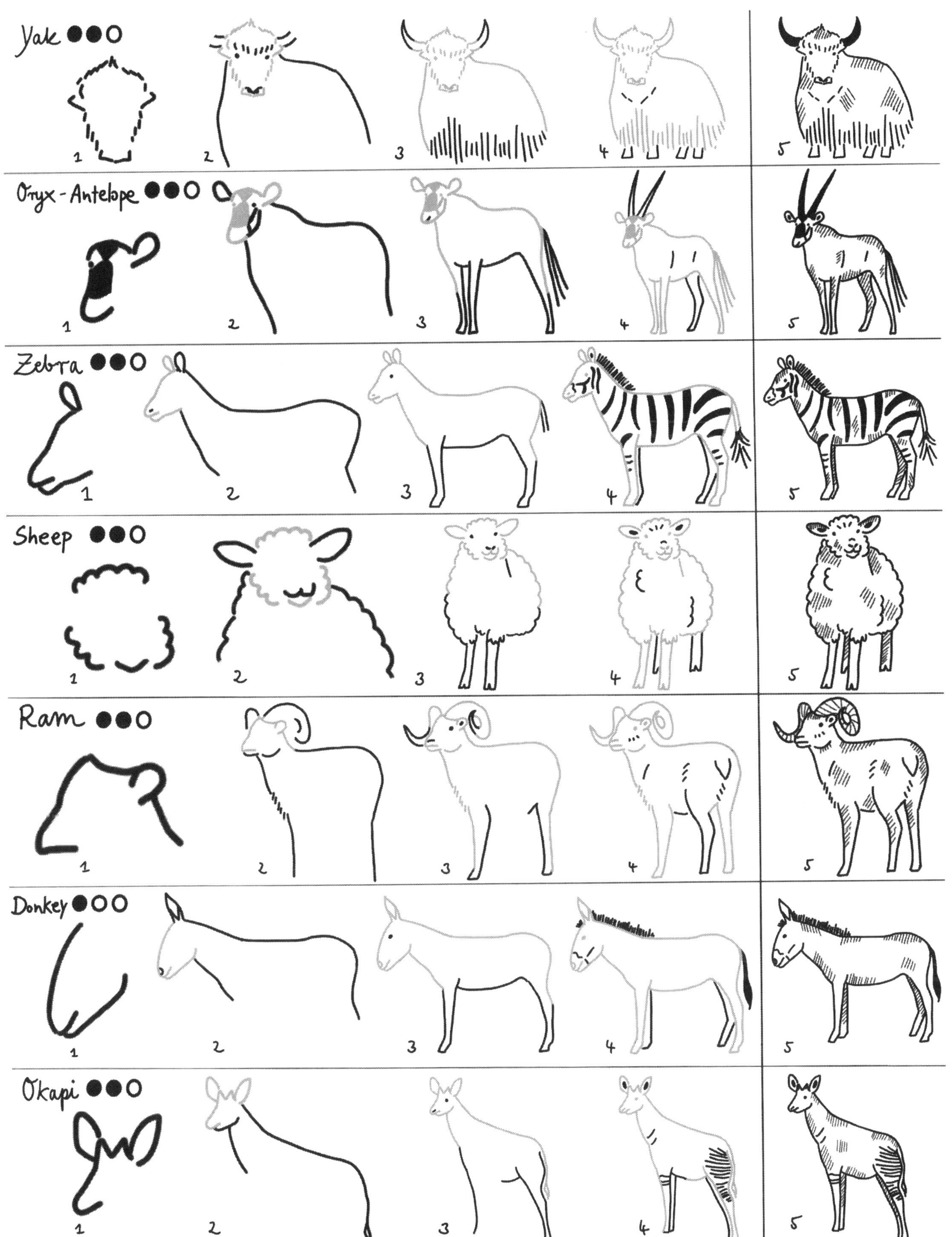

Yak
1
2
3
4
5
Oryx-Antelope
1
2
3
4
5
Zebra
1
2
3
4
5
Sheep
1
2
3
4
5
Ram
1
2
3
4
5
Donkey
1
2
3
4
5
Okapi
1
2
3
4
5

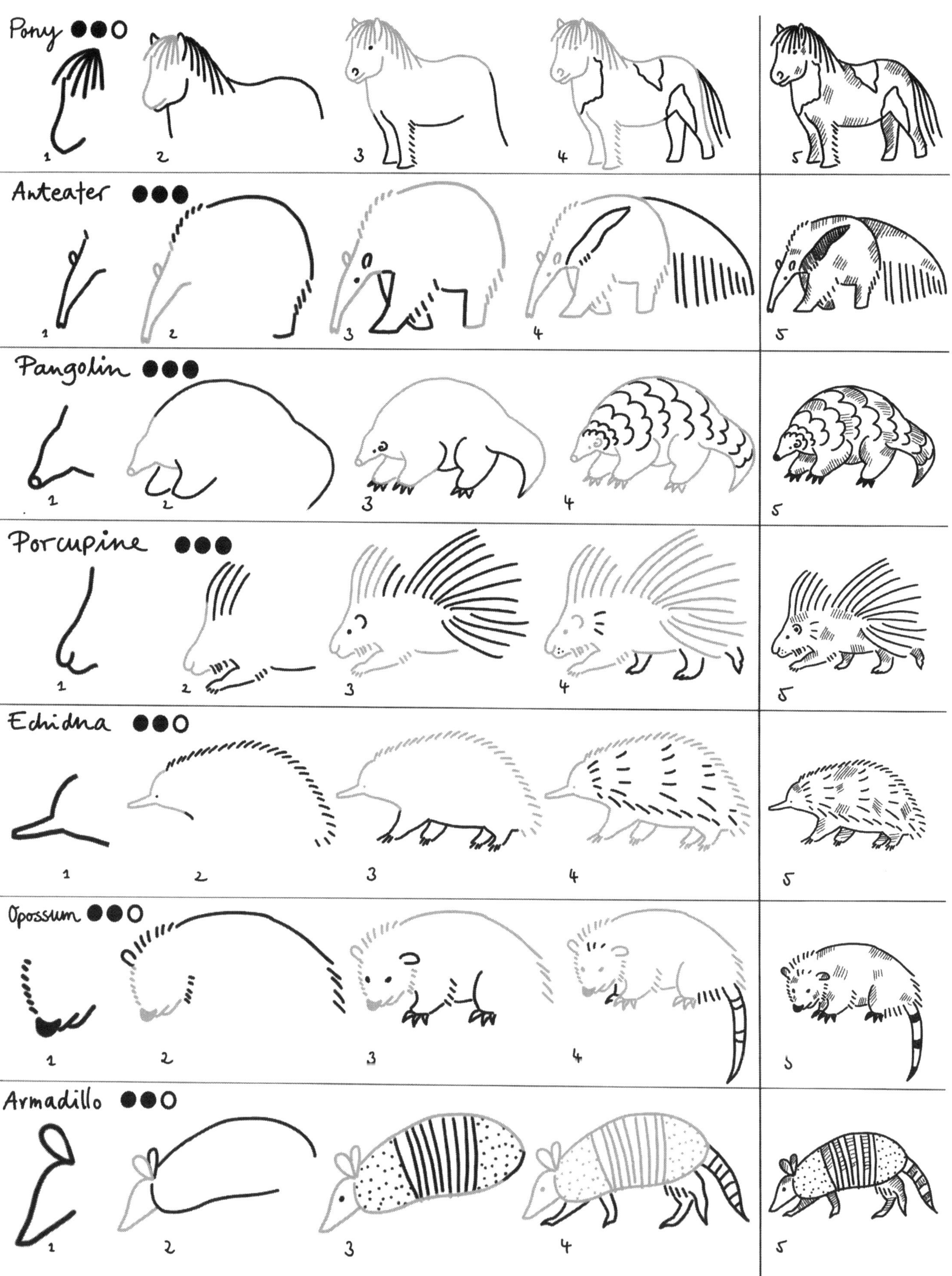
Pony
1
2
3
4
5
Anteater
1
2
3
4
5
Pangolin
1
2
3
4
5
Porcupine
1
2
3
4
5
Echidna
1
2
3
4
5
Opossum
1
2
3
4
5
Armadillo
1
2
3
4
5

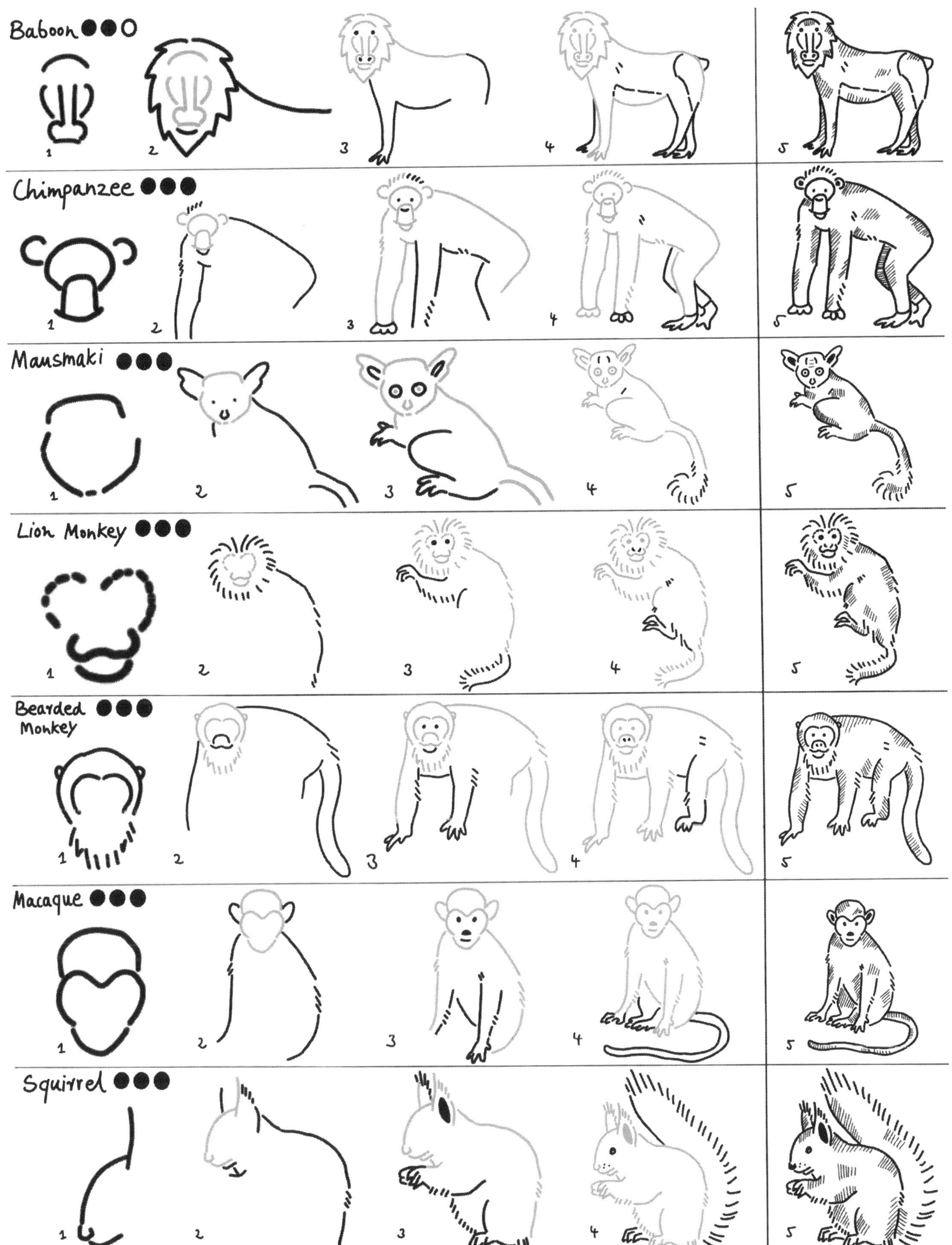

Baboon
1
2
3
4
5
Chimpanzee
1
2
3
4
5
Mausmaki
1
2
3
4
5
Lion Monkey
1
2
3
4
5
Bearded Monkey
1
2
3
4
5
Macaque
1
2
3
4
5
Squirrel
1
2
3
4
5

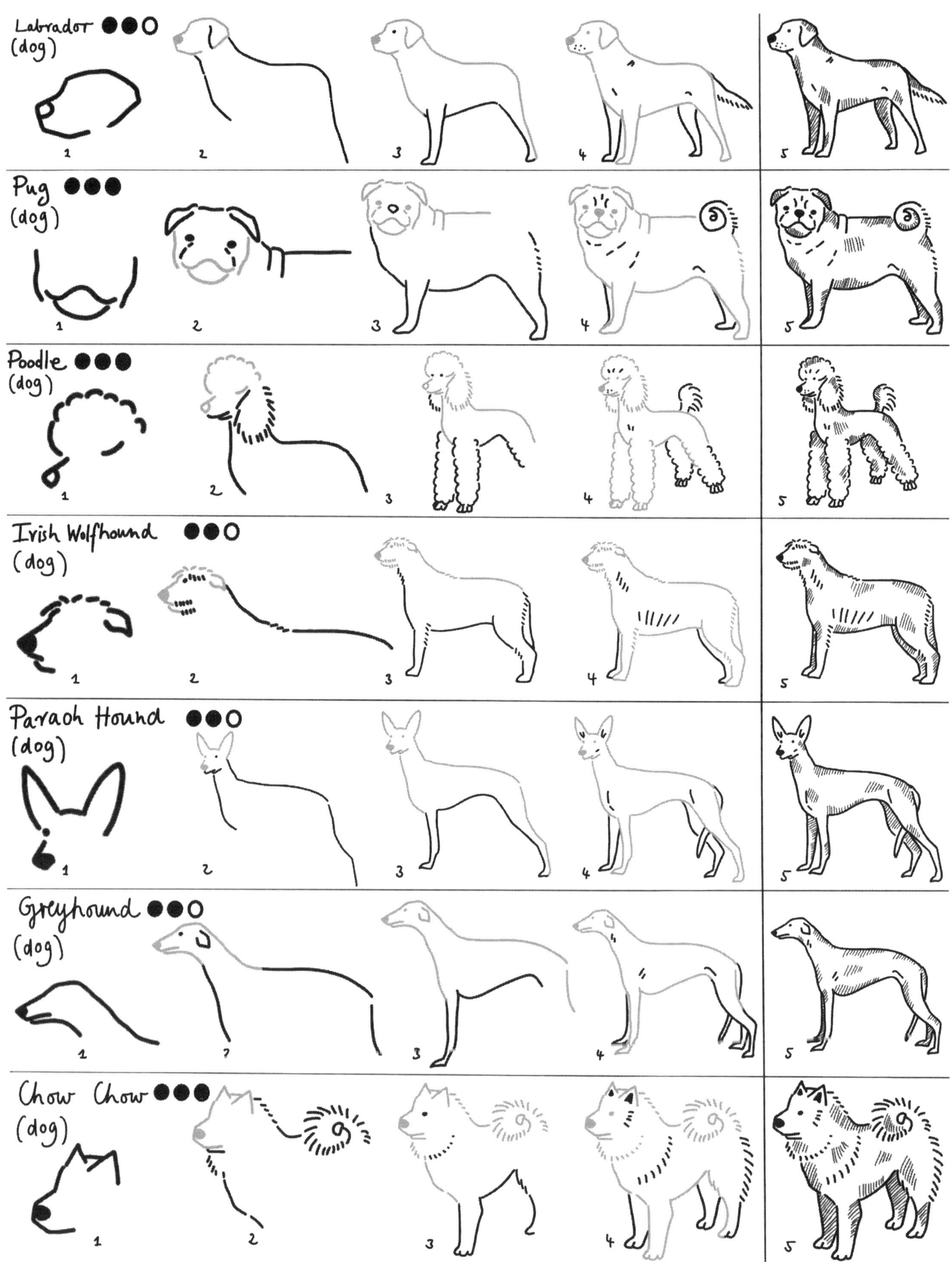
Labrador
(dog)
1
2
3
4
5
Pug
(dog)
1
2
3
4
5
Poodle
(dog)
1
2
3
4
5
Irish Wolfhound
(dog)
1
2
3
4
5
Paraoh Hound
(dog)
1
2
3
4
5
Greyhound
(dog)
1
7
3
4
5
Chow Chow
(dog)
1
2
3
4
5

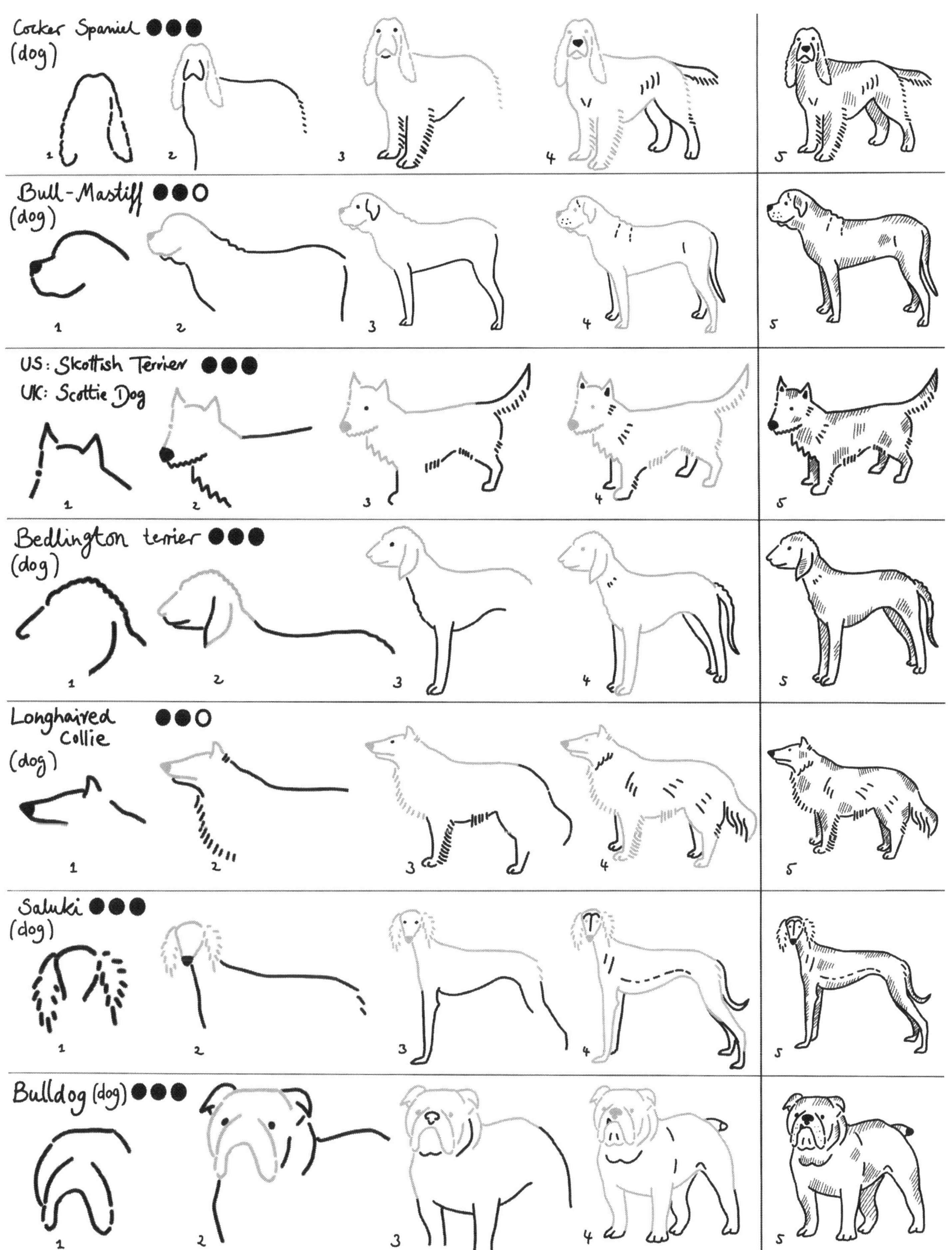
Cocker Spaniel (dog)
Bull-Mastiff (dog)
US: Skottish Terrier
UK: Scottie Dog
Bedlington terrier (dog)
Longhaired Collie (dog)
Saluki (dog)
Bulldog (dog)

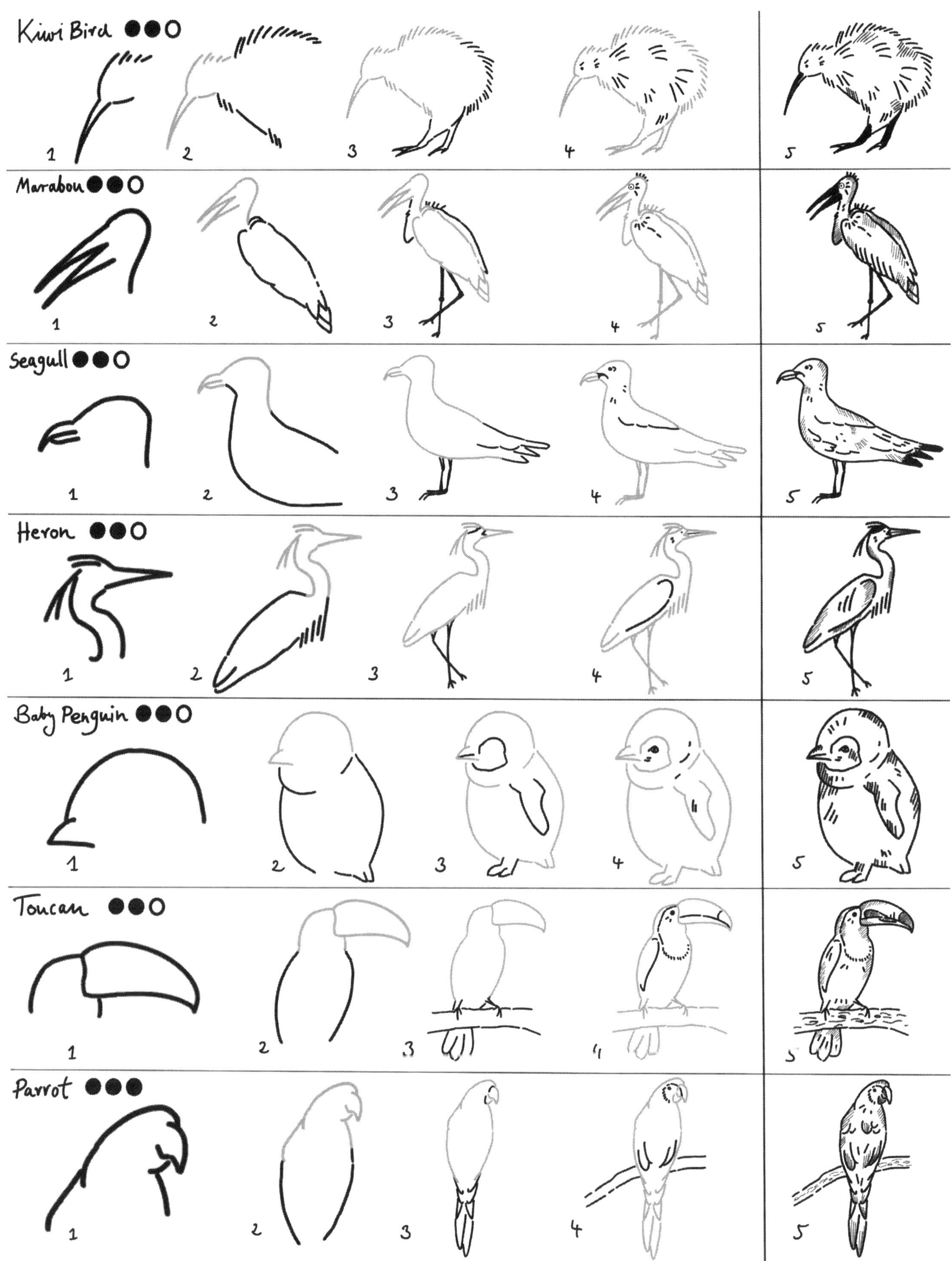
Kiwi Bird
1
2
3
4
5
Marabou
1
2
3
4
5
Seagull
1
2
3
4
5
Heron
1
2
3
4
5
Baby Penguin
1
2
3
4
5
Toucan
1
2
3
4
5
Parrot
1
2
3
4
5

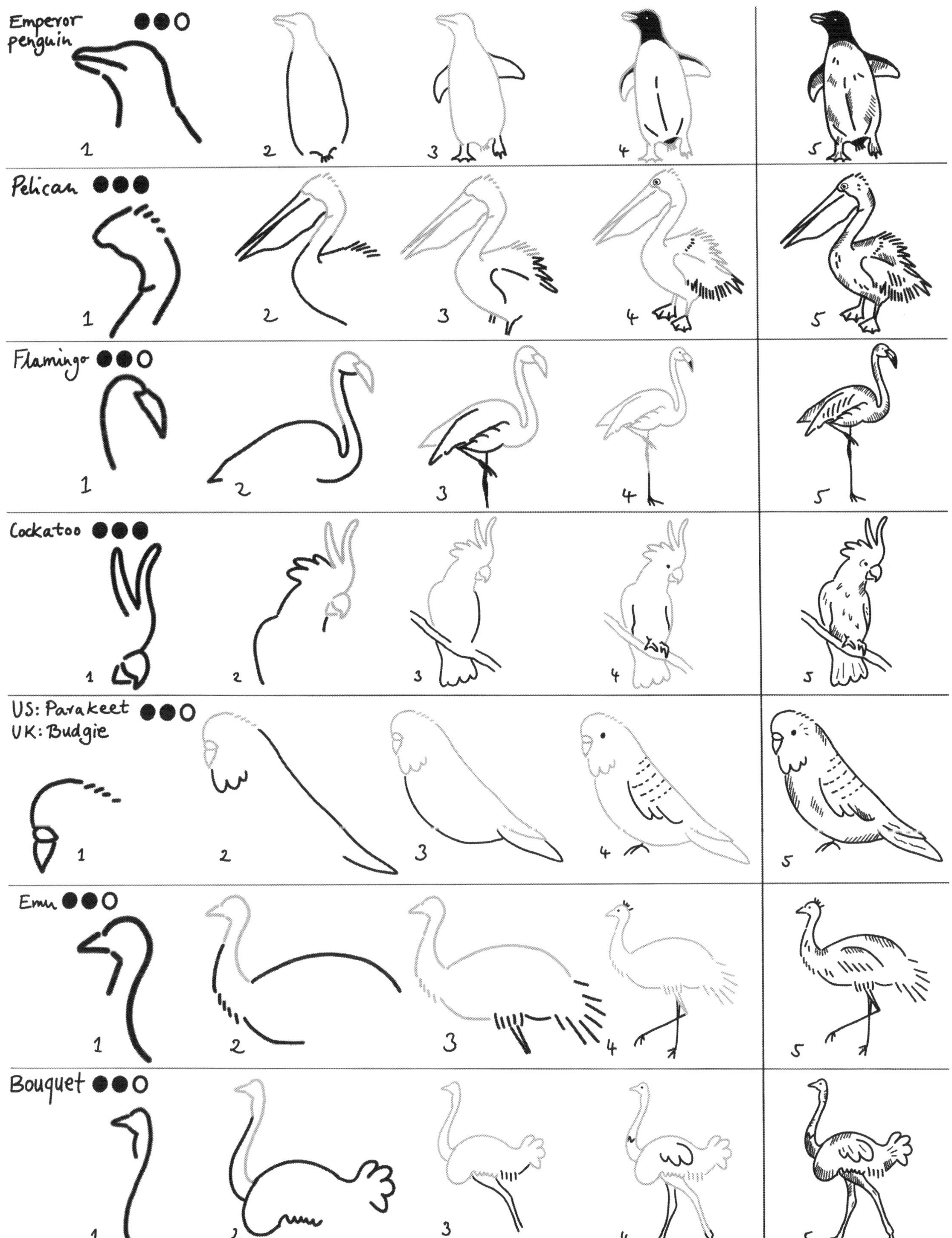

Emperor penguin
1
2
3
4
5
Pelican
1
2
3
4
5
Flamingo
1
2
3
4
5
Cockatoo
1
2
3
4
5
US: Parakeet
UK: Budgie
1
2
3
4
5
Emu
1
2
3
4
5
Bouquet
1
2
3
4
5

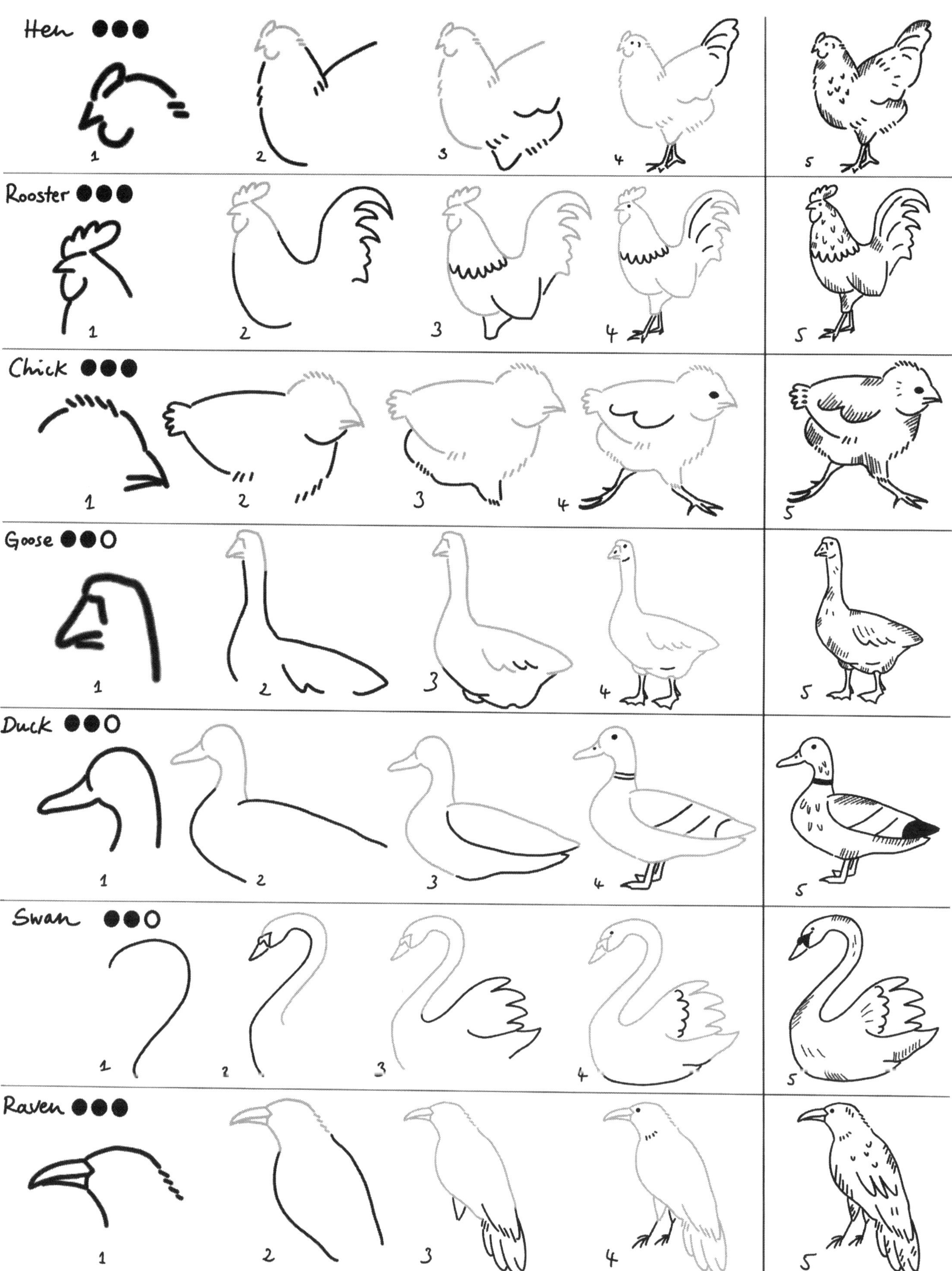
Hen
1
2
3
4
5
Rooster
1
2
3
4
5
Chick
1
2
3
4
5
Goose
1
2
3
4
5
Duck
1
2
3
4
5
Swan
1
2
3
4
5
Raven
1
2
3
4
5

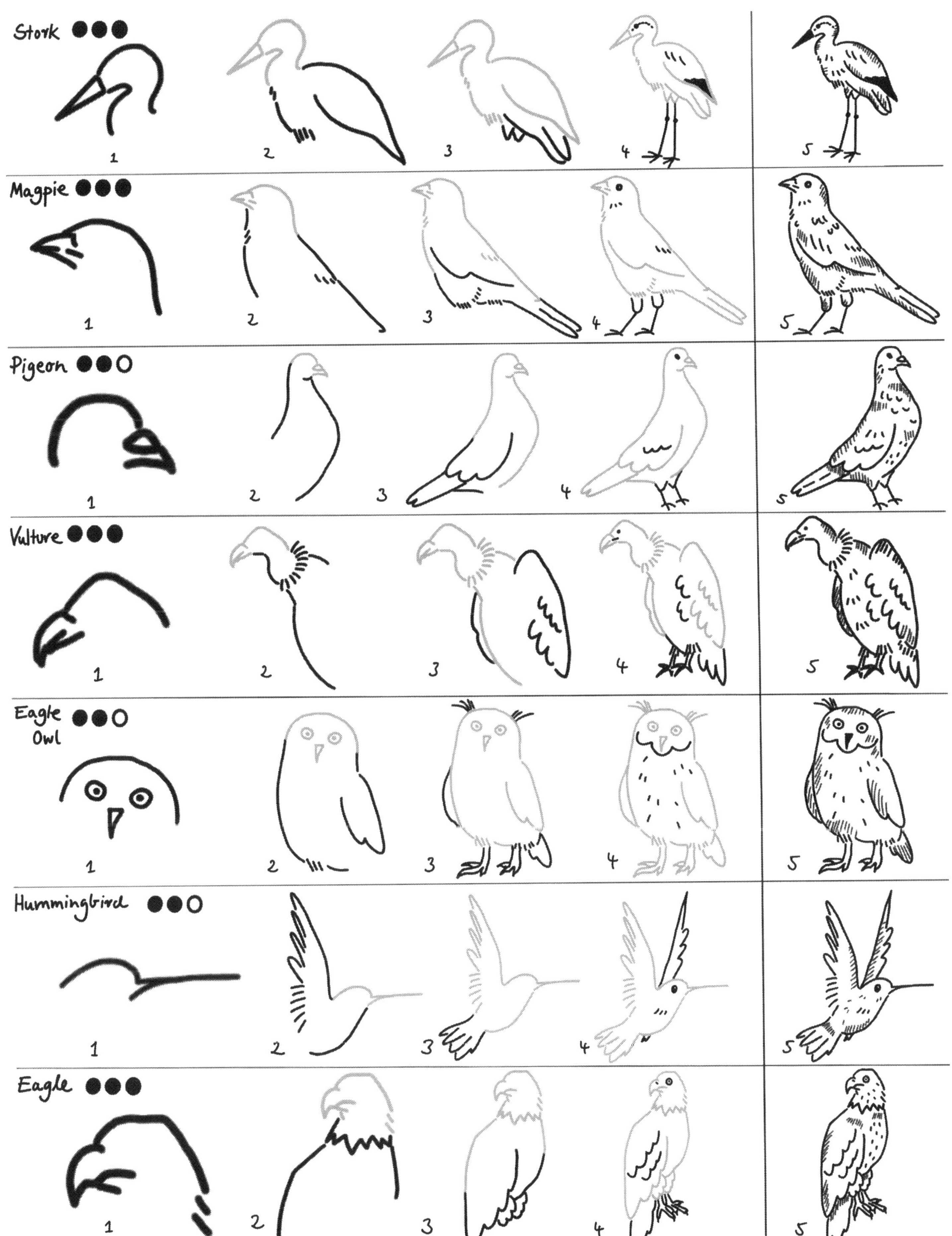
Stork
1
2
3
4
5
Magpie
1
2
3
4
5
Pigeon
1
2
3
4
5
Vulture
1
2
3
4
5
Eagle Owl
1
2
3
4
5
Hummingbird
1
2
3
4
5
Eagle
1
2
3
4
5

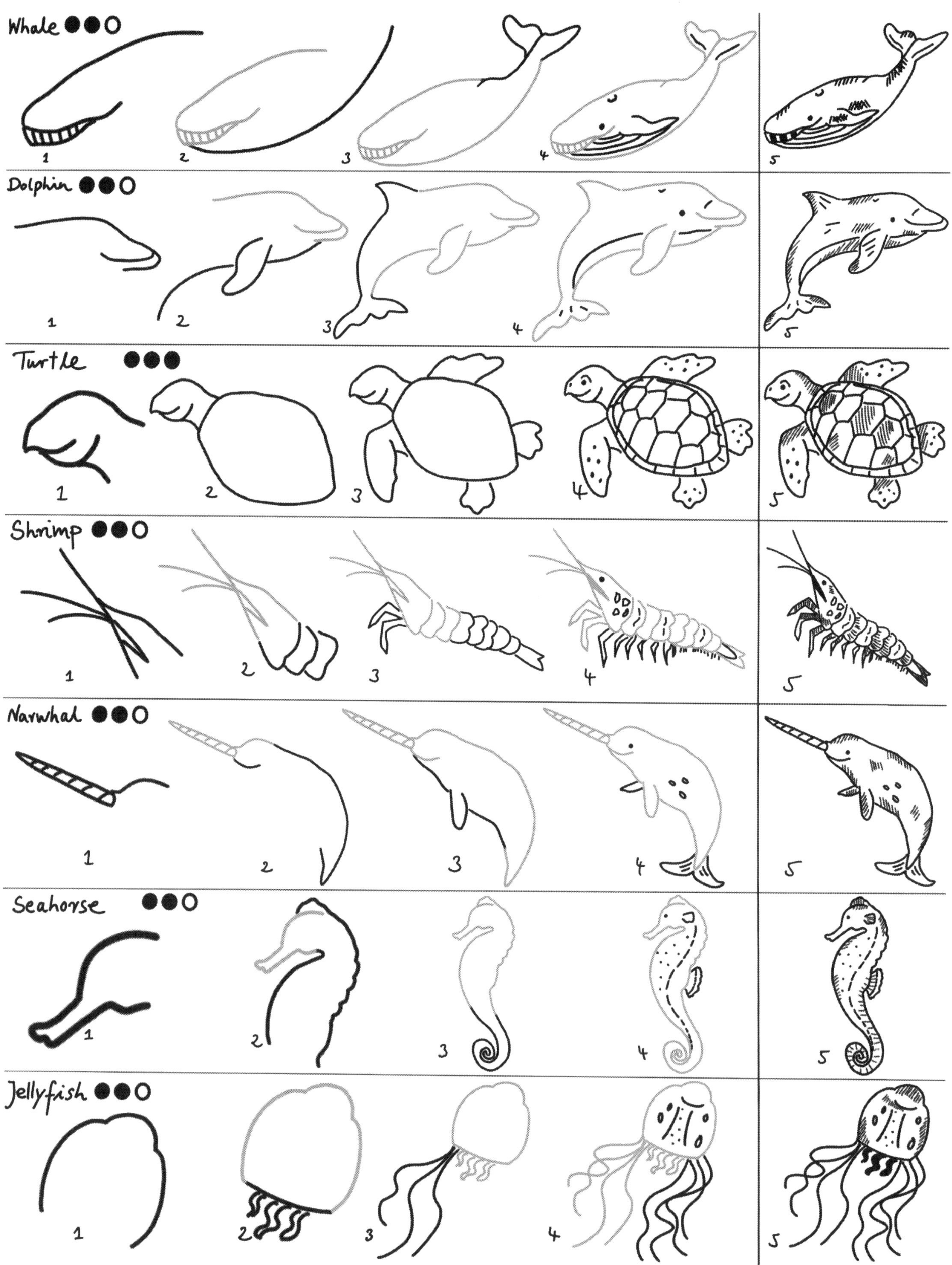

Whale
1
2
3
4
5
Dolphin
1
2
3
4
5
Turtle
1
2
3
4
5
Shrimp
1
2
3
4
5
Narwhal
1
2
3
4
5
Seahorse
1
2
3
4
5
Jellyfish
1
2
3
4
5

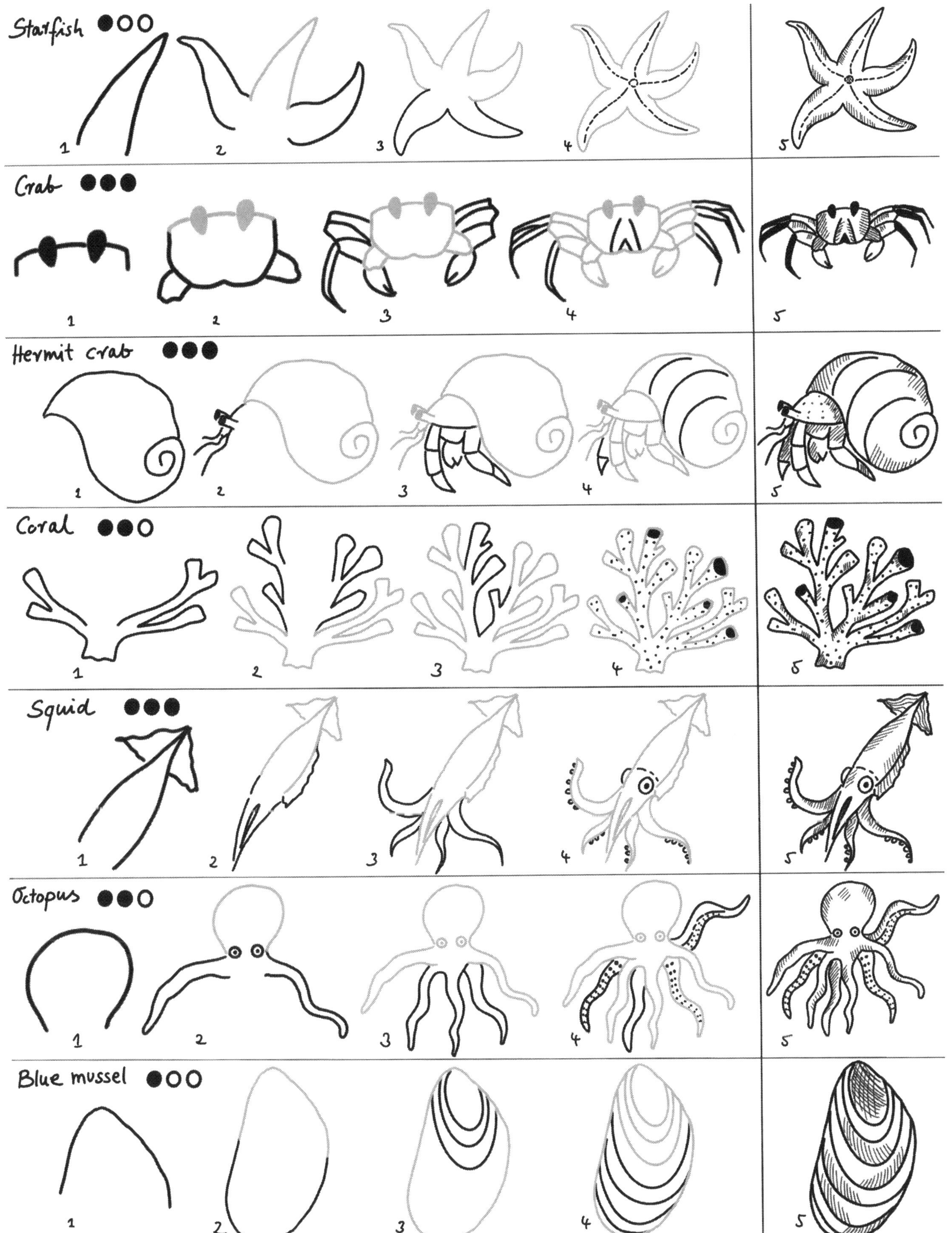
Starfish
1
2
3
4
5
Crab
1
2
3
4
5
Hermit crab
1
2
3
4
5
Coral
1
2
3
4
5
Squid
1
2
3
4
5
Octopus
1
2
3
4
5
Blue mussel
1
2
3
4
5

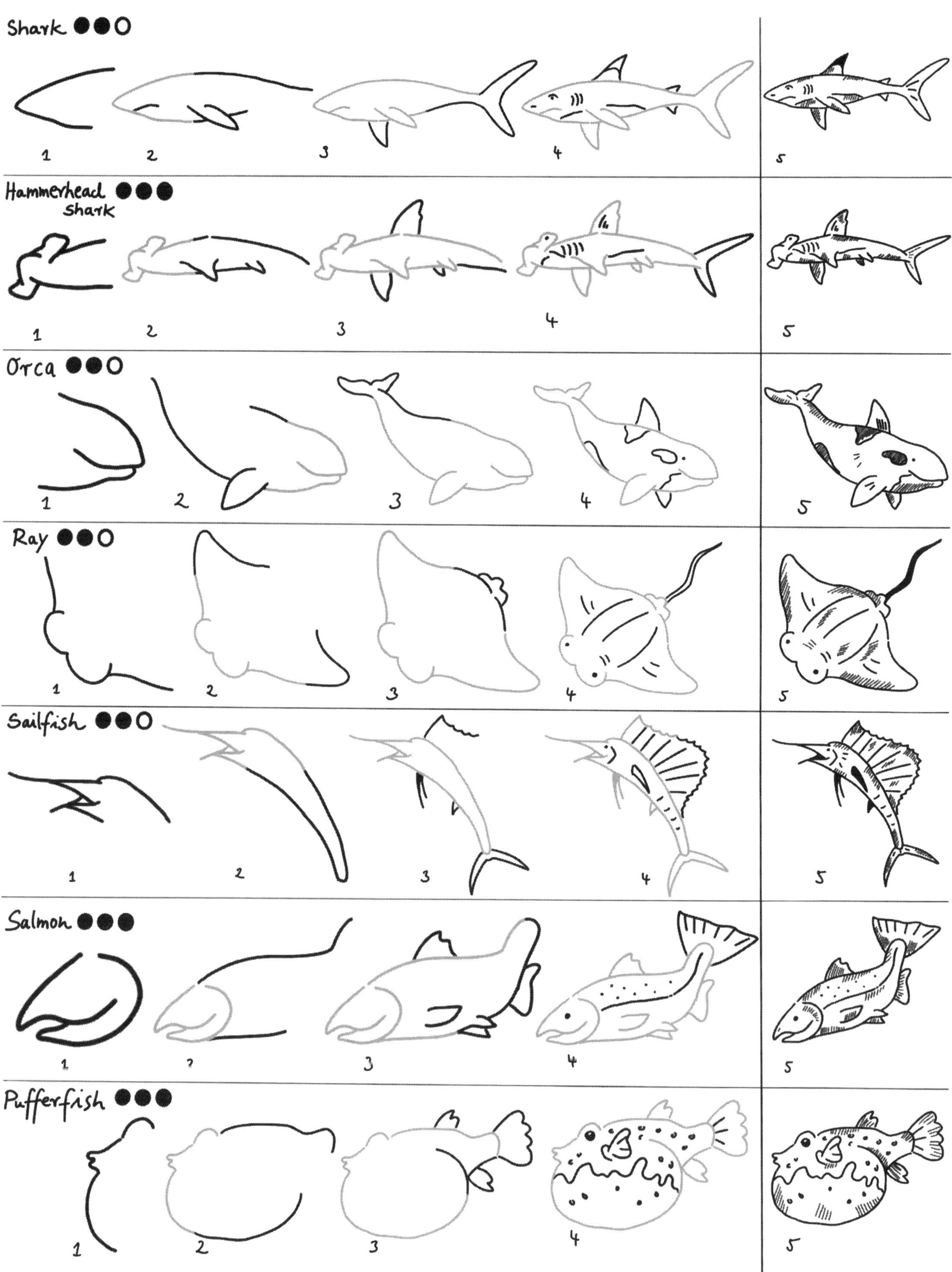
Shark
1
2
3
4
5
Hammerhead shark
1
2
3
4
5
Orca
1
2
3
4
5
Ray
1
2
3
4
5
Sailfish
1
2
3
4
5
Salmon
1
3
4
5
Pufferfish
1
2
3
4
5

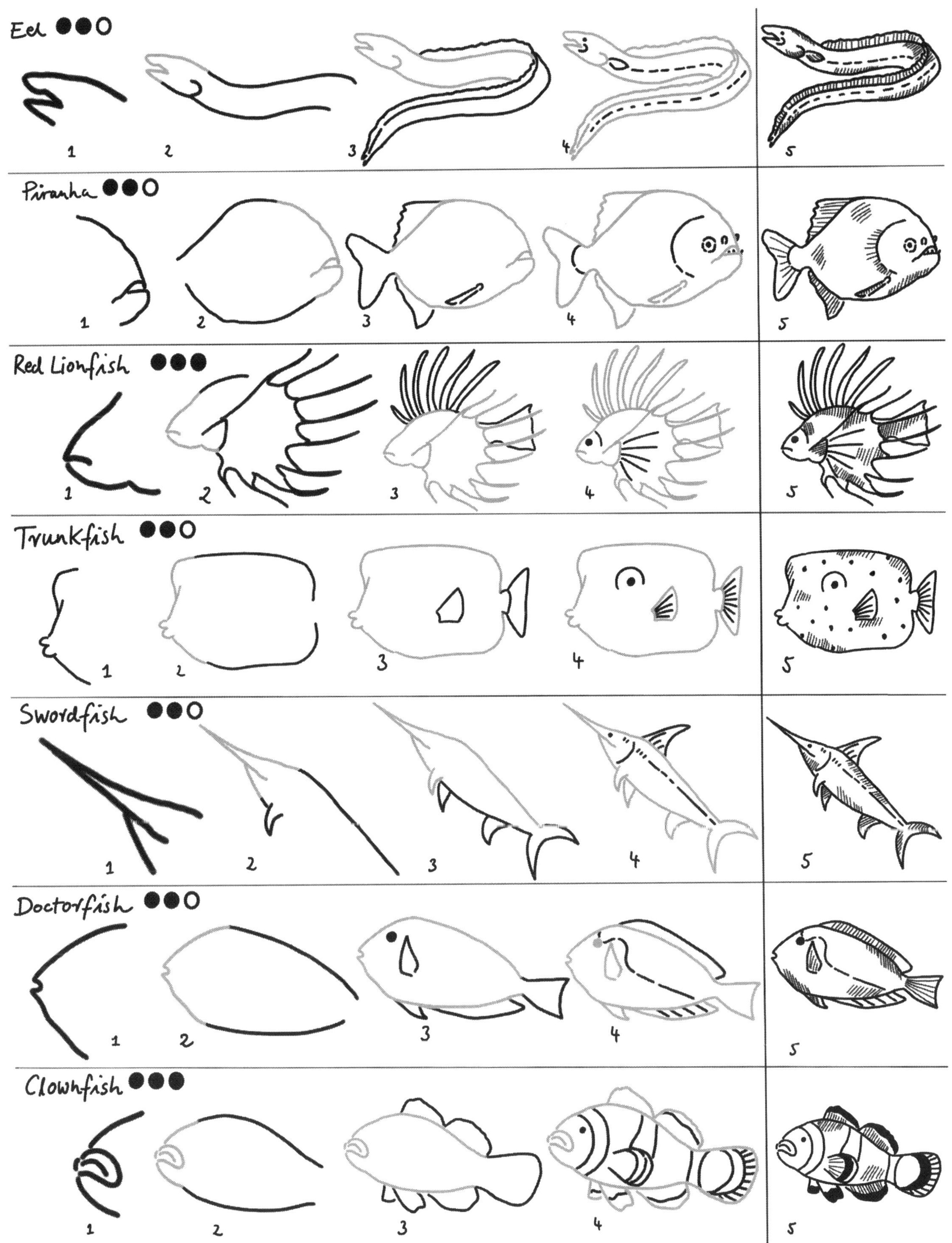
Eel
1
2
3
4
5
Piranha
1
2
3
4
5
Red Lionfish
1
2
3
4
5
Trunkfish
1
2
3
4
5
Swordfish
1
2
3
4
5
Doctorfish
1
2
3
4
5
Clownfish
1
2
3
4
5

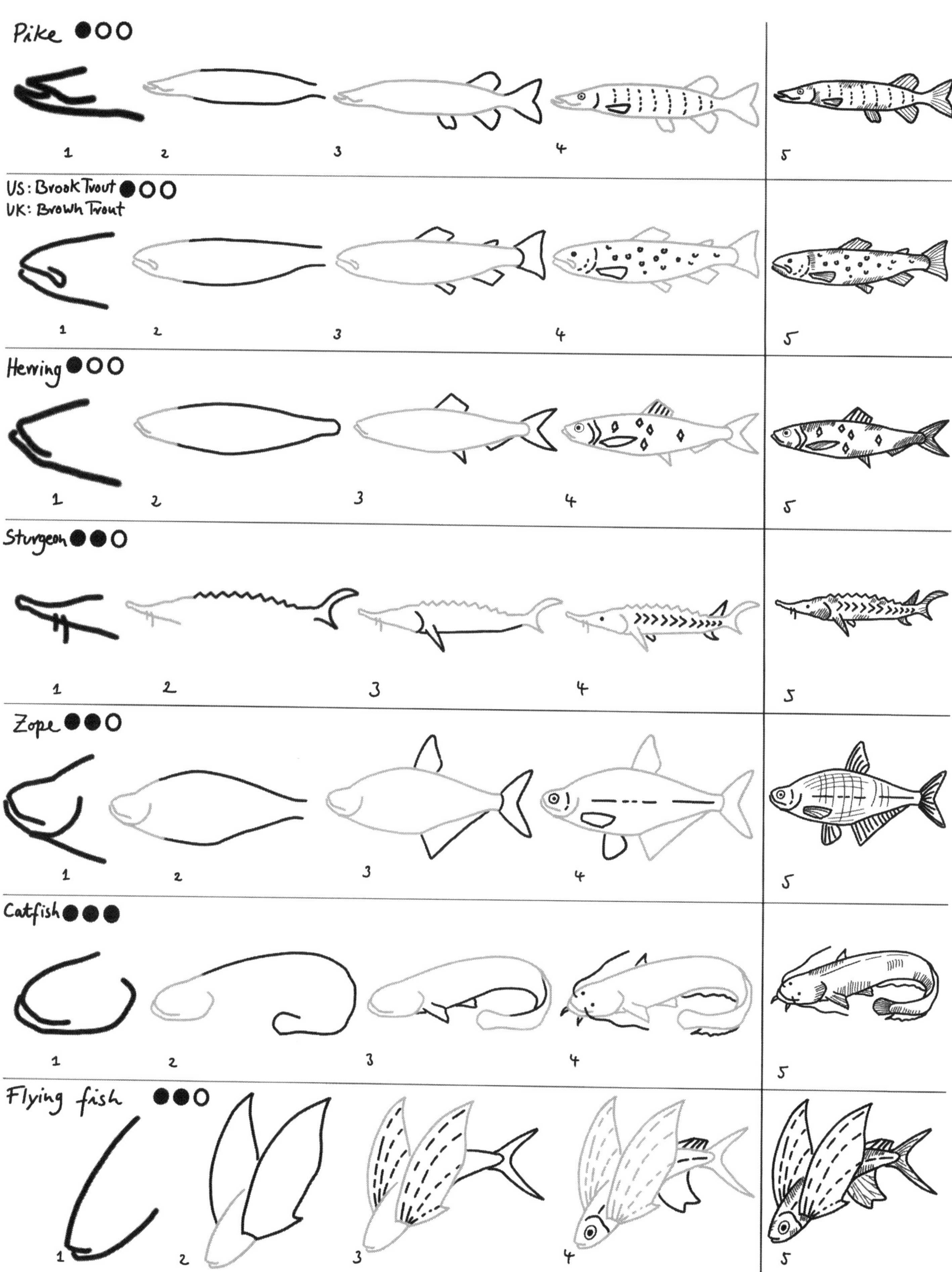
Pike ●○○
1
2
3
4
5
US: Brook Trout ●○○
UK: Brown Trout
1
2
3
4
5
Herring ●○○
1
2
3
4
5
Sturgeon ●●○
1
2
3
4
5
Zope ●●○
1
2
3
4
5
Catfish ●●●
1
2
3
4
5
Flying fish ●●○
1
2
3
4
5

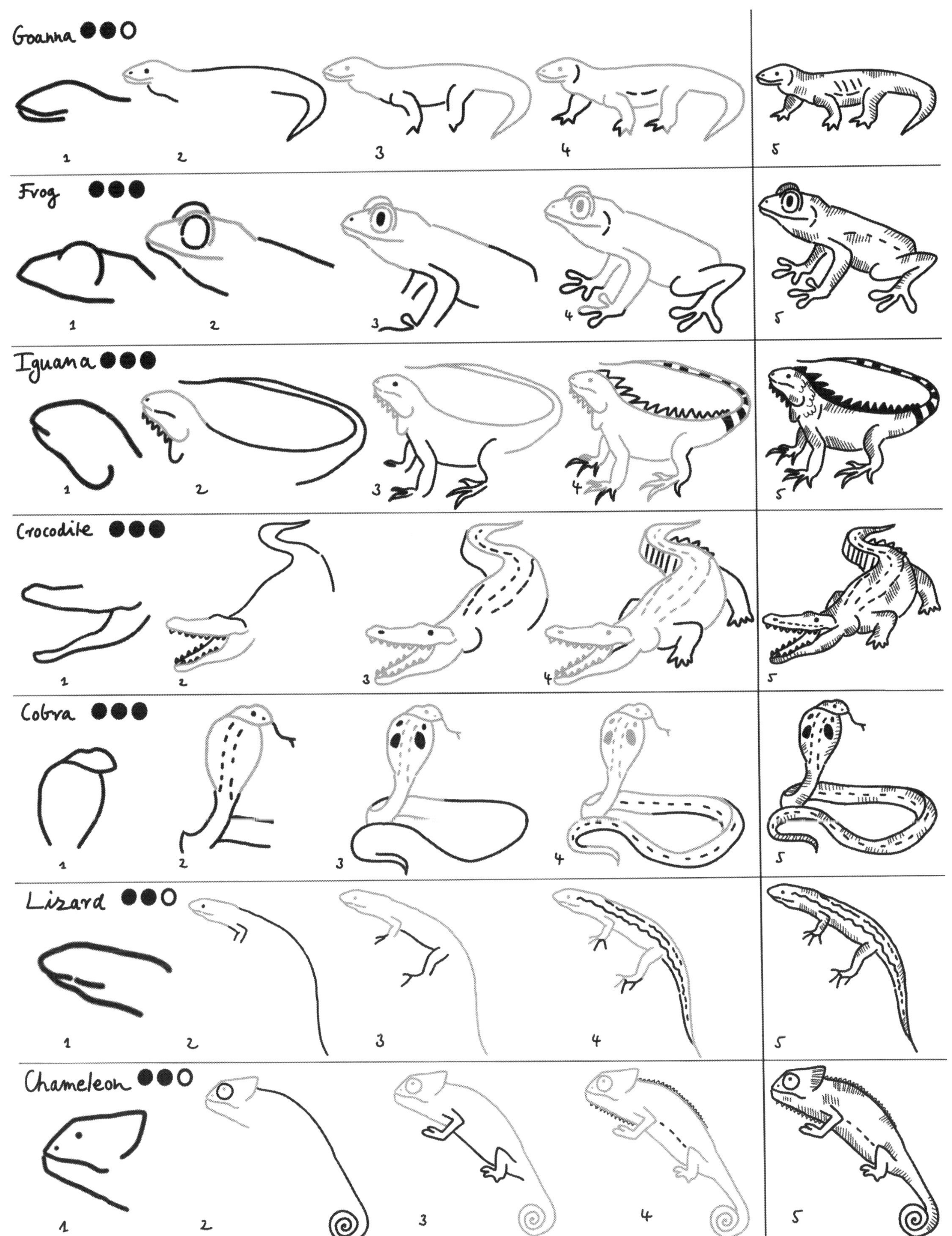
Goanna
1
2
3
4
5
Frog
1
2
3
4
5
Iguana
1
2
3
4
5
Crocodile
1
2
3
4
5
Cobra
1
2
3
4
5
Lizard
1
2
3
4
5
Chameleon
1
2
3
4
5

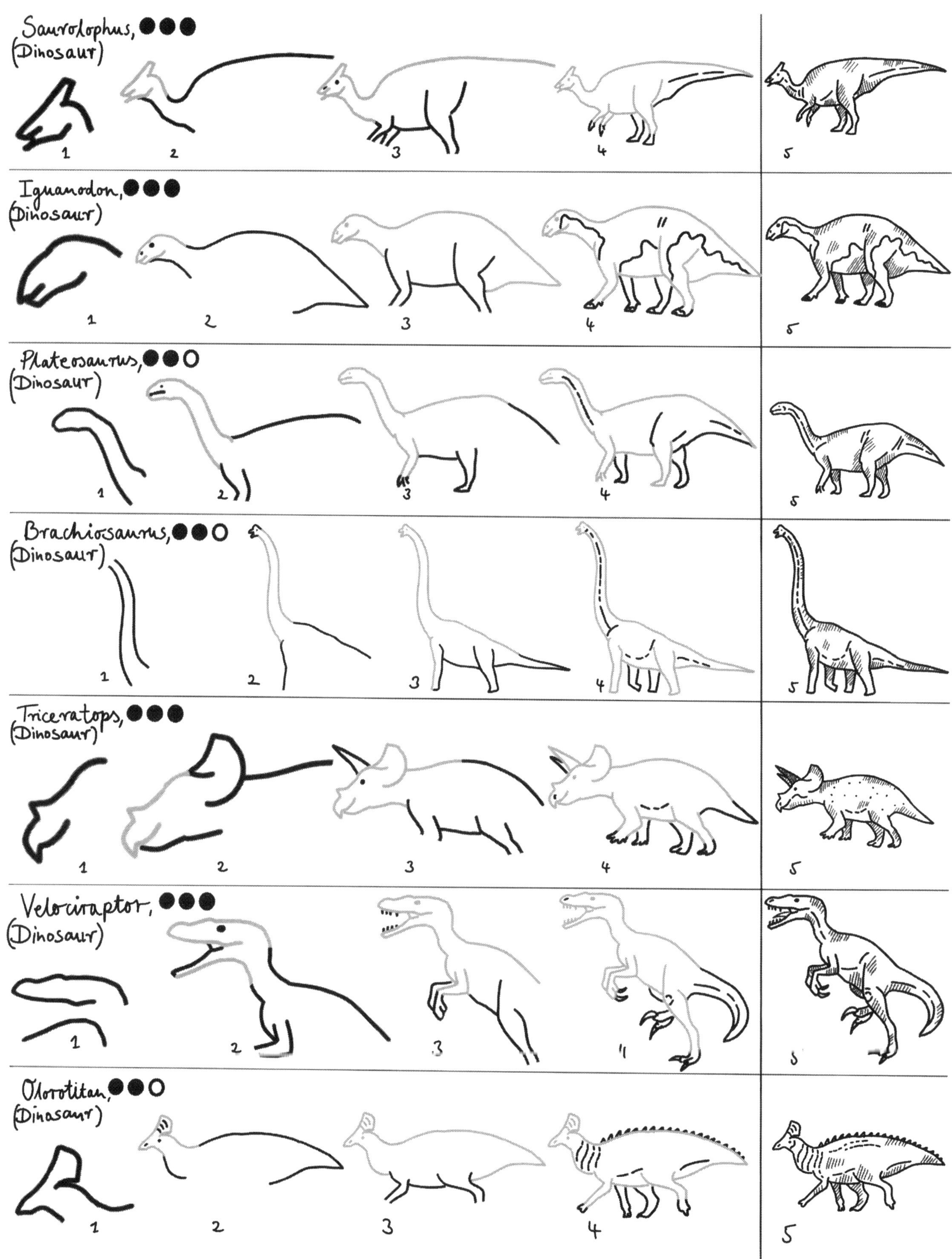

Saurolophus, ●●●
(Dinosaur)
1
2
3
4
5
Iguanodon, ●●●
(Dinosaur)
1
2
3
4
5
Plateosaurus, ●●○
(Dinosaur)
1
2
3
4
5
Brachiosaurus, ●●○
(Dinosaur)
1
2
3
4
5
Triceratops, ●●●
(Dinosaur)
1
2
3
4
5
Velociraptor, ●●●
(Dinosaur)
1
2
3
4
5
Olorotitan, ●●○
(Dinosaur)
1
2
3
4
5

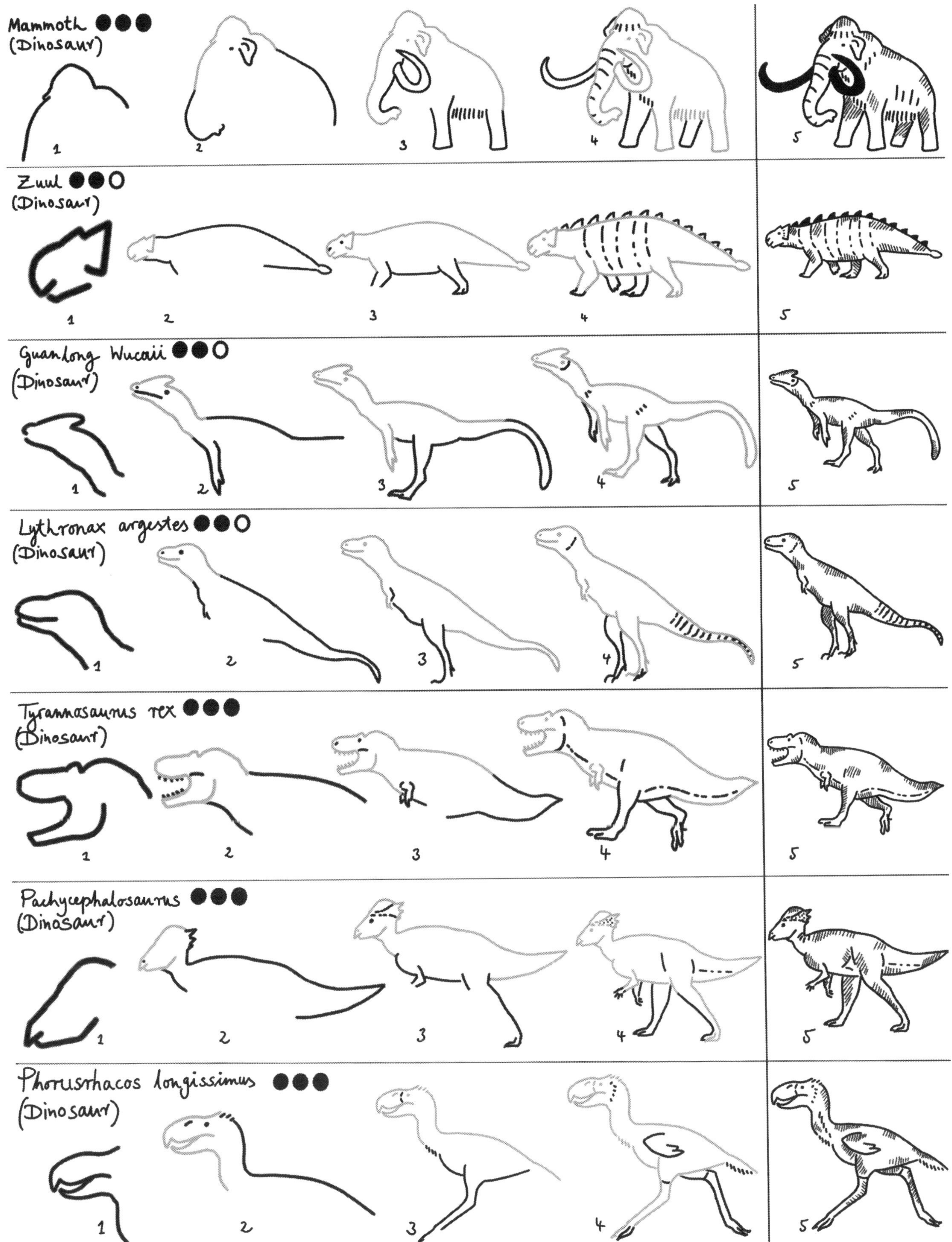
Mammoth
(Dinosaur)
1
2
3
4
5
Zuul
(Dinosaur)
1
2
3
4
5
Guanlong Wucaii
(Dinosaur)
1
2
3
4
5
Lythronax argestes
(Dinosaur)
1
2
3
4
5
Tyrannosaurus rex
(Dinosaur)
1
2
3
4
5
Pachycephalosaurus
(Dinosaur)
1
2
3
4
5
Phorusrhacos longissimus
(Dinosaur)
1
2
3
4
5

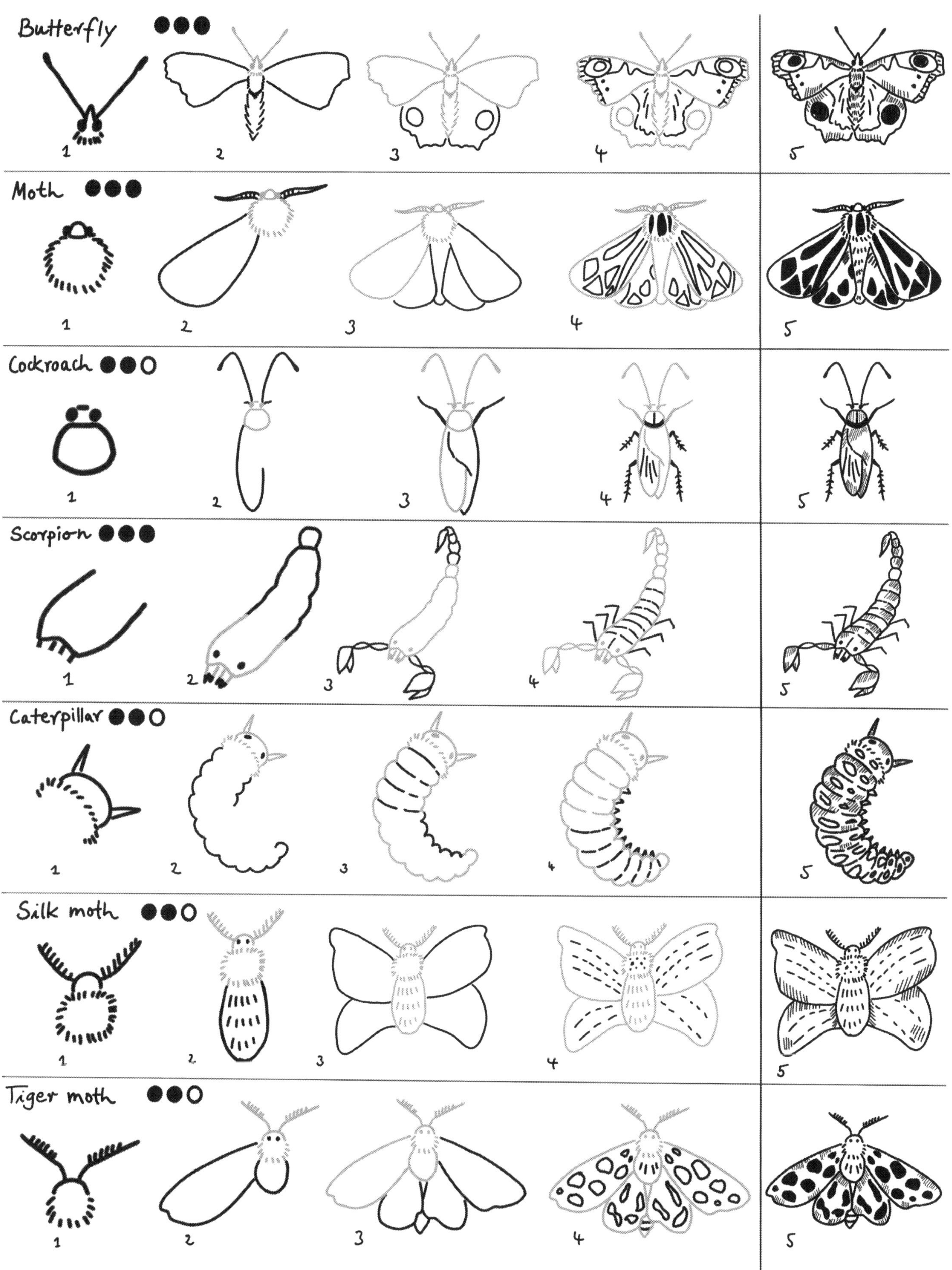
Butterfly
1
2
3
4
5
Moth
1
2
3
4
5
Cockroach
1
2
3
4
5
Scorpion
1
2
3
4
5
Caterpillar
1
2
3
4
5
Silk moth
1
2
3
4
5
Tiger moth
1
2
3
4
5

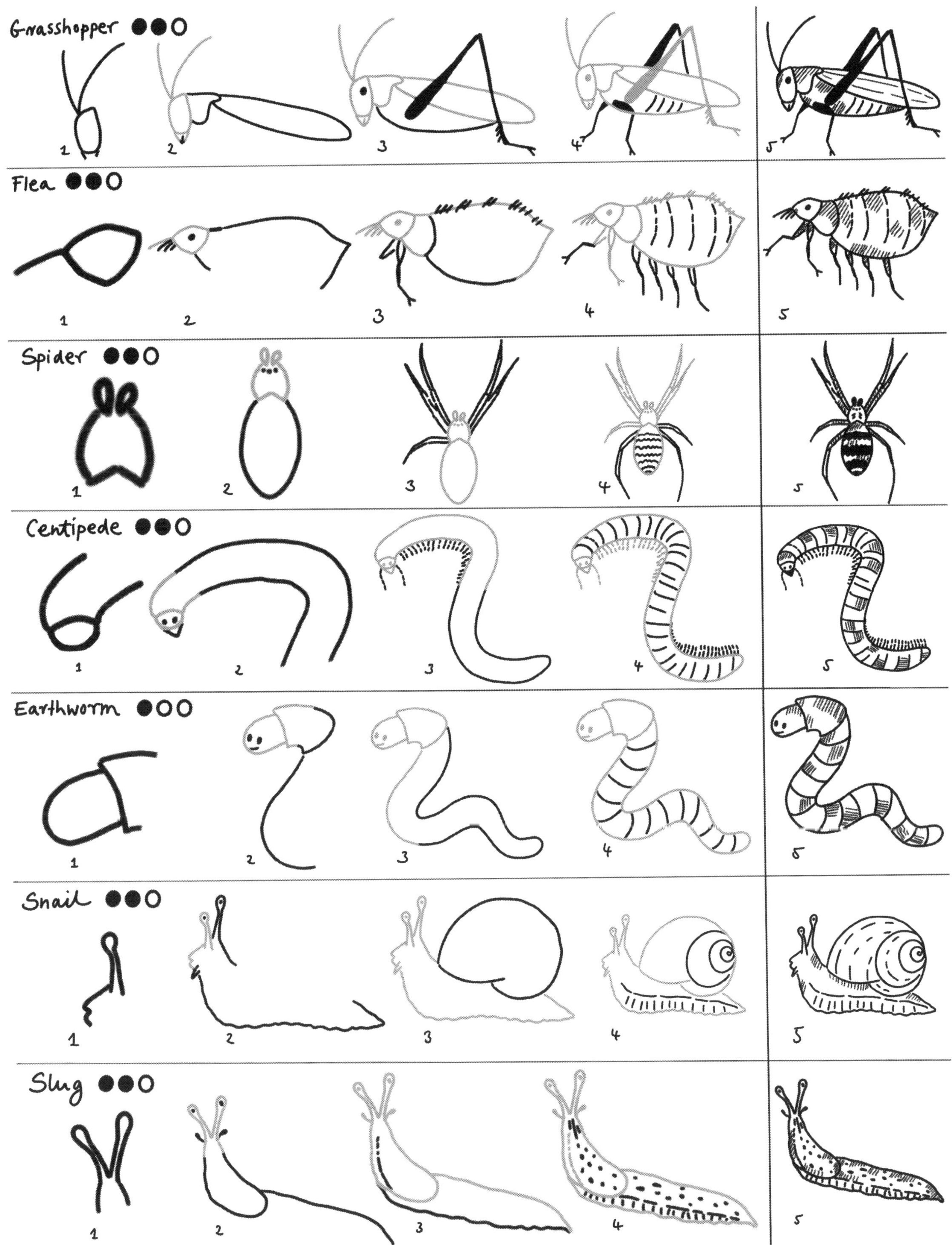
Grasshopper
1
2
3
4
5
Flea
1
2
3
4
5
Spider
1
2
3
4
5
Centipede
1
2
3
4
5
Earthworm
1
2
3
4
5
Snail
1
2
3
4
5
Slug
1
2
3
4
5

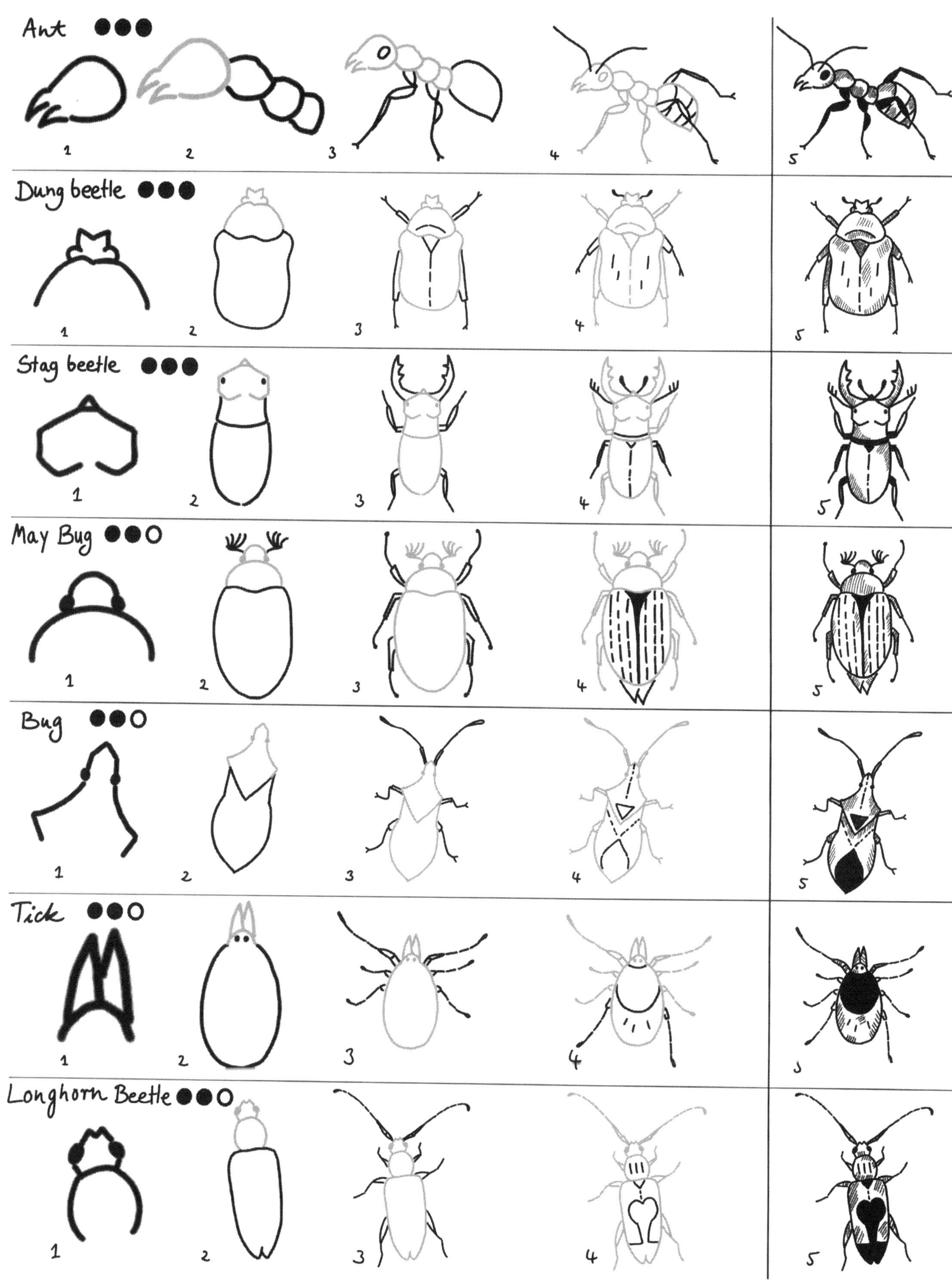
Ant ●●●
1
2
3
4
5
Dung beetle ●●●
1
2
3
4
5
Stag beetle ●●●
1
2
3
4
5
May Bug ●●○
1
2
3
4
5
Bug ●●○
1
2
3
4
5
Tick ●●○
1
2
3
4
5
Longhorn Beetle ●●○
1
2
3
4
5

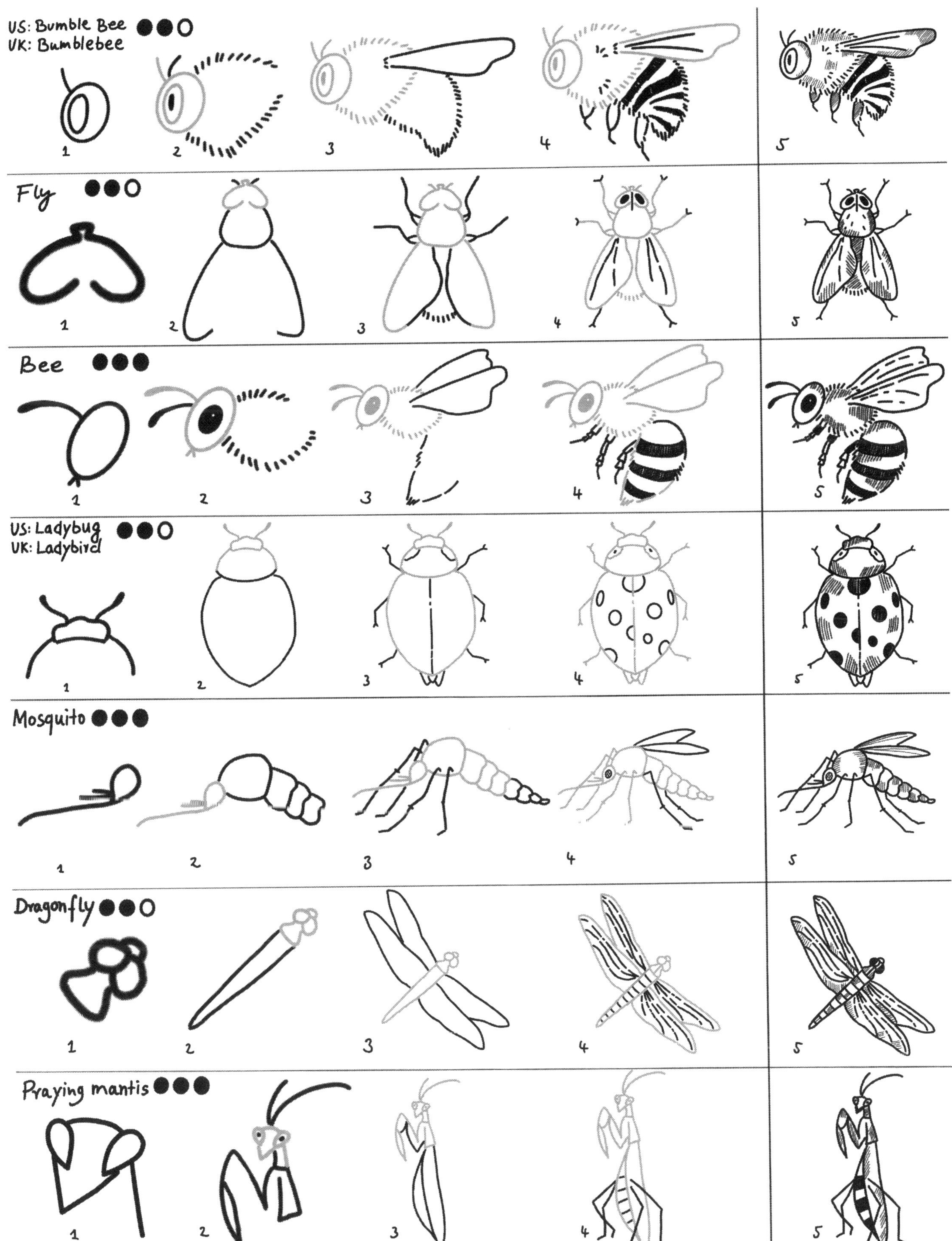
US: Bumble Bee
UK: Bumblebee
1
2
3
4
5
Fly
1
2
3
4
5
Bee
1
2
3
4
5
US: Ladybug
UK: Ladybird
1
2
3
4
5
Mosquito
1
2
3
4
5
Dragonfly
1
2
3
4
5
Praying mantis
1
2
3
4
5

# NATURE / PLANTS

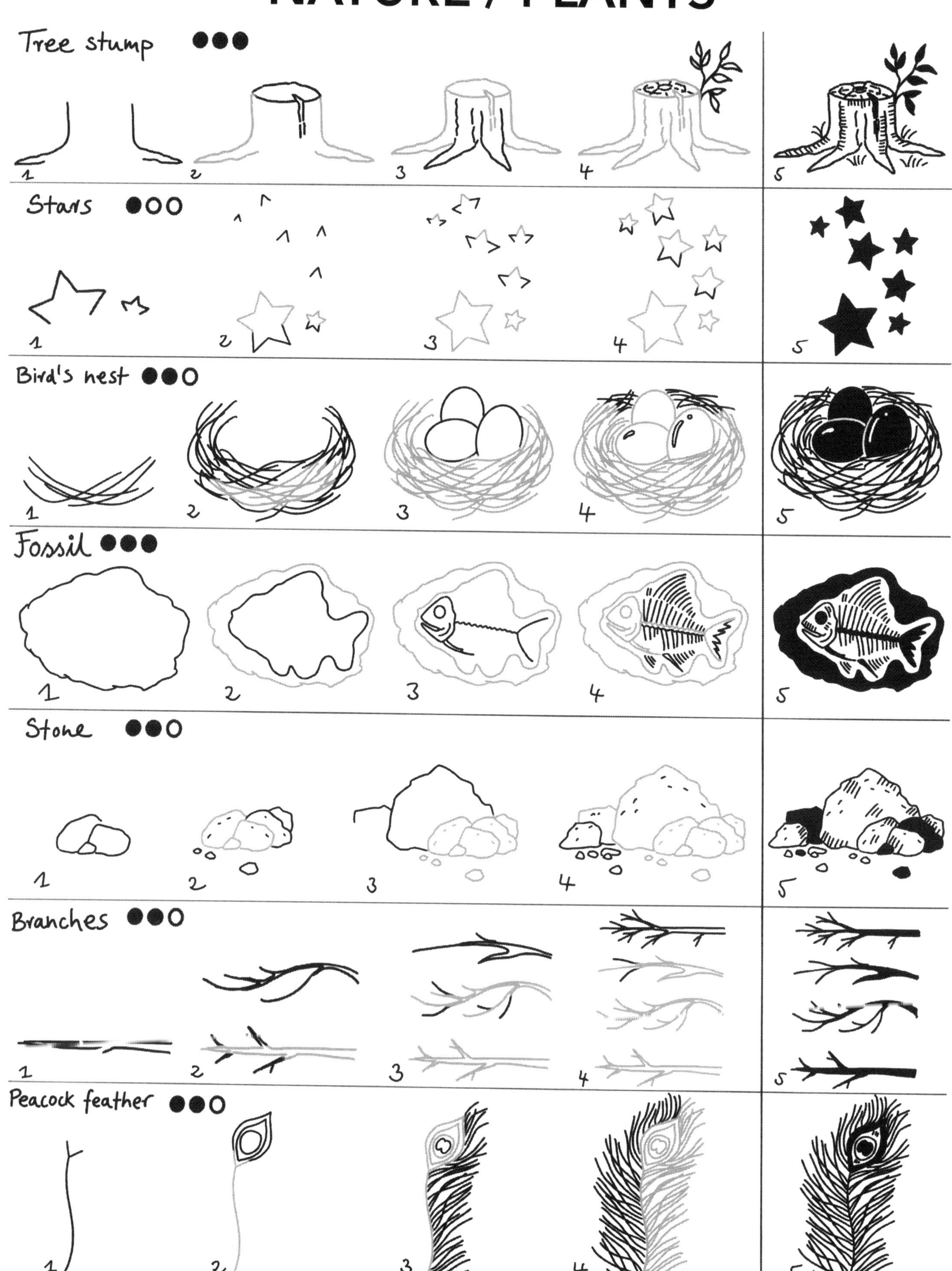

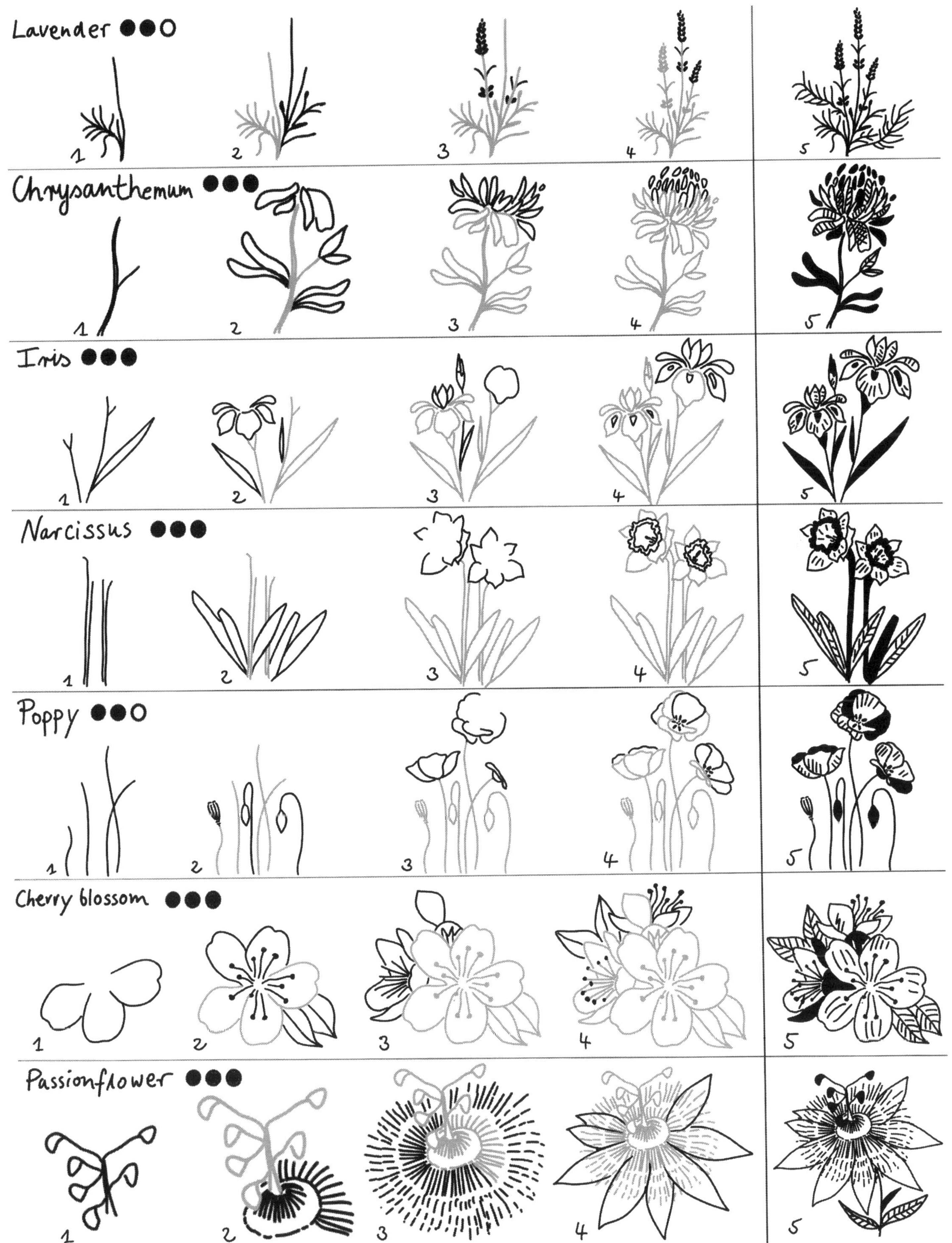
Lavender
1
2
3
4
5
Chrysanthemum
1
2
3
4
5
Iris
1
2
3
4
5
Narcissus
1
2
3
4
5
Poppy
1
2
3
4
5
Cherry blossom
1
2
3
4
5
Passionflower
1
2
3
4
5

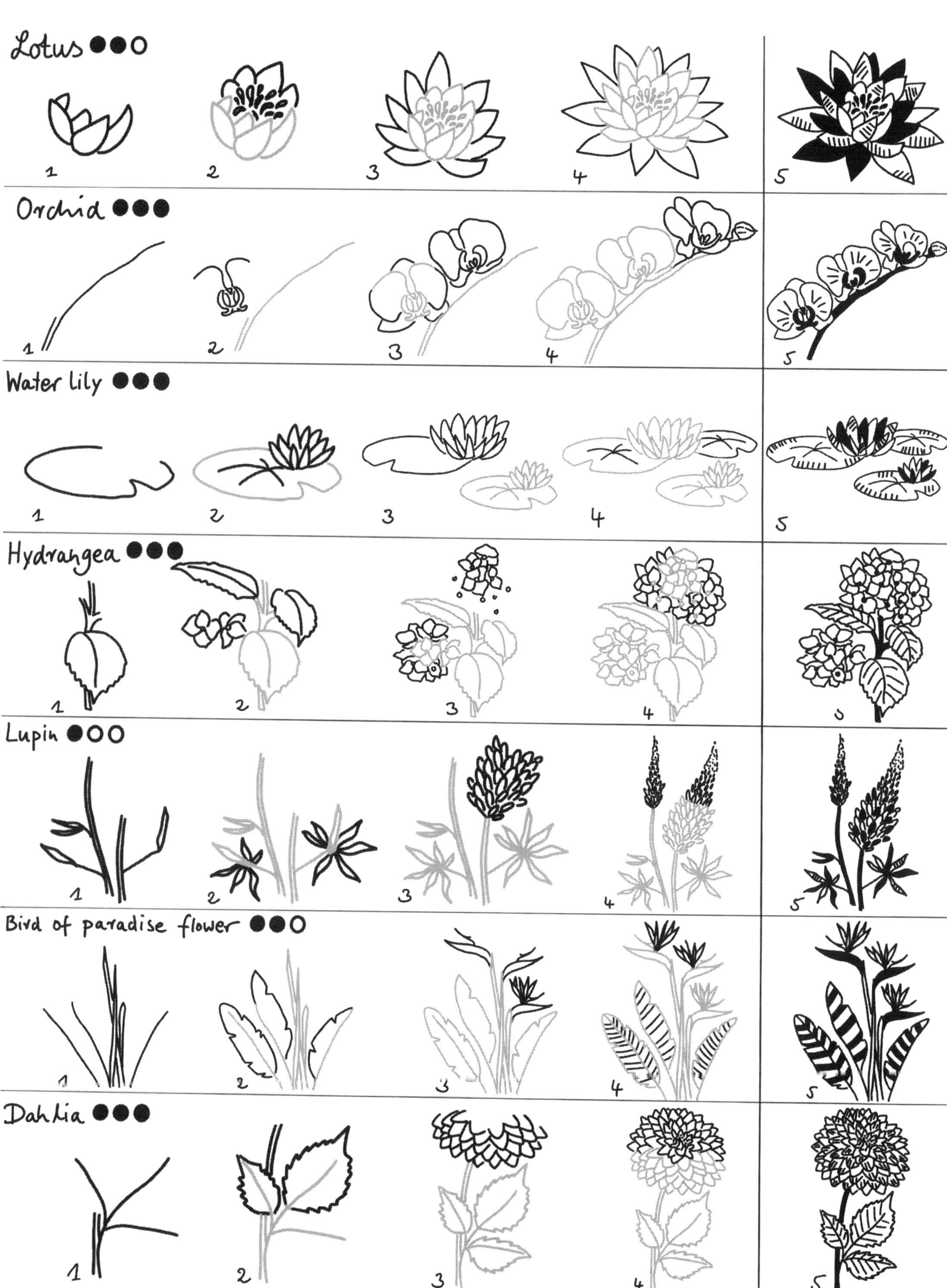
Lotus
1
2
3
4
5
Orchid
1
2
3
4
5
Water Lily
1
2
3
4
5
Hydrangea
1
2
3
4
5
Lupin
1
2
3
4
5
Bird of paradise flower
1
2
3
4
5
Dahlia
1
2
3
4
5

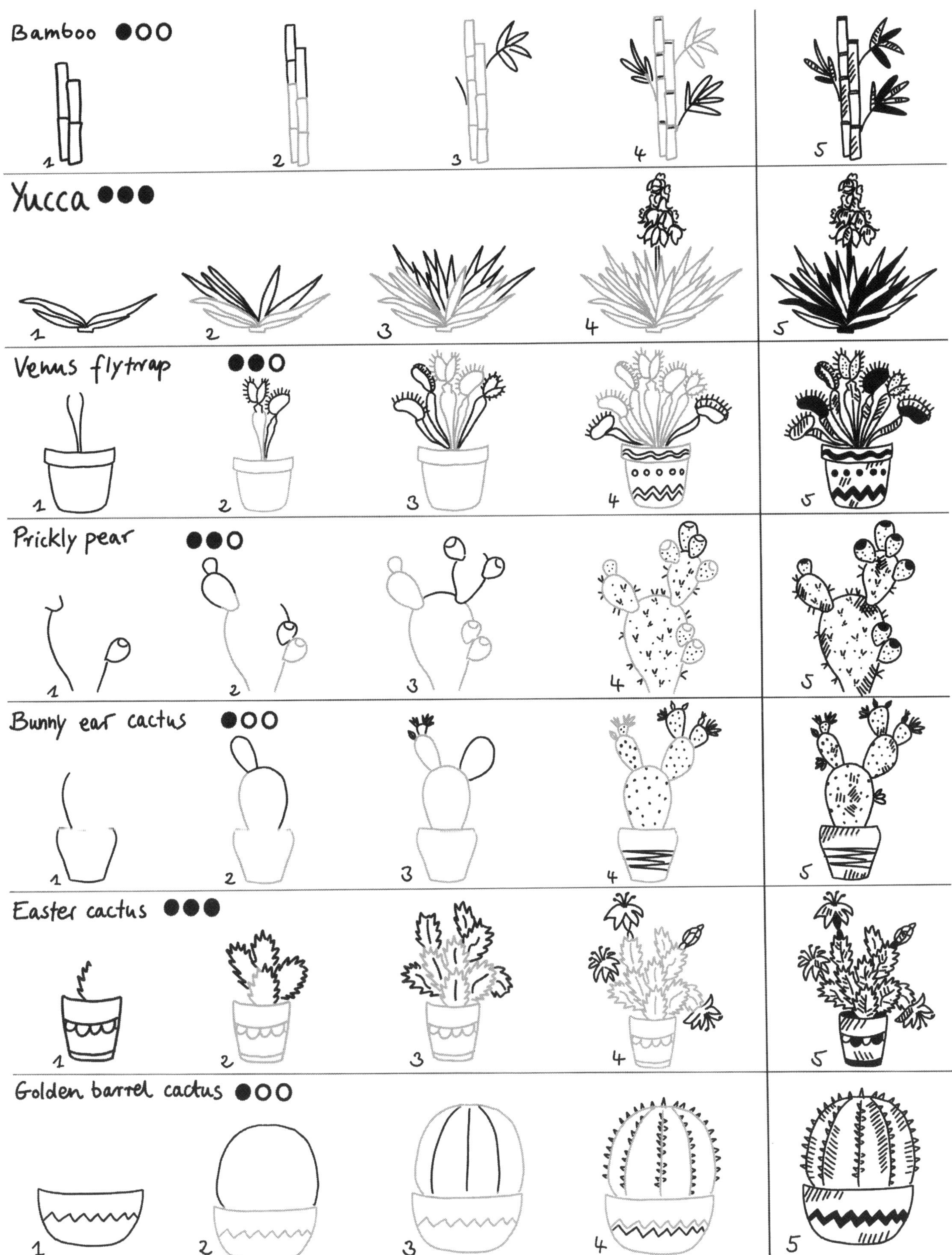
Bamboo
1
2
3
4
5
Yucca
1
2
3
4
5
Venus flytrap
1
2
3
4
5
Prickly pear
1
2
3
4
5
Bunny ear cactus
1
2
3
4
5
Easter cactus
1
2
3
4
5
Golden barrel cactus
1
2
3
4
5

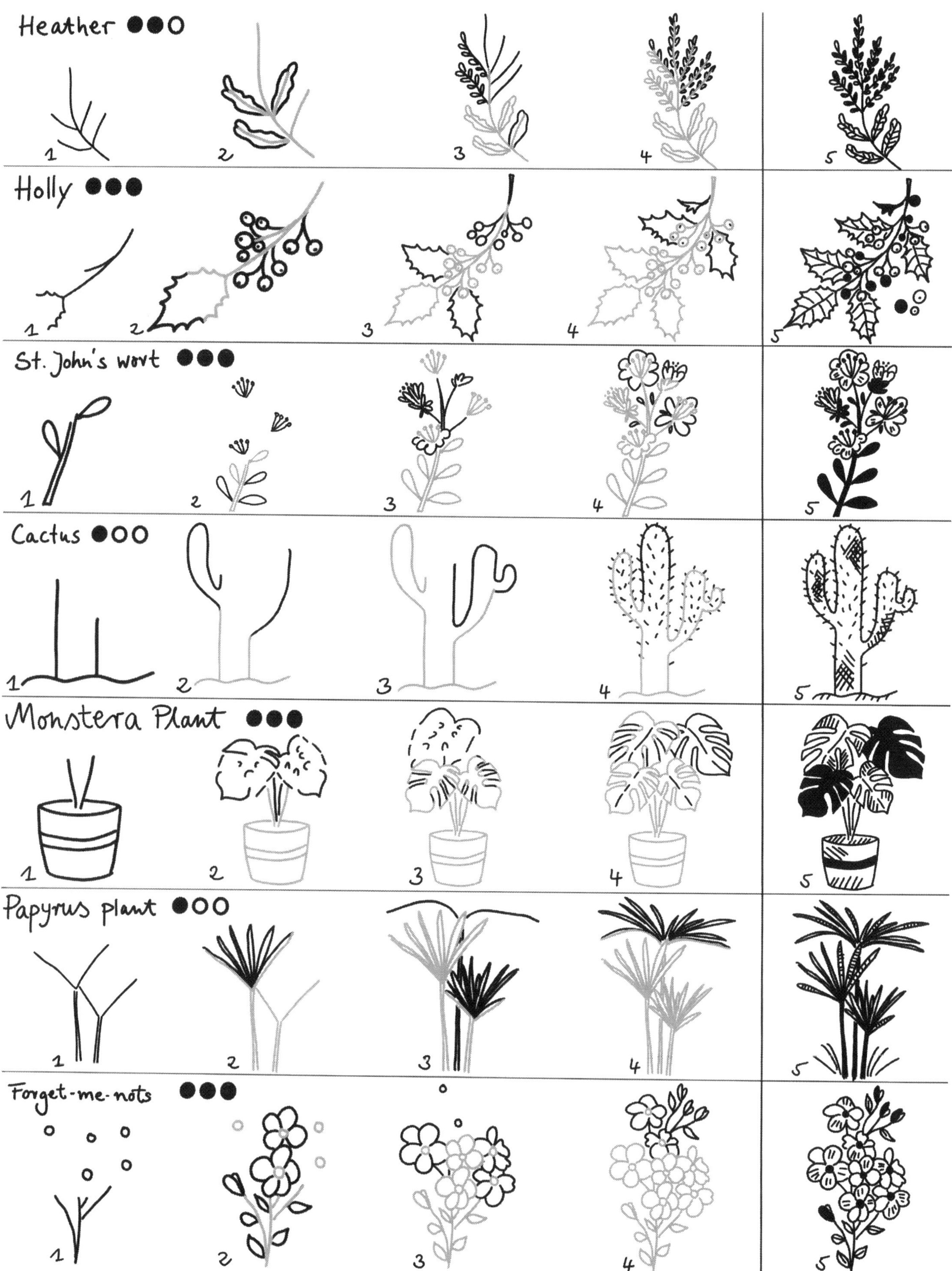
Heather
1
2
3
4
5
Holly
1
2
3
4
5
St. John's wort
1
2
3
4
5
Cactus
1
2
3
4
5
Monstera Plant
1
2
3
4
5
Papyrus plant
1
2
3
4
5
Forget-me-nots
1
2
3
4
5

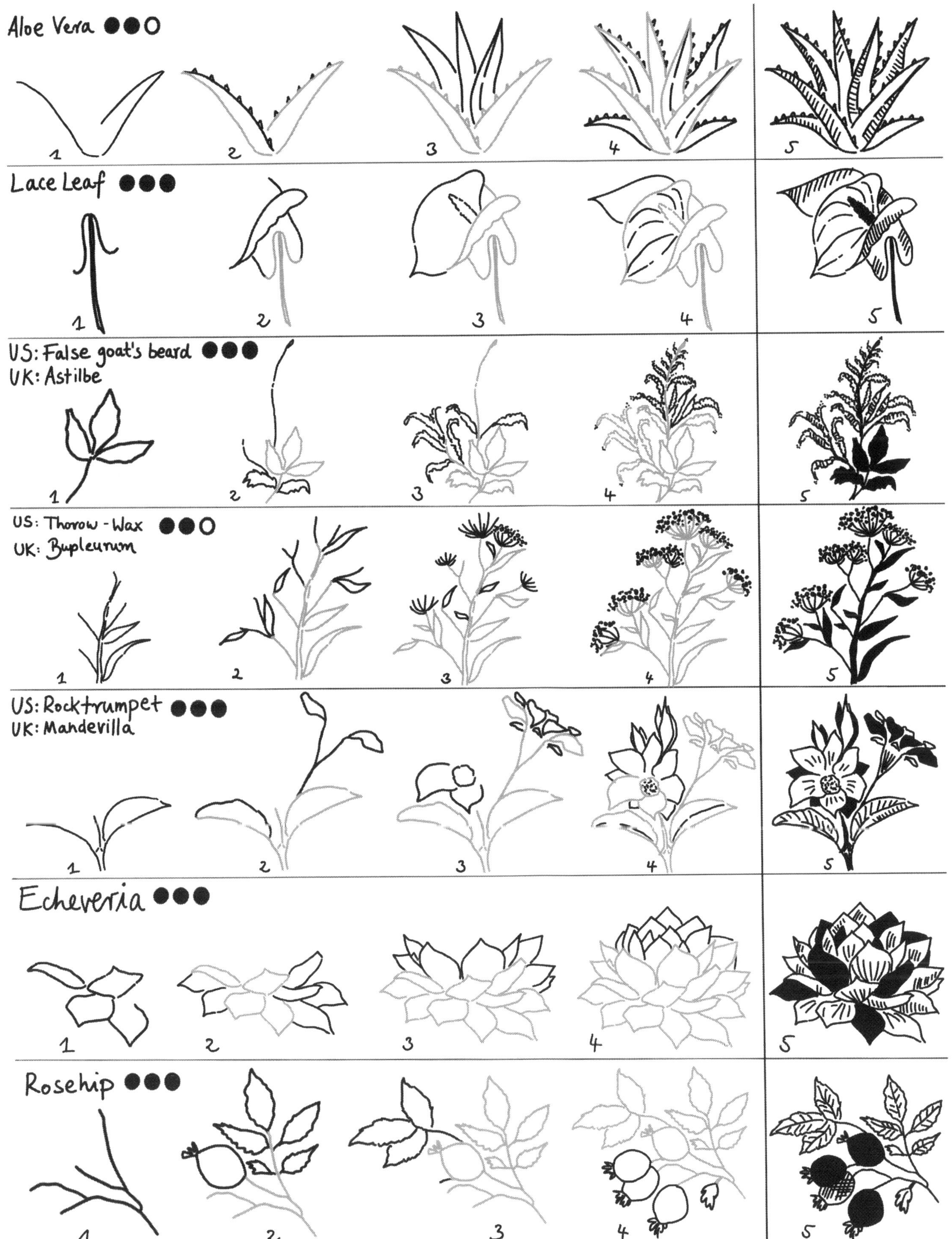
Aloe Vera
1
2
3
4
5
Lace Leaf
1
2
3
4
5
US: False goat's beard
UK: Astilbe
1
2
3
4
5
US: Thorow-Wax
UK: Bupleurum
1
2
3
4
5
US: Rocktrumpet
UK: Mandevilla
1
2
3
4
5
Echeveria
1
2
3
4
5
Rosehip
1
2
3
4
5

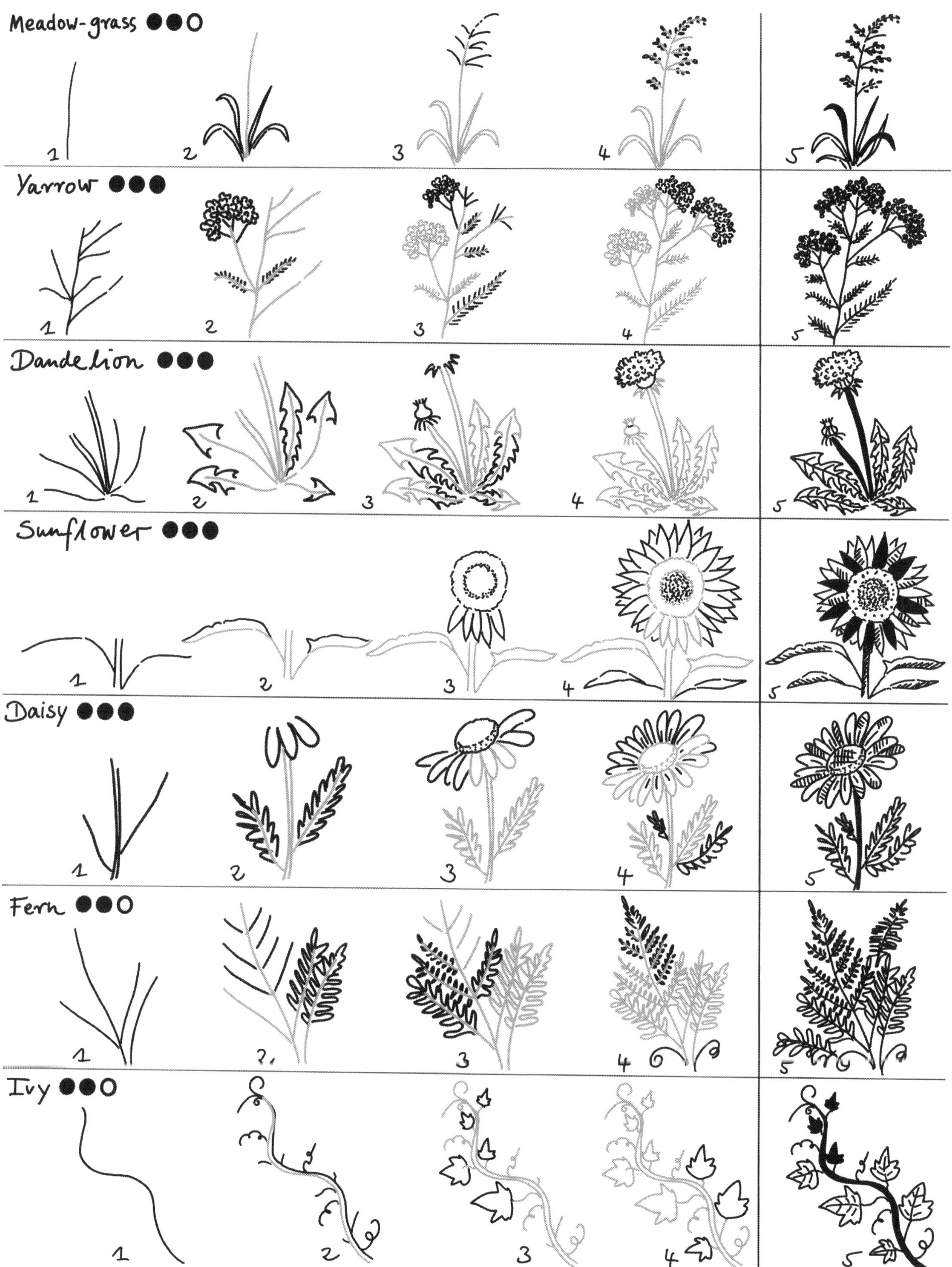
Meadow-grass ●●○
1
2
3
4
5
Yarrow ●●●
1
2
3
4
5
Dandelion ●●●
1
2
3
4
5
Sunflower ●●●
1
2
3
4
5
Daisy ●●●
1
2
3
4
5
Fern ●●○
1
2
3
4
5
Ivy ●●○
1
2
3
4
5

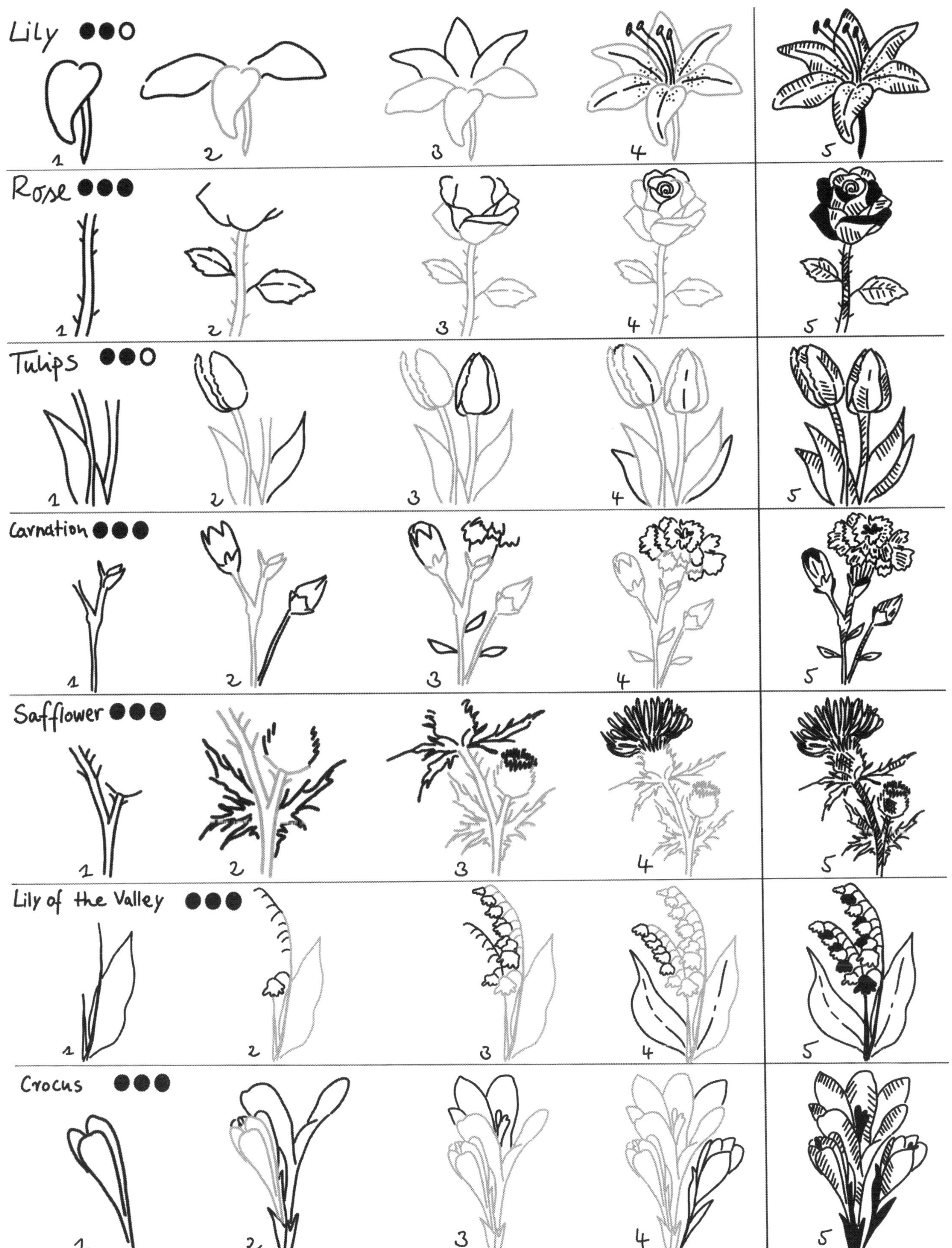
Lily
1
2
3
4
5
Rose
1
2
3
4
5
Tulips
1
2
3
4
5
Carnation
1
2
3
4
5
Safflower
1
2
3
4
5
Lily of the Valley
1
2
3
4
5
Crocus
1
2
3
4
5

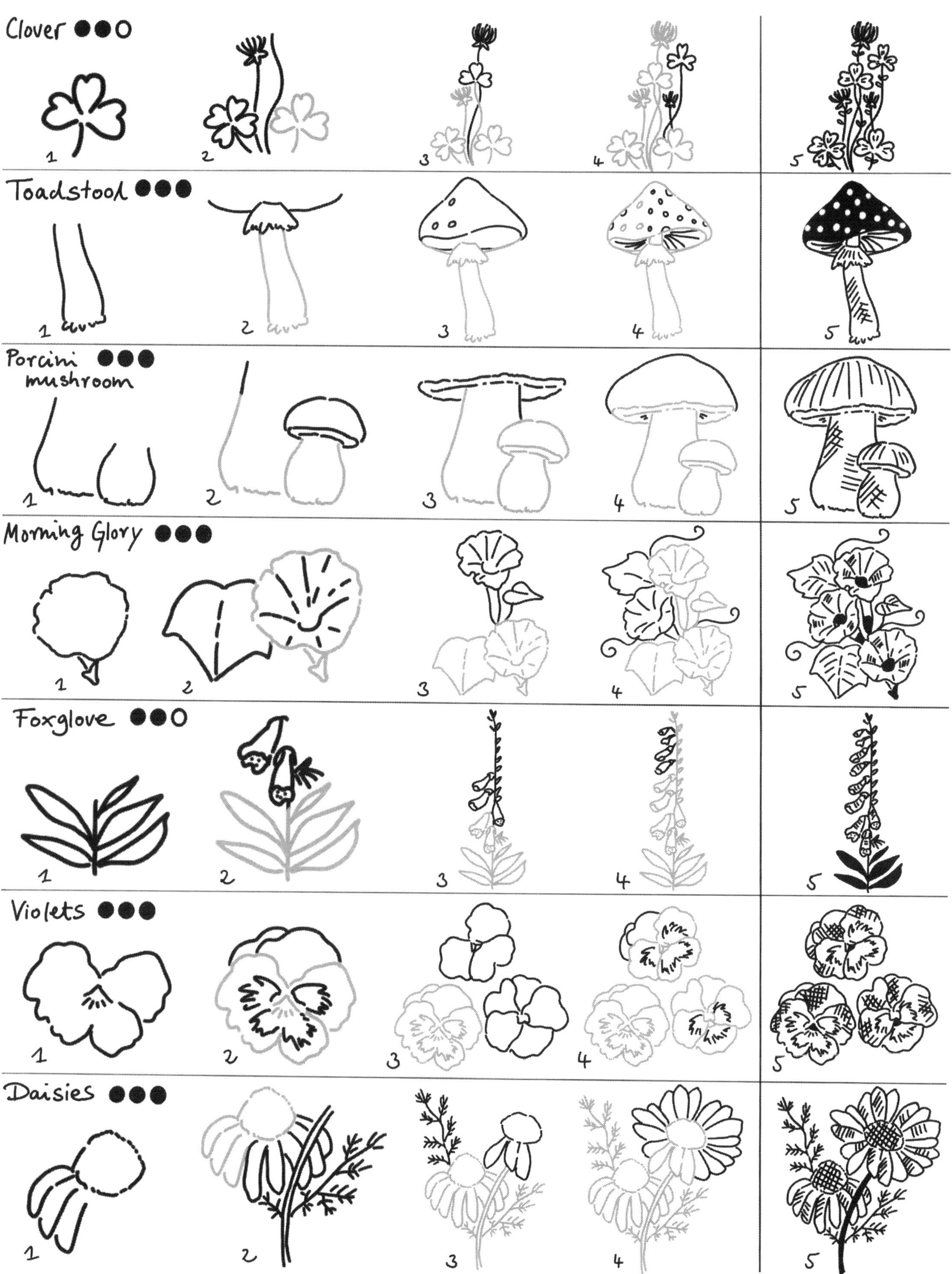
Clover ●●○
1
2
3
4
5
Toadstool ●●●
1
2
3
4
5
Porcini mushroom ●●●
1
2
3
4
5
Morning Glory ●●●
1
2
3
4
5
Foxglove ●●○
1
2
3
4
5
Violets ●●●
1
2
3
4
5
Daisies ●●●
1
2
3
4
5

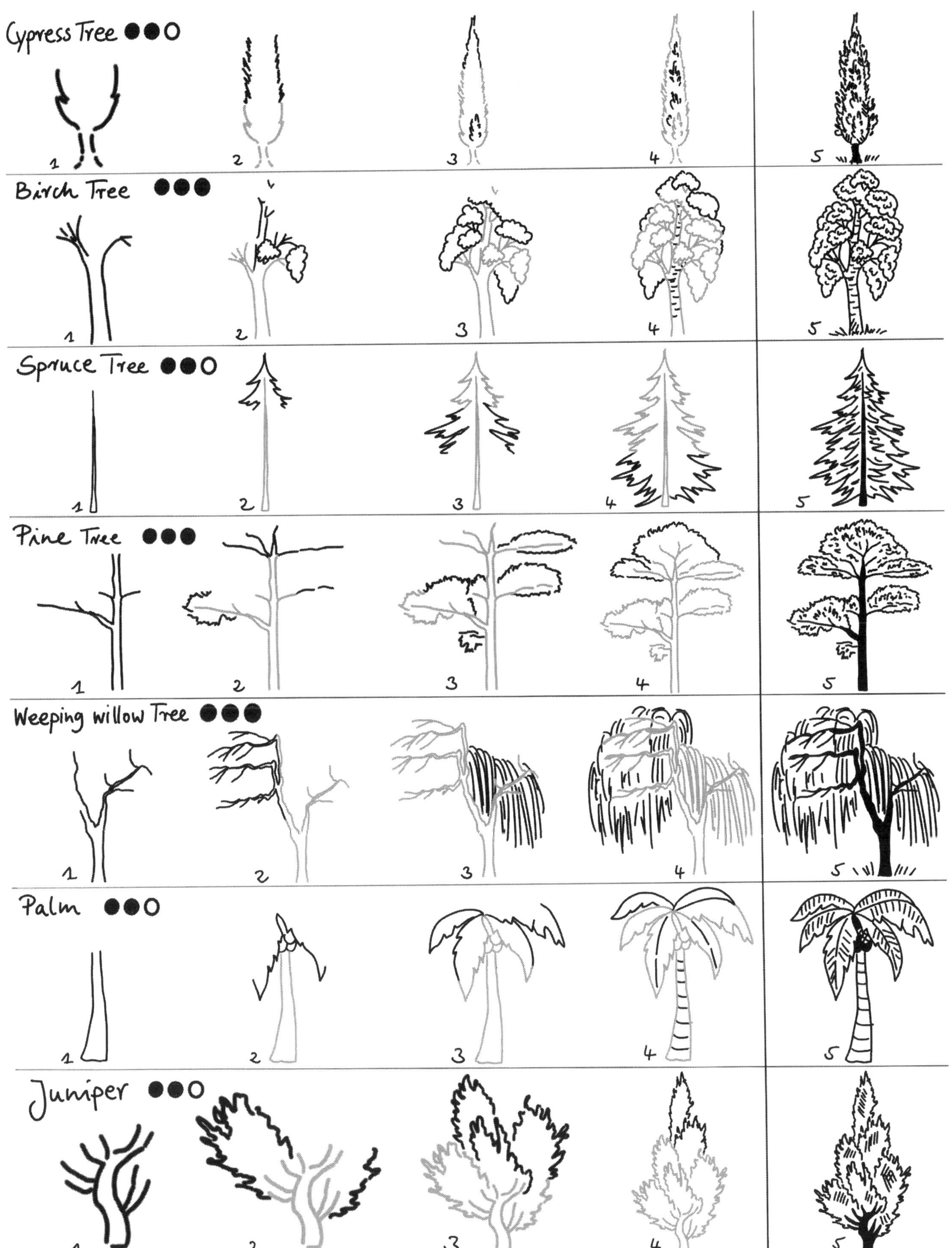
Cypress Tree
1
2
3
4
5
Birch Tree
1
2
3
4
5
Spruce Tree
1
2
3
4
5
Pine Tree
1
2
3
4
5
Weeping willow Tree
1
2
3
4
5
Palm
1
2
3
4
5
Juniper
1
2
3
4
5

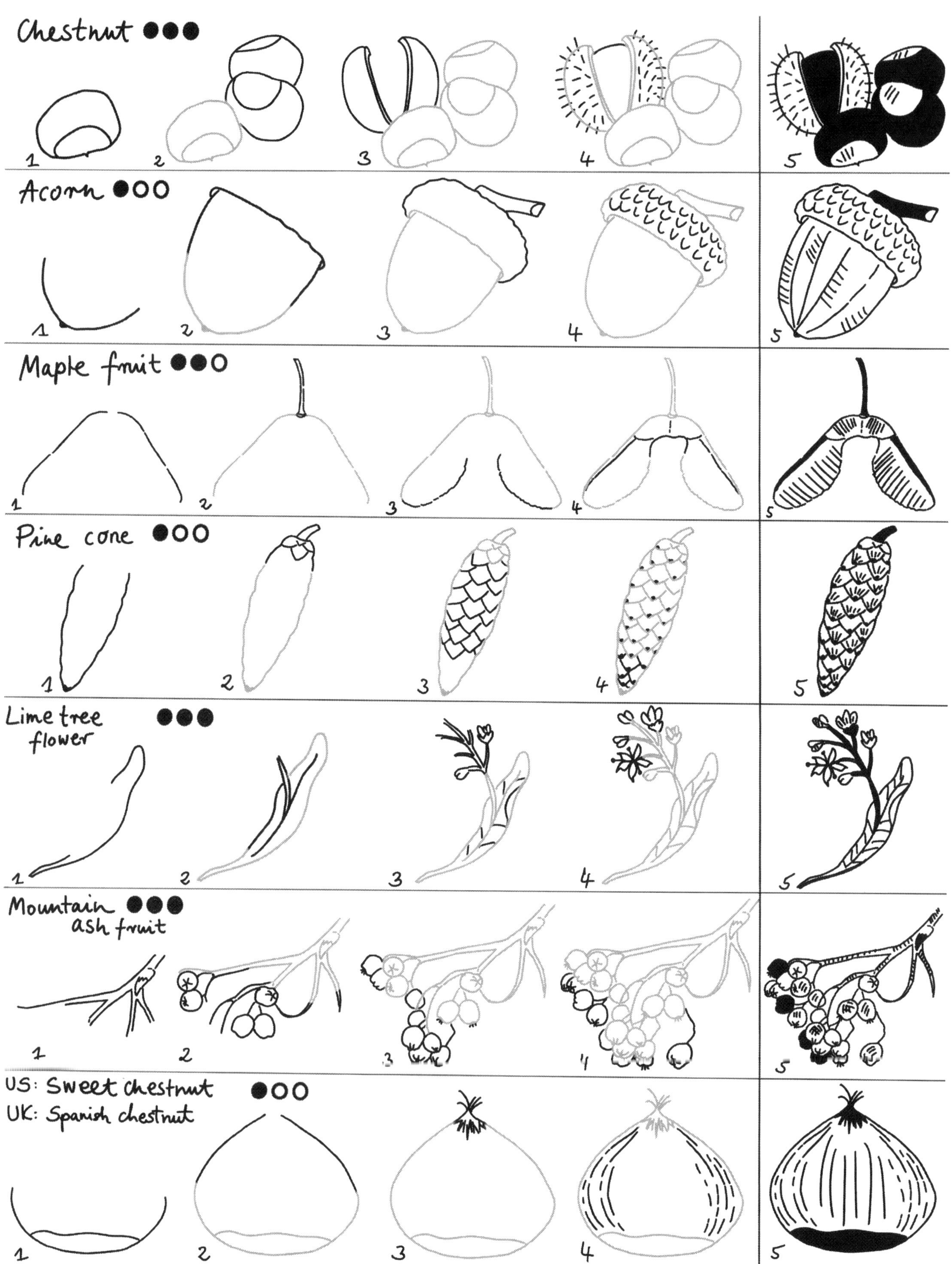
Chestnut ●●●
1
2
3
4
5
Acorn ●○○
1
2
3
4
5
Maple fruit ●●○
1
2
3
4
5
Pine cone ●○○
1
2
3
4
5
Lime tree flower ●●●
1
2
3
4
5
Mountain ash fruit ●●●
1
2
3
4
5
US: Sweet chestnut
UK: Spanish chestnut ●○○
1
2
3
4
5

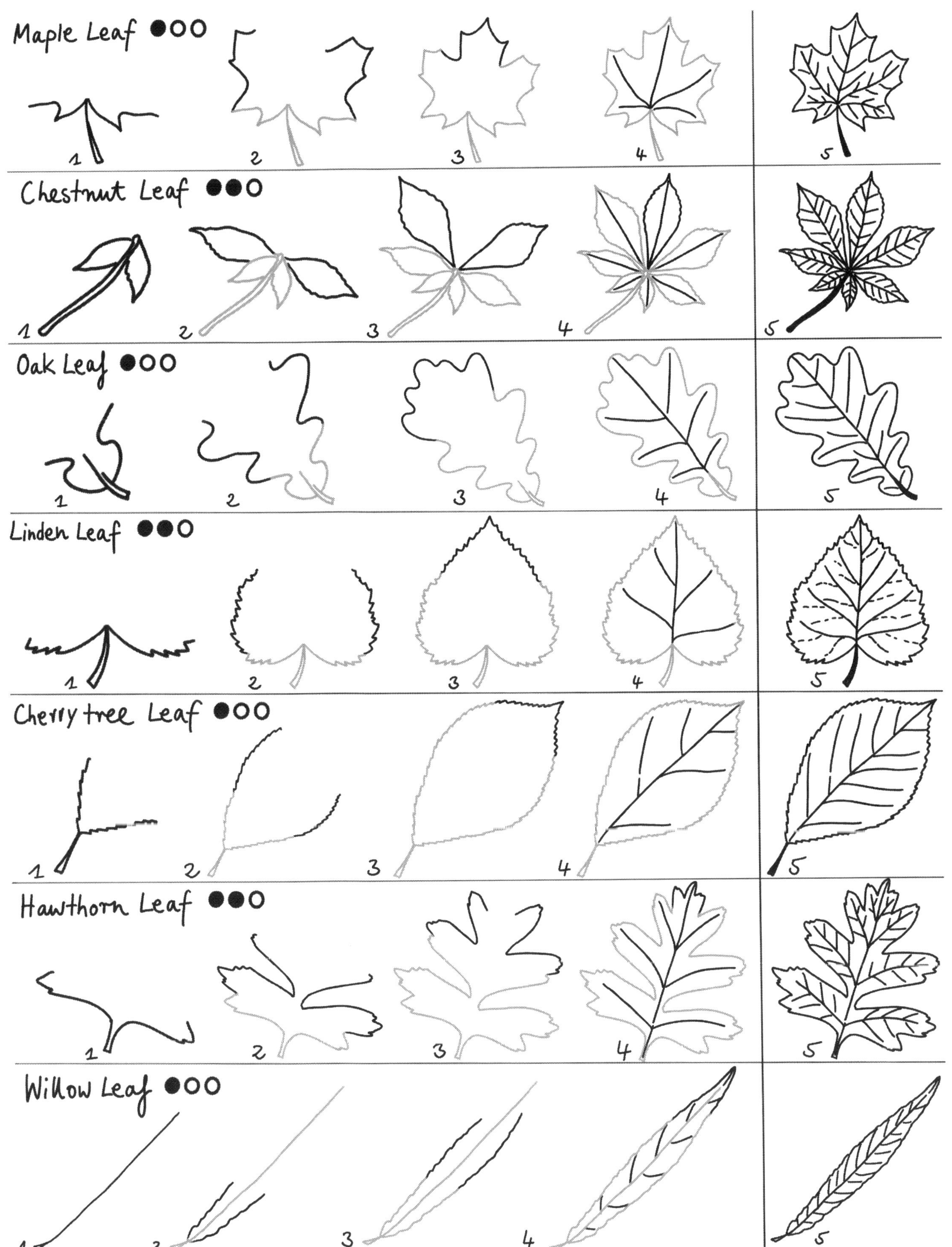
Maple Leaf
Chestnut Leaf
Oak Leaf
Linden Leaf
Cherry tree Leaf
Hawthorn Leaf
Willow Leaf

# FOOD

Carrots
Tomato
Pea Pod
Cucumber
Red pepper
Asparagus
US: Zucchini
UK: Courgette

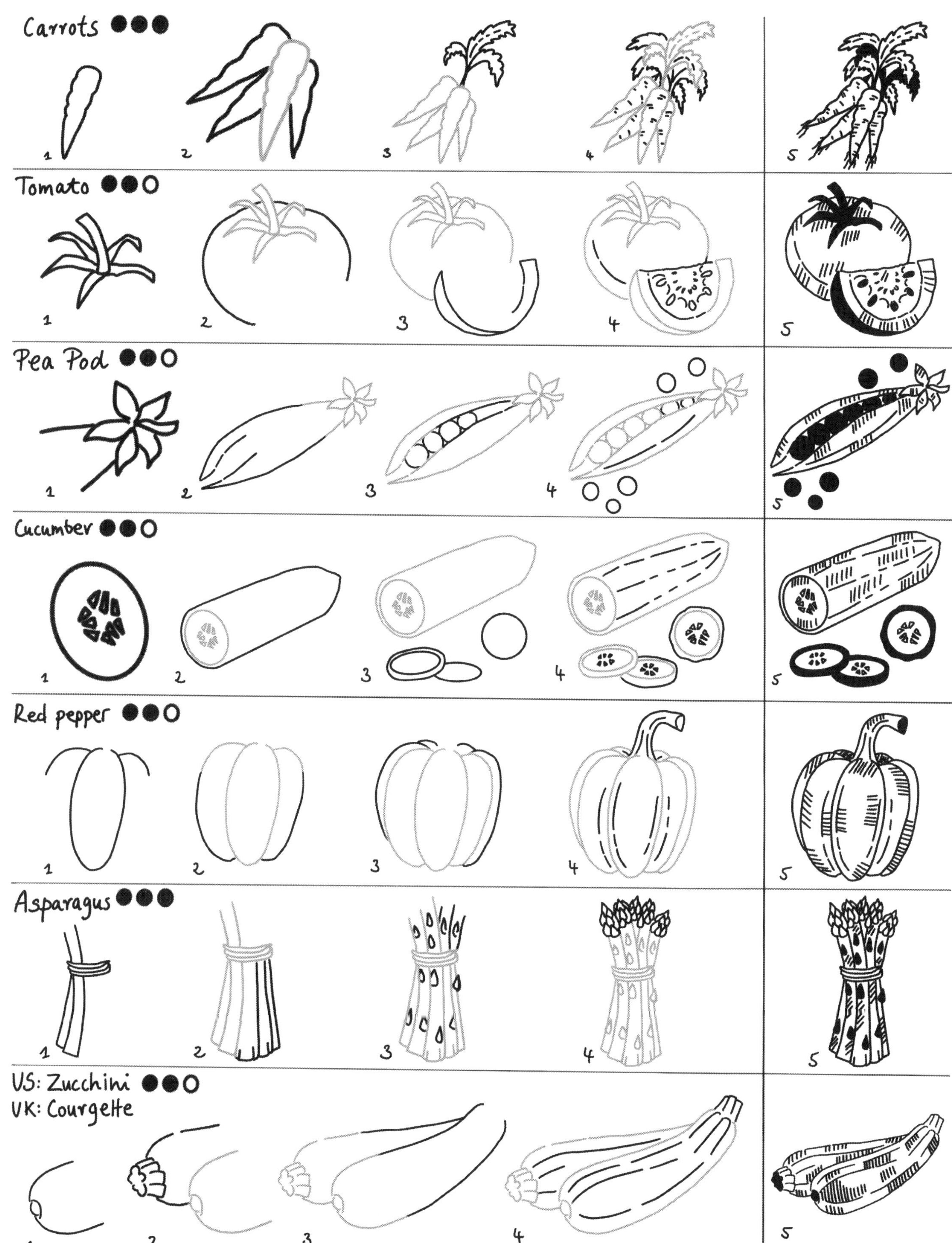

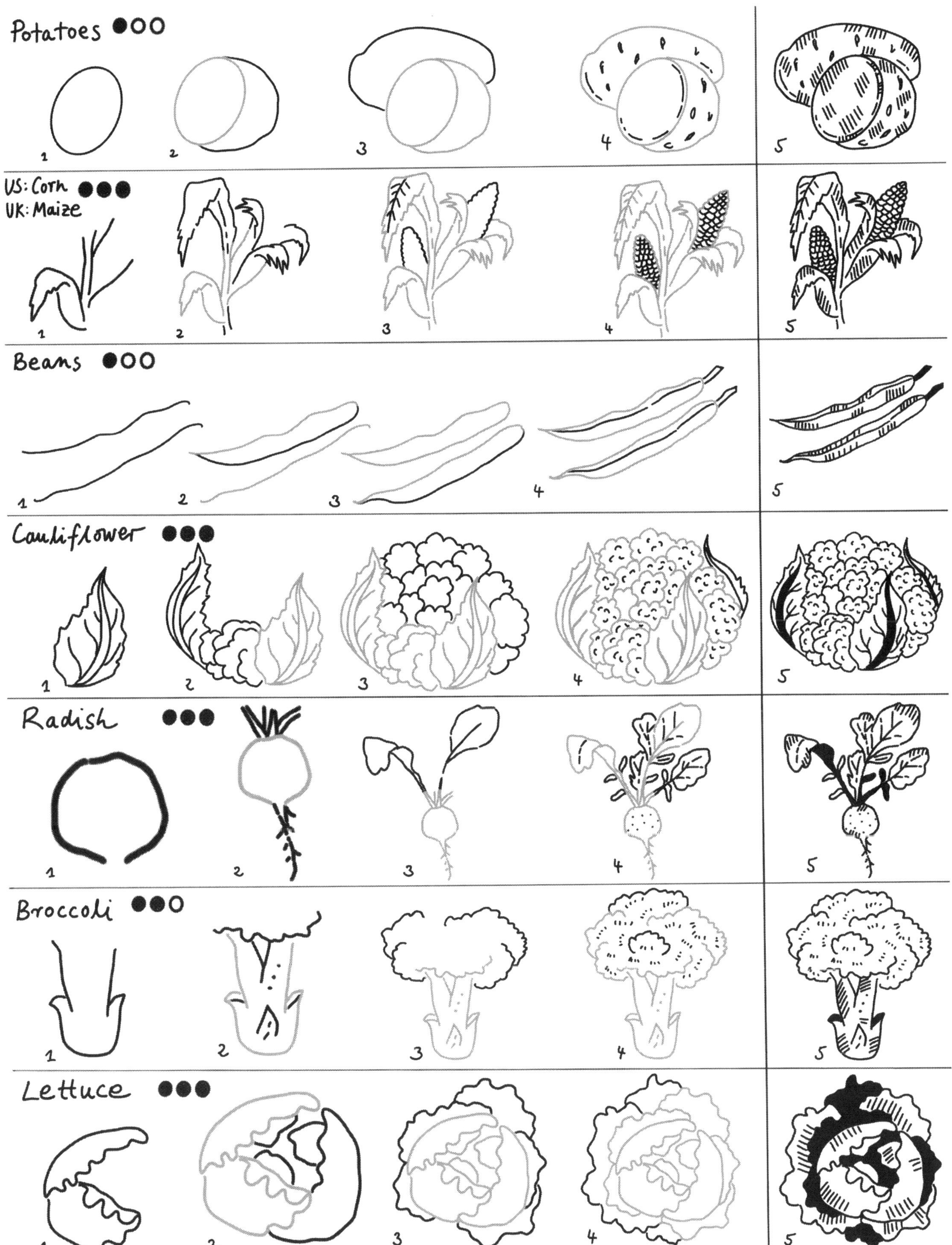

Potatoes
1
2
3
4
5
US: Corn
UK: Maize
1
2
3
4
5
Beans
1
2
3
4
5
Cauliflower
1
2
3
4
5
Radish
1
2
3
4
5
Broccoli
1
2
3
4
5
Lettuce
1
2
3
4
5

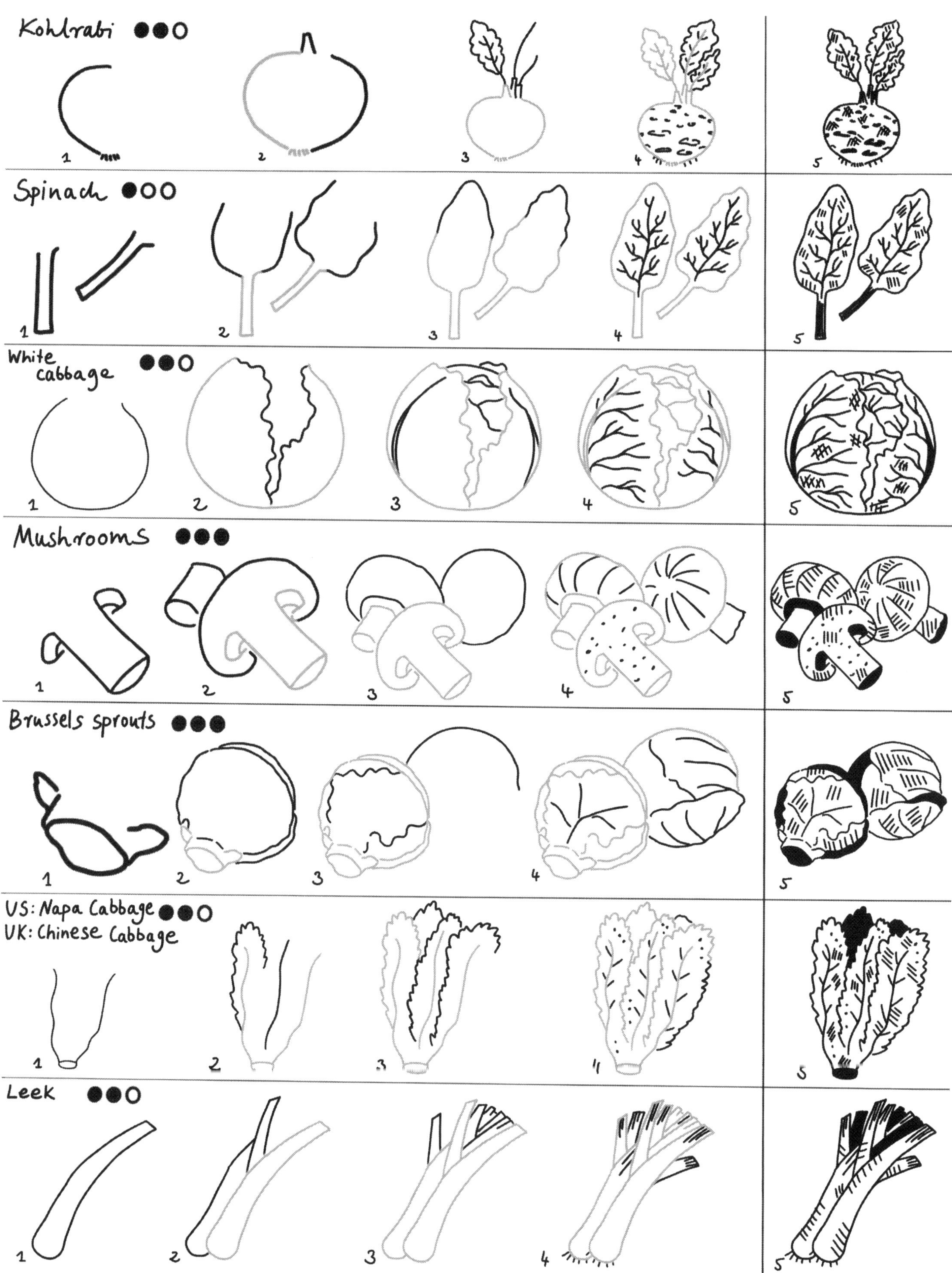
Kohlrabi
Spinach
White cabbage
Mushrooms
Brussels sprouts
US: Napa Cabbage
UK: Chinese Cabbage
Leek

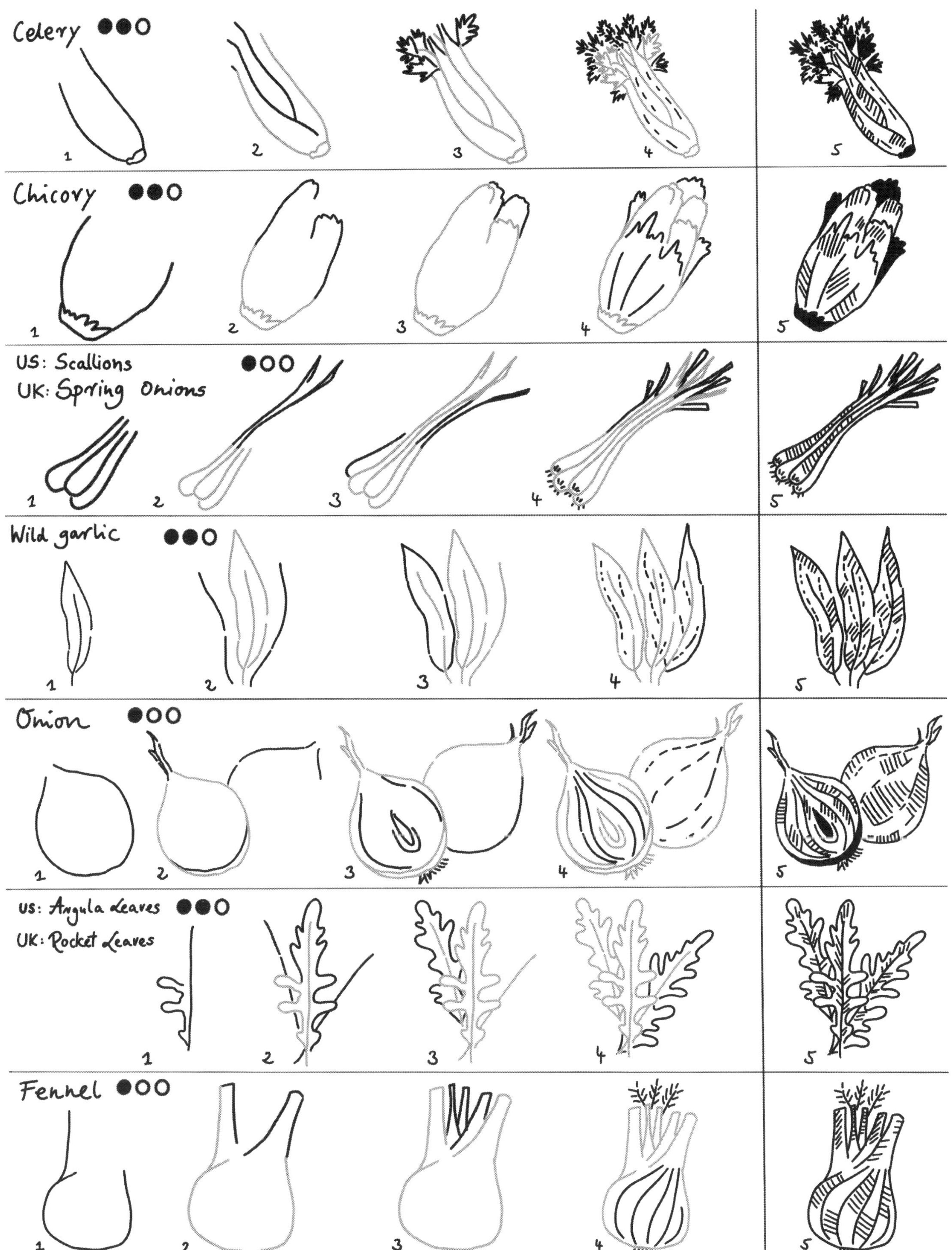
Celery
1
2
3
4
5
Chicory
1
2
3
4
5
US: Scallions
UK: Spring onions
1
2
3
4
5
Wild garlic
1
2
3
4
5
Onion
1
2
3
4
5
US: Arugula Leaves
UK: Rocket Leaves
1
2
3
4
5
Fennel
1
2
3
4
5

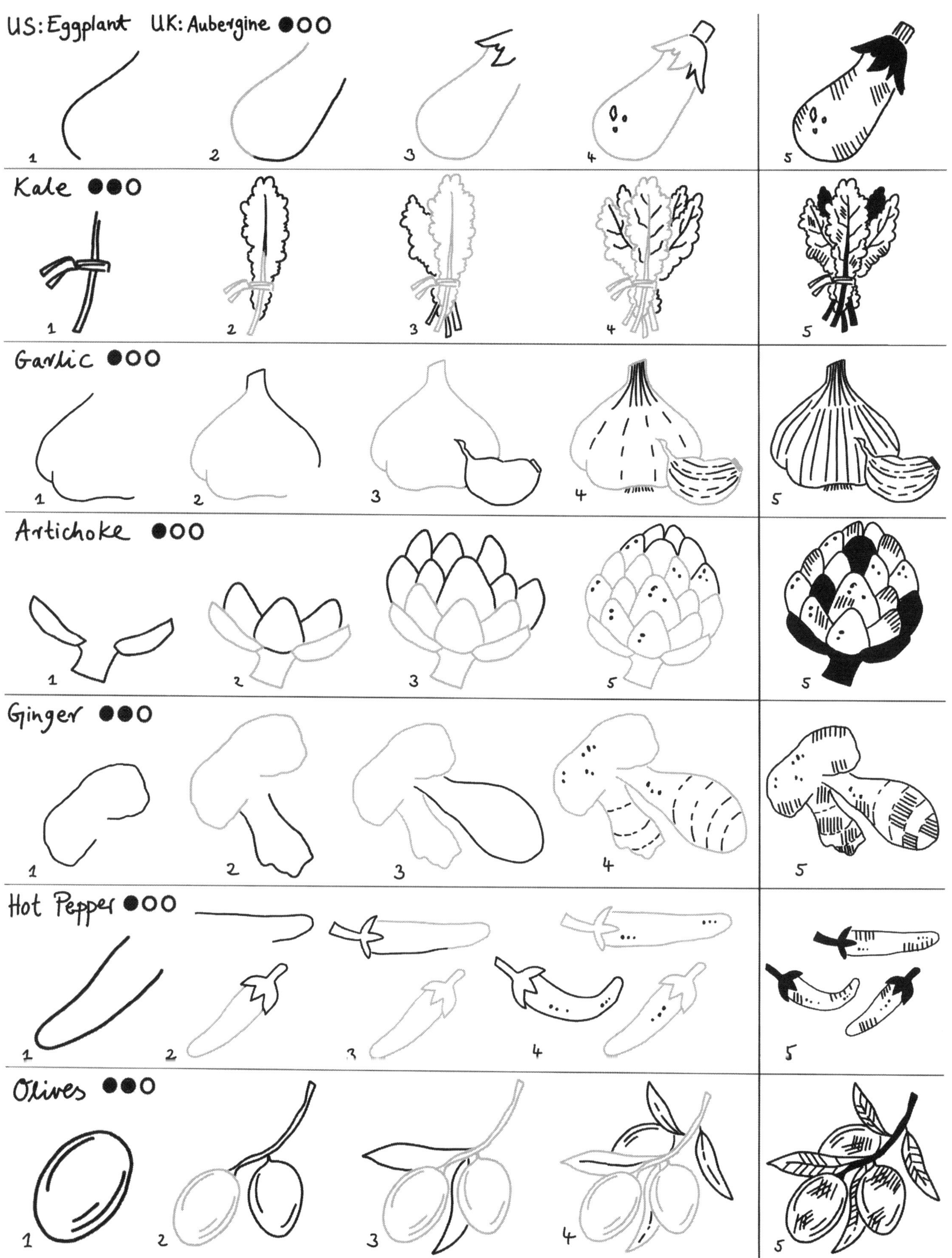
US: Eggplant UK: Aubergine
Kale
Garlic
Artichoke
Ginger
Hot Pepper
Olives

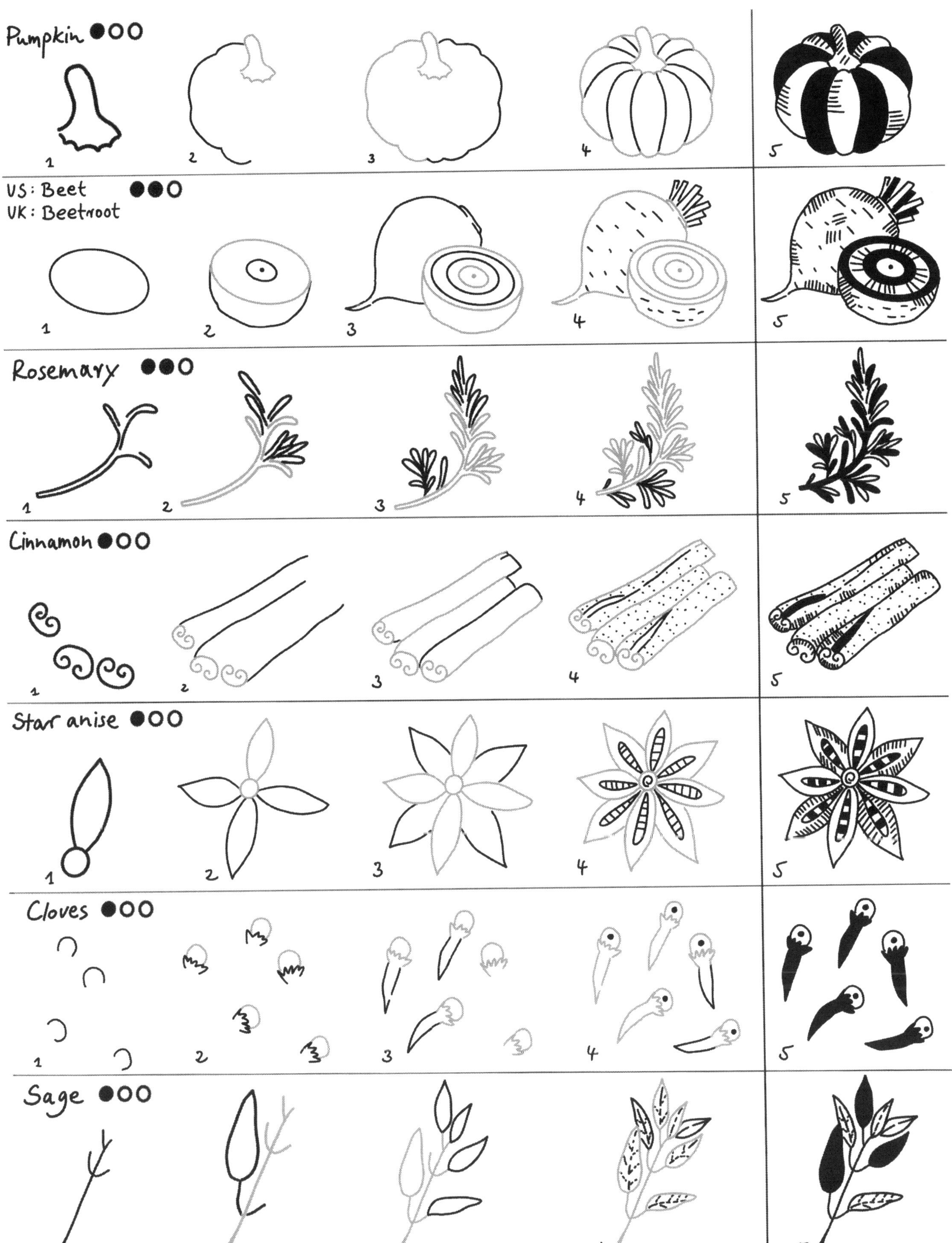
Pumpkin
1
2
3
4
5
US: Beet
UK: Beetroot
1
2
3
4
5
Rosemary
1
2
3
4
5
Cinnamon
1
2
3
4
5
Star anise
1
2
3
4
5
Cloves
1
2
3
4
5
Sage
1
2
3
4
5

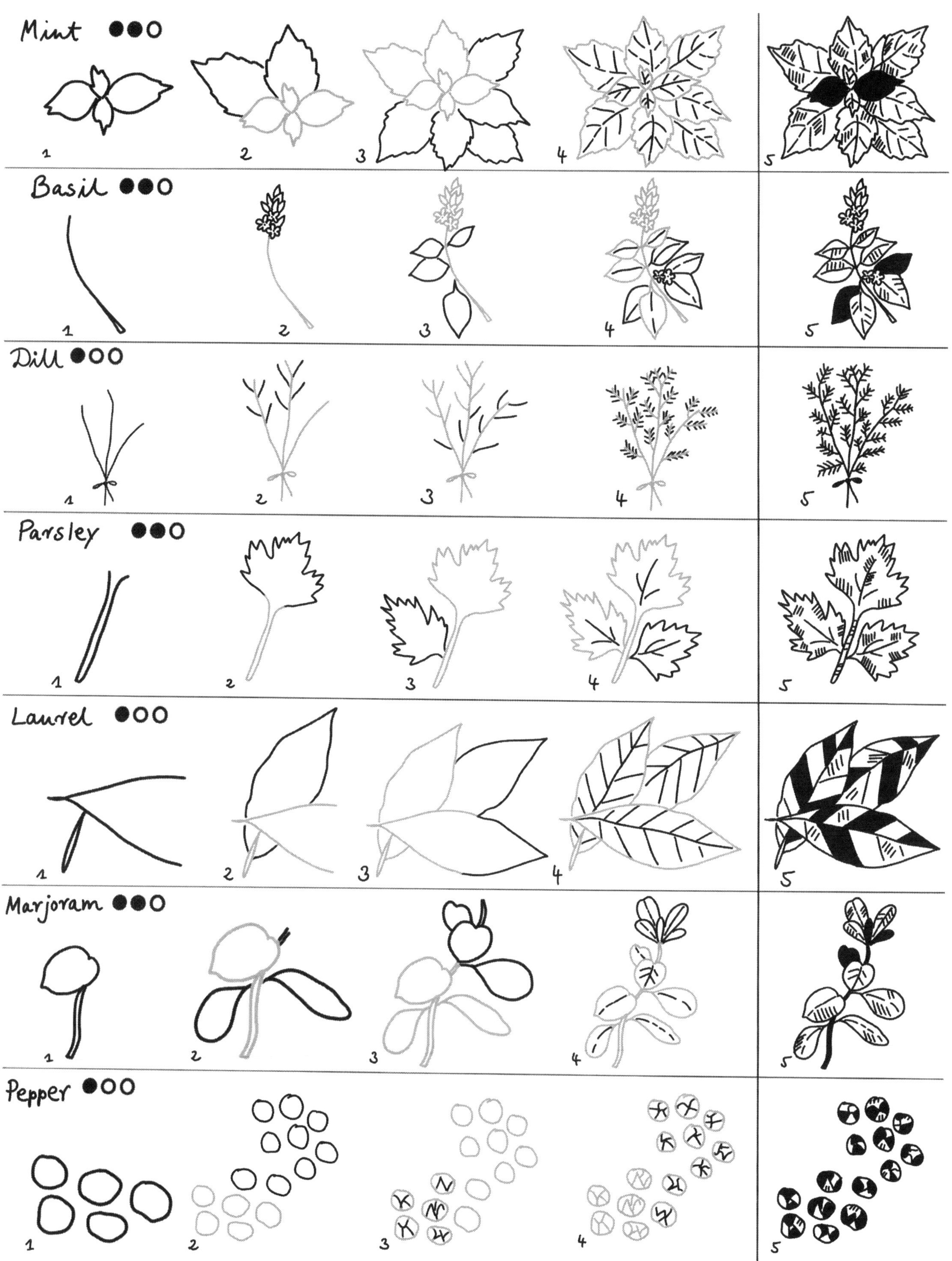
Mint
1
2
3
4
5
Basil
1
2
3
4
5
Dill
1
2
3
4
5
Parsley
1
2
3
4
5
Laurel
1
2
3
4
5
Marjoram
1
2
3
4
5
Pepper
1
2
3
4
5

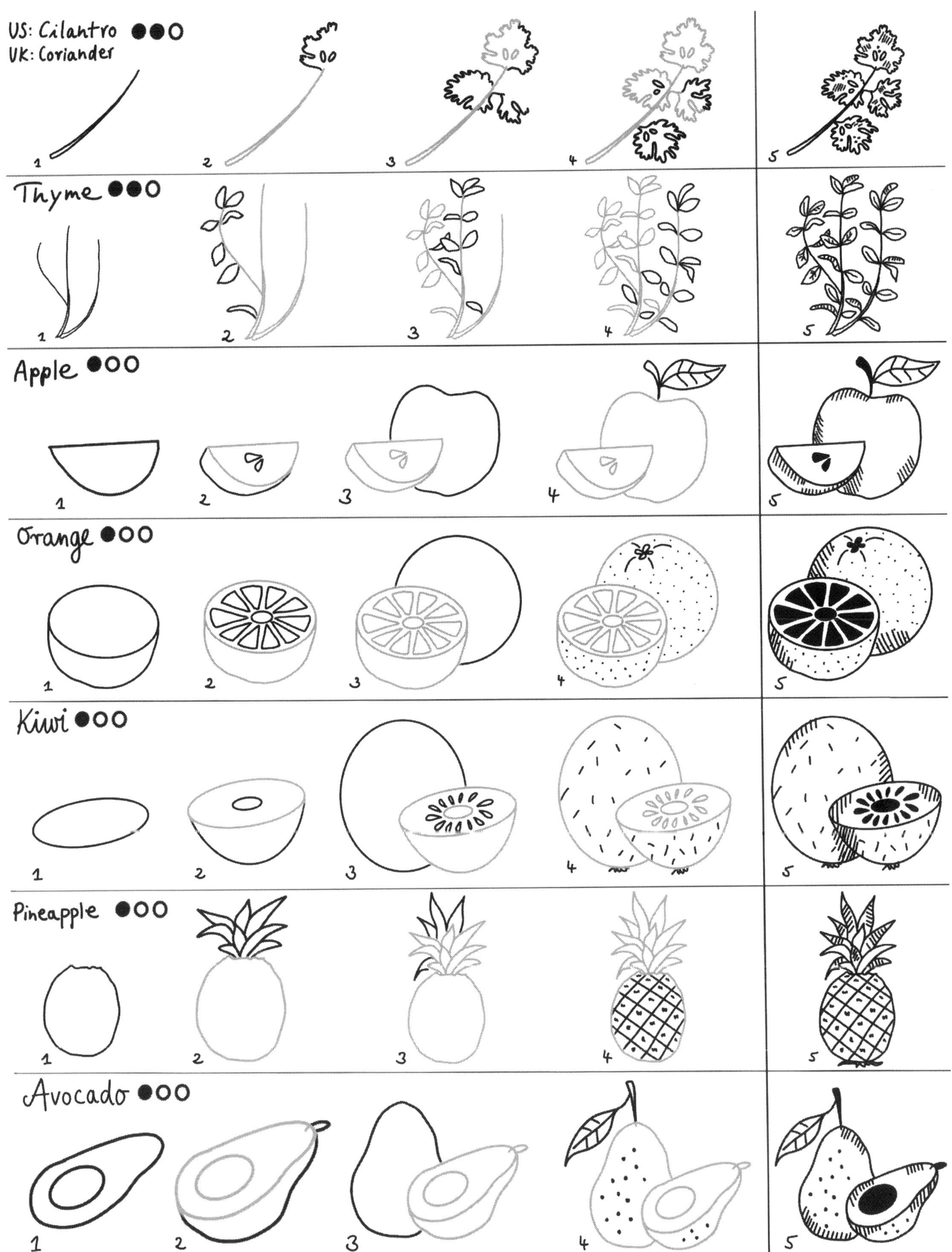
US: Cilantro
UK: Coriander
1
2
3
4
5
Thyme
1
2
3
4
5
Apple
1
2
3
4
5
Orange
1
2
3
4
5
Kiwi
1
2
3
4
5
Pineapple
1
2
3
4
5
Avocado
1
2
3
4
5

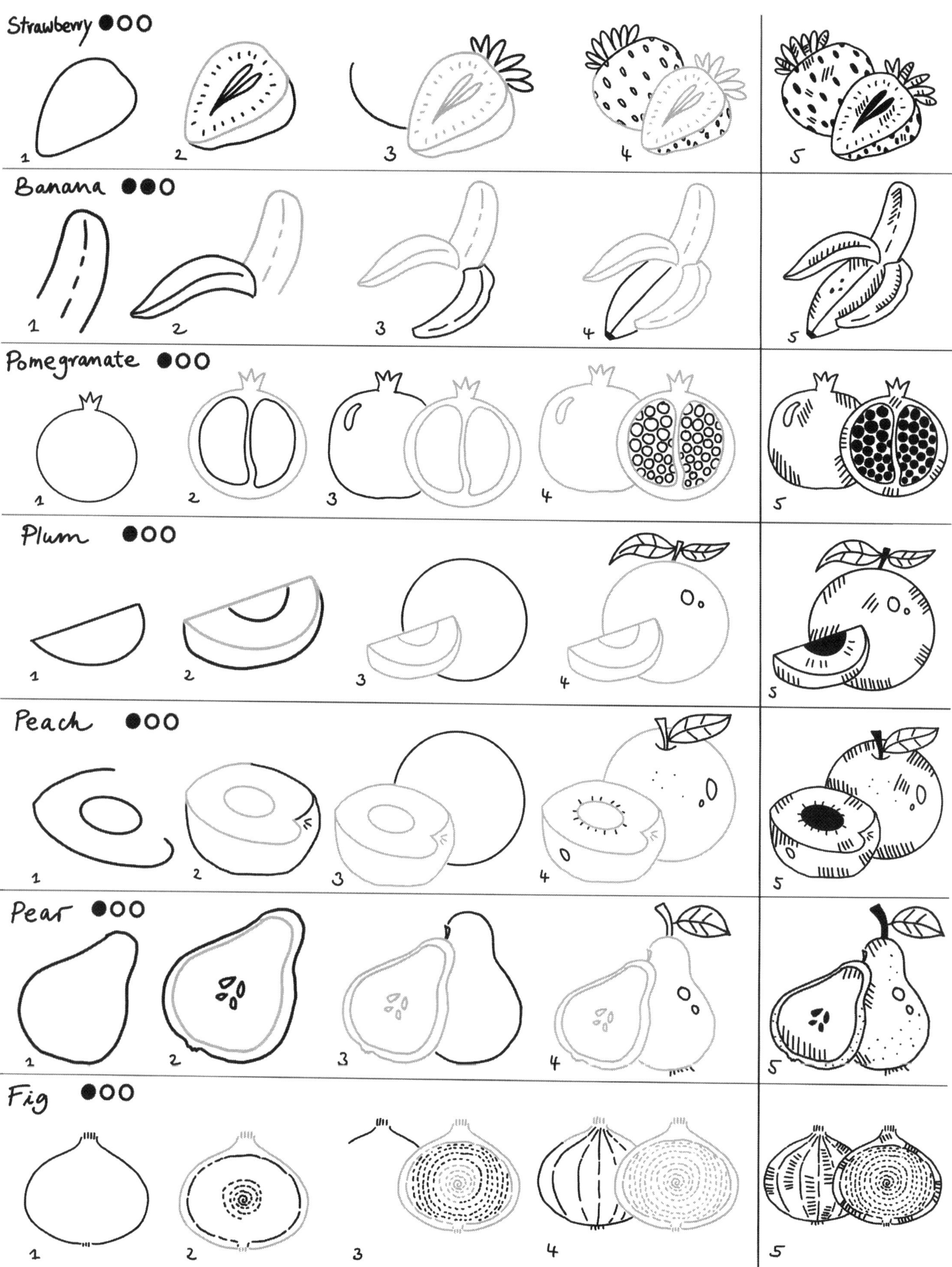
Strawberry
1
2
3
4
5
Banana
1
2
3
4
5
Pomegranate
1
2
3
4
5
Plum
1
2
3
4
5
Peach
1
2
3
4
5
Pear
1
2
3
4
5
Fig
1
2
3
4
5

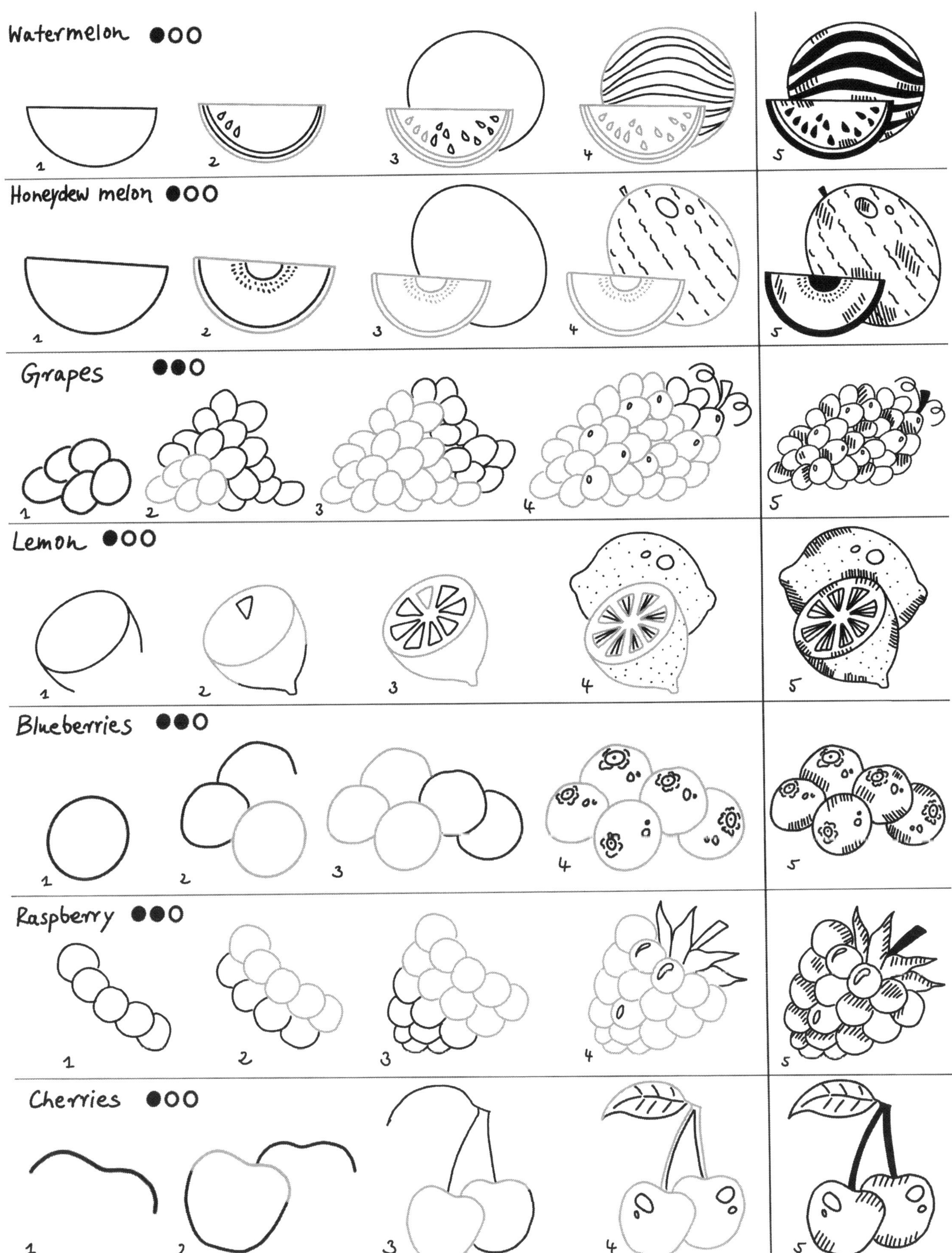
Watermelon ●○○
1
2
3
4
5
Honeydew melon ●○○
1
2
3
4
5
Grapes ●●○
1
2
3
4
5
Lemon ●○○
1
2
3
4
5
Blueberries ●●○
1
2
3
4
5
Raspberry ●●○
1
2
3
4
5
Cherries ●○○
1
2
3
4
5

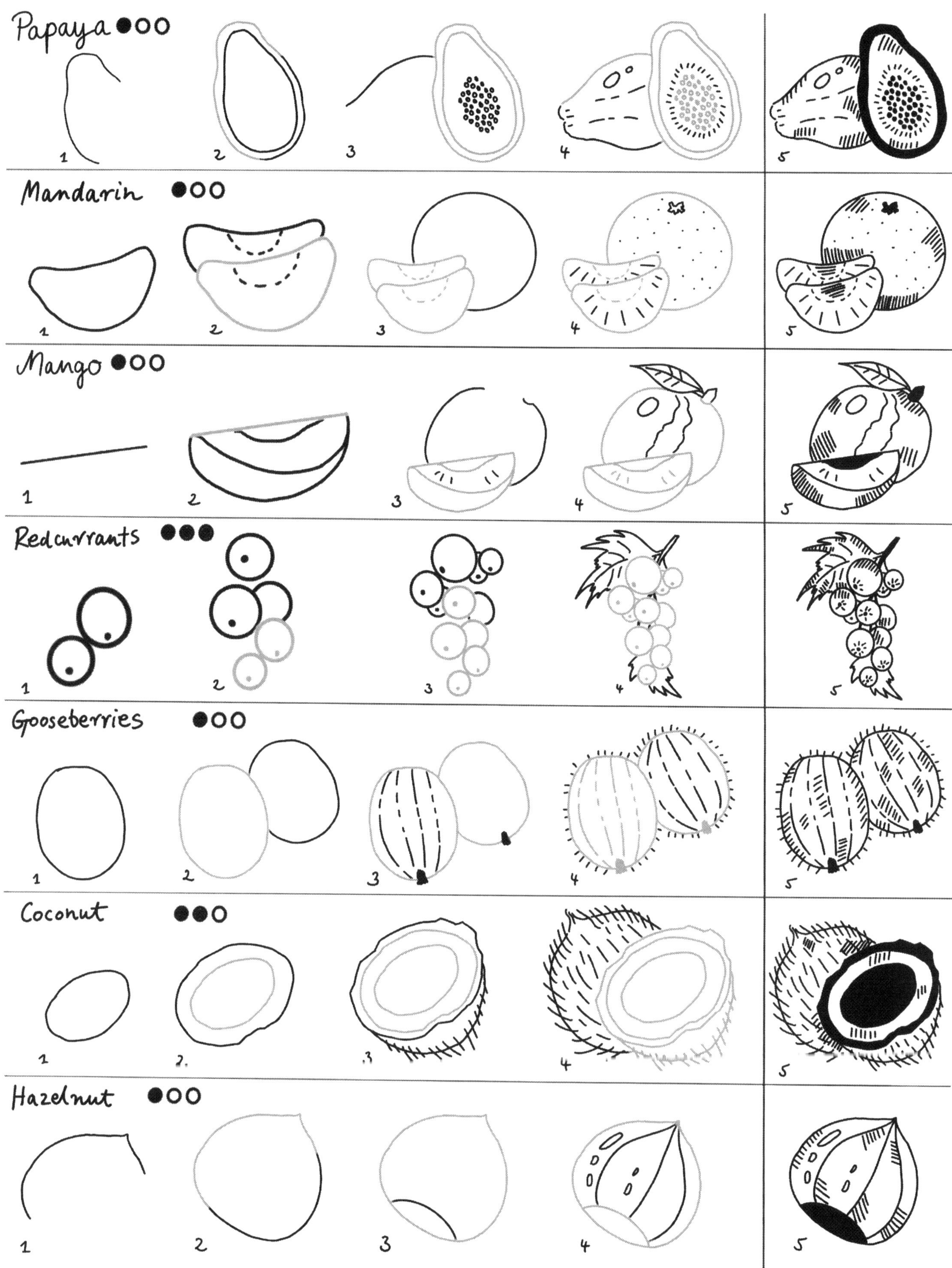
Papaya
1
2
3
4
5
Mandarin
1
2
3
4
5
Mango
1
2
3
4
5
Redcurrants
1
2
3
4
5
Gooseberries
1
2
3
4
5
Coconut
1
2
3
4
5
Hazelnut
1
2
3
4
5

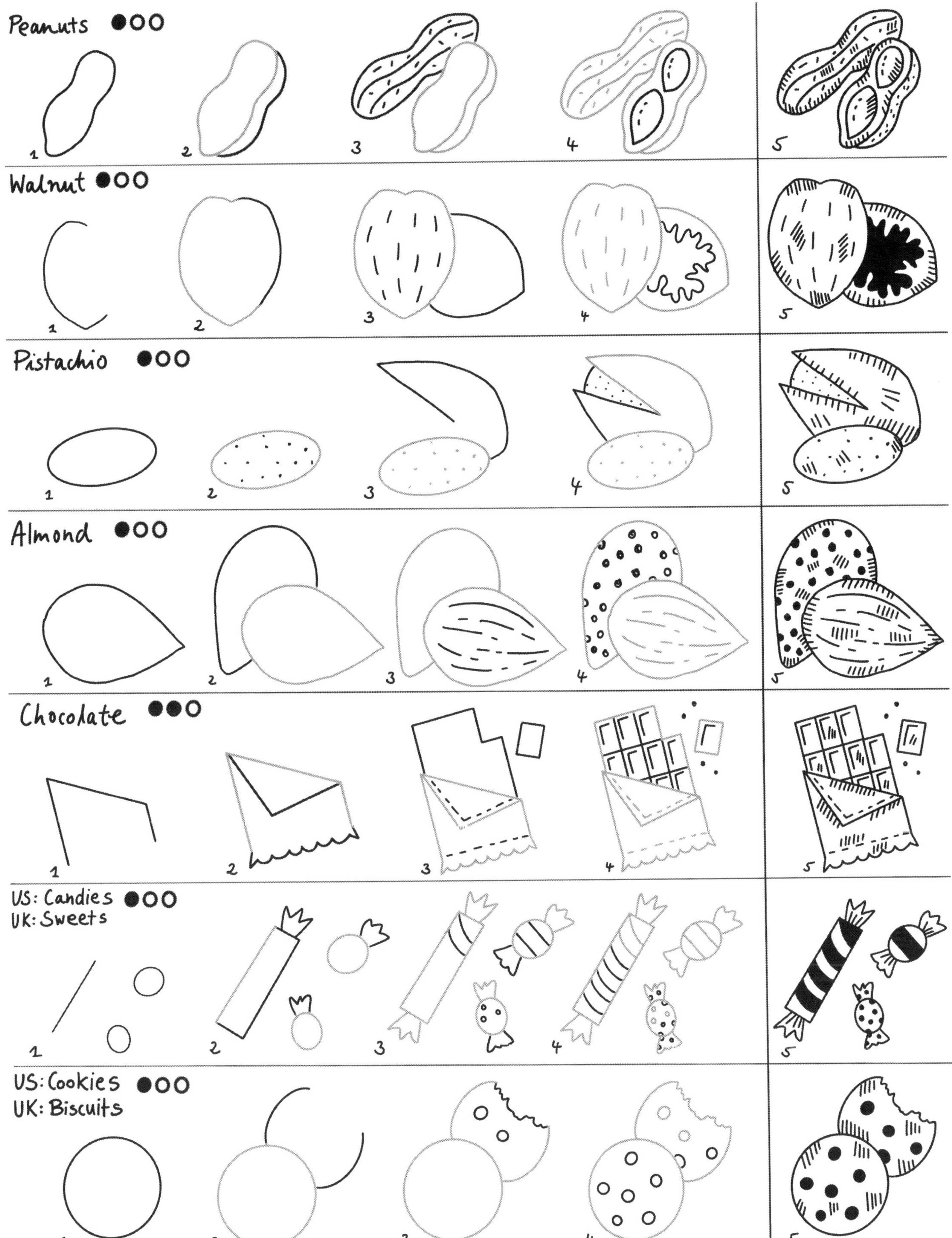
Peanuts
1
2
3
4
5
Walnut
1
2
3
4
5
Pistachio
1
2
3
4
5
Almond
1
2
3
4
5
Chocolate
1
2
3
4
5
US: Candies
UK: Sweets
1
2
3
4
5
US: Cookies
UK: Biscuits
1
2
3
4
5

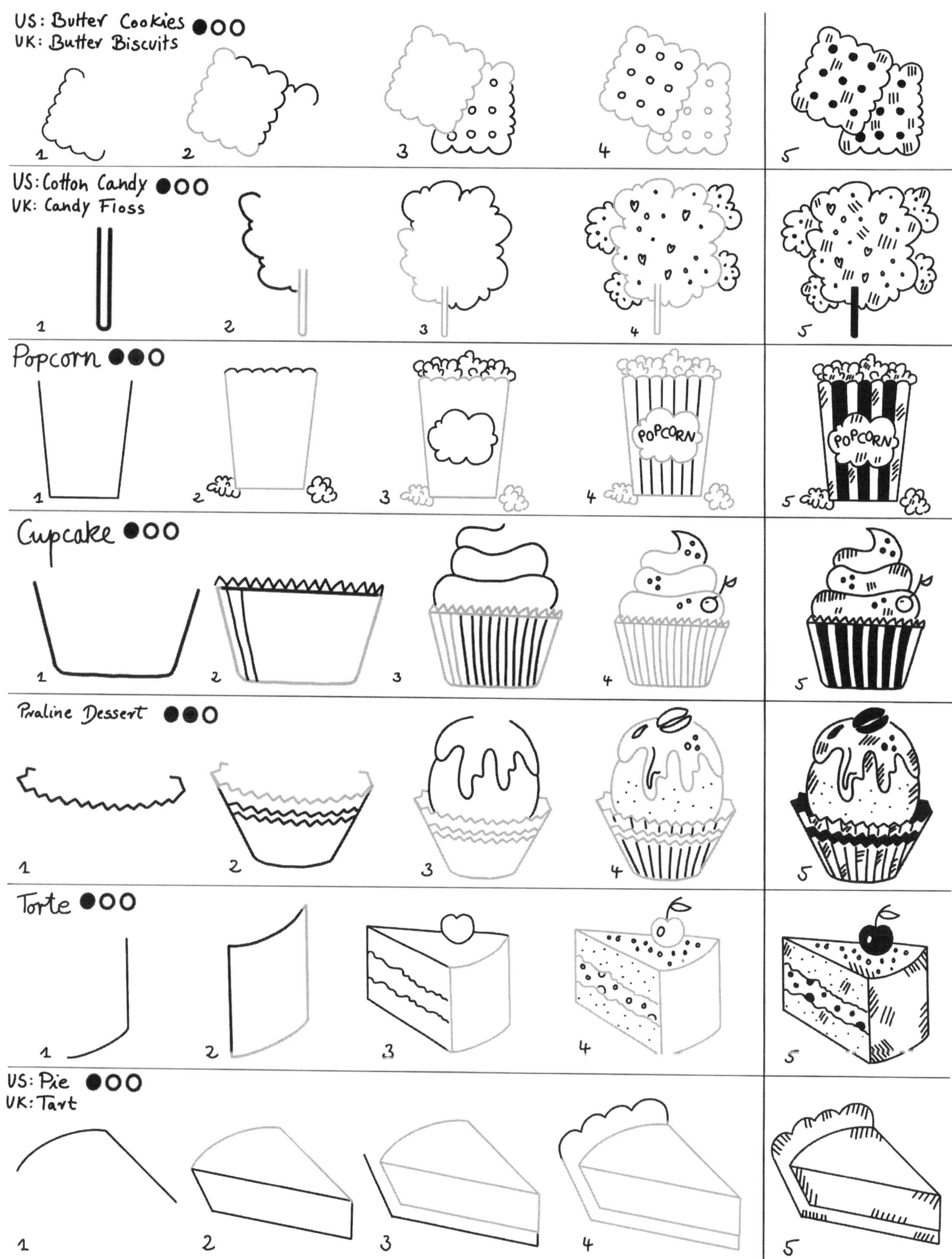
US: Butter Cookies
UK: Butter Biscuits
1
2
3
4
5
US: Cotton Candy
UK: Candy Floss
1
2
3
4
5
Popcorn
1
2
3
POPCORN
4
POPCORN
5
Cupcake
1
2
3
4
5
Praline Dessert
1
2
3
4
5
Torte
1
2
3
4
5
US: Pie
UK: Tart
1
2
3
4
5

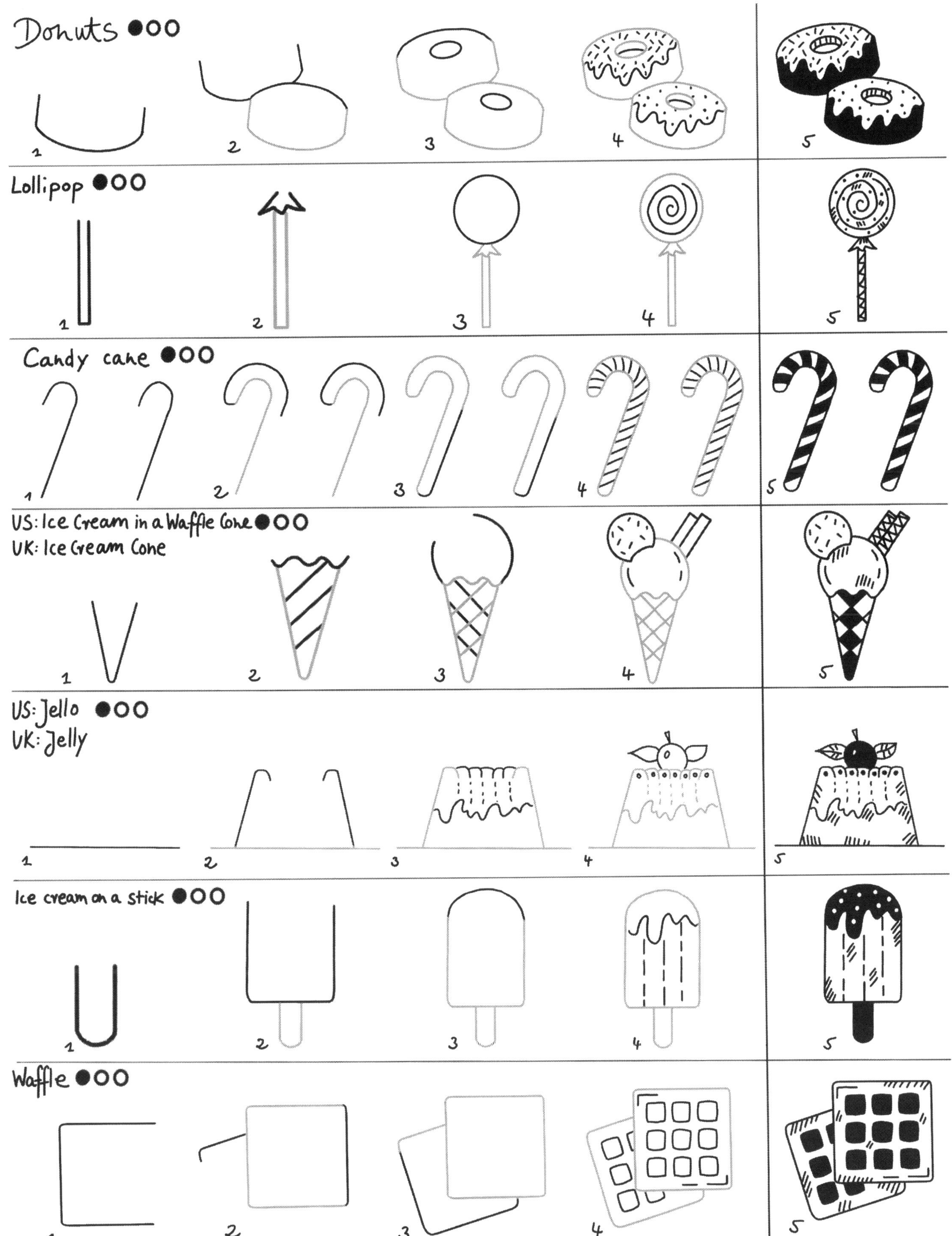

Donuts
1
2
3
4
5
Lollipop
1
2
3
4
5
Candy cane
1
2
3
4
5
US: Ice Cream in a Waffle Cone
UK: Ice Cream Cone
1
2
3
4
5
US: Jello
UK: Jelly
1
2
3
4
5
Ice cream on a stick
1
2
3
4
5
Waffle
1
2
3
4
5

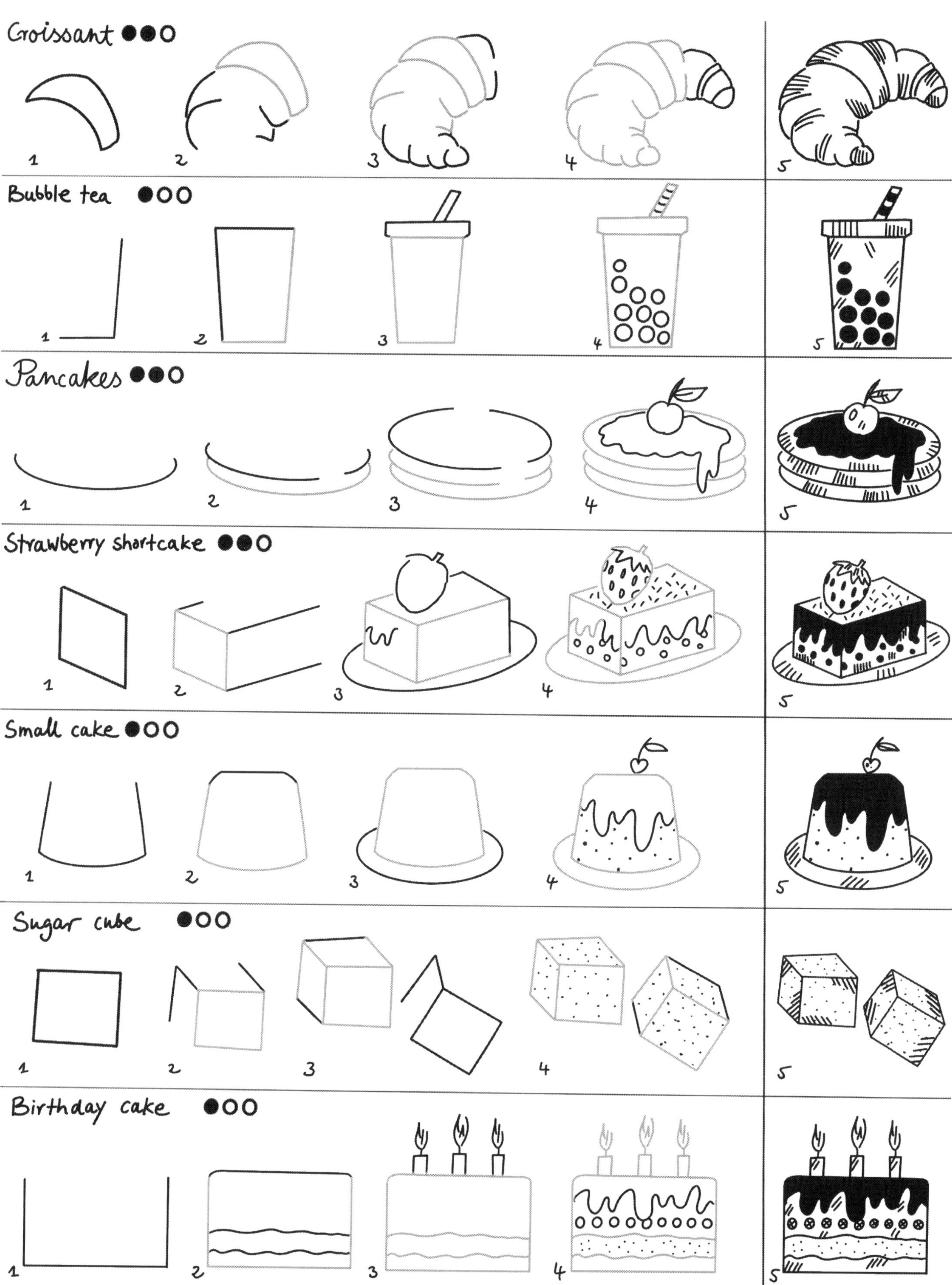
Croissant
1
2
3
4
5
Bubble tea
1
2
3
4
5
Pancakes
1
2
3
4
5
Strawberry shortcake
1
2
3
4
5
Small cake
1
2
3
4
5
Sugar cube
1
2
3
4
5
Birthday cake
1
2
3
4
5

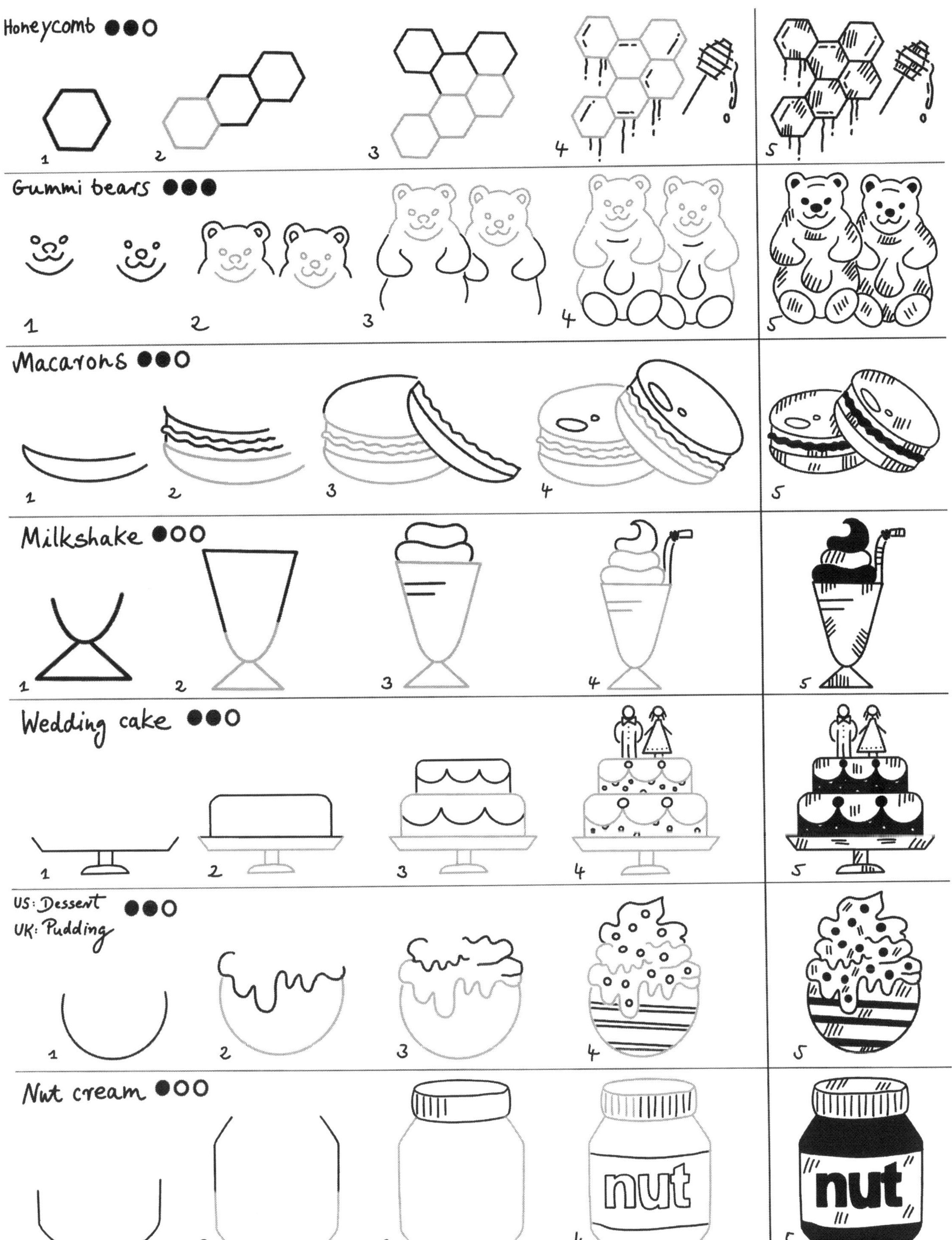
Honeycomb
Gummi bears
Macarons
Milkshake
Wedding cake
US: Dessert
UK: Pudding
Nut cream
nut
nut

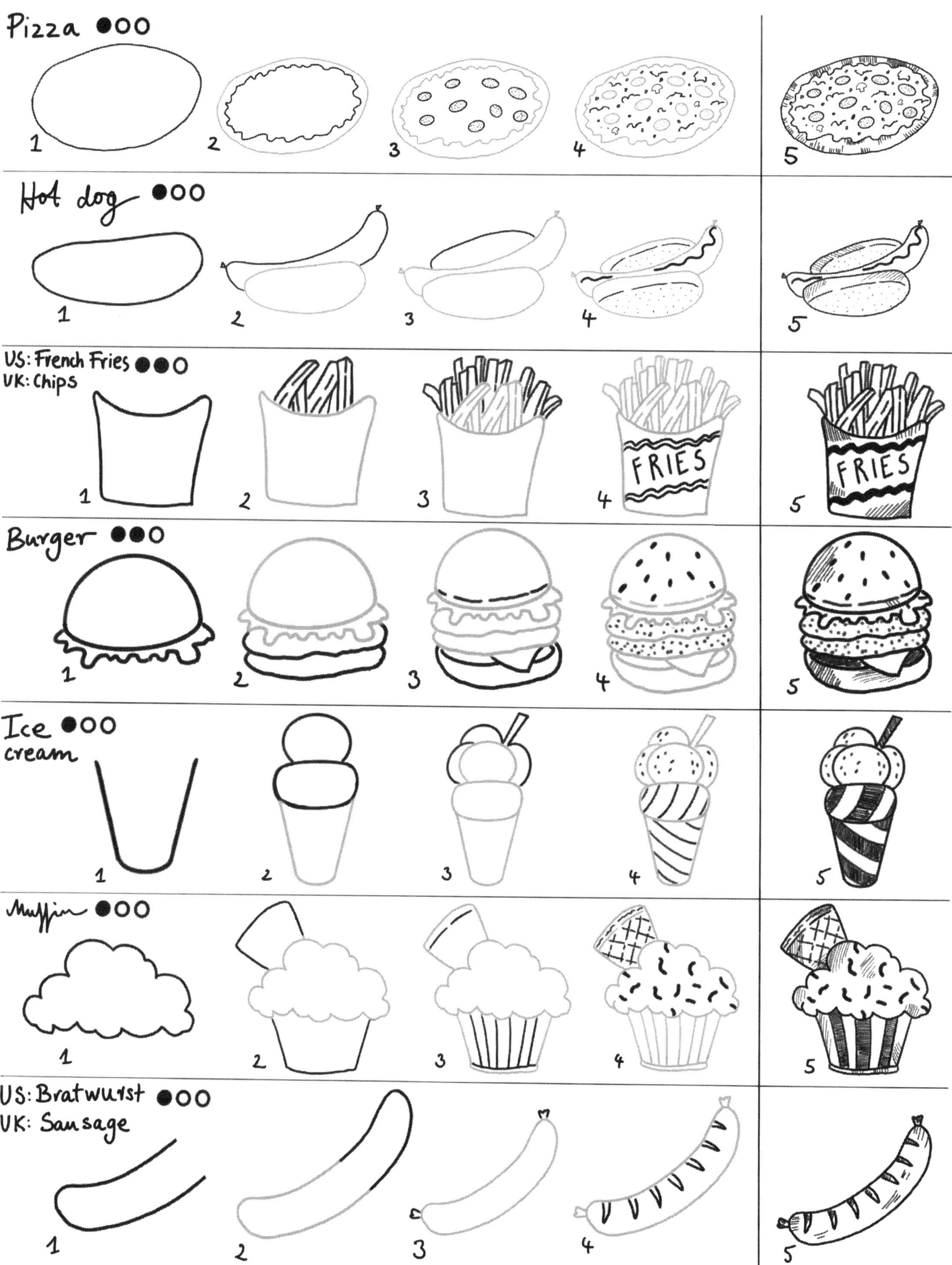
Pizza
1
2
3
4
5
Hot dog
1
2
3
4
5
US: French Fries
UK: Chips
1
2
3
FRIES
4
FRIES
5
Burger
1
2
3
4
5
Ice cream
1
2
3
4
5
Muffin
1
2
3
4
5
US: Bratwurst
UK: Sausage
1
2
3
4
5

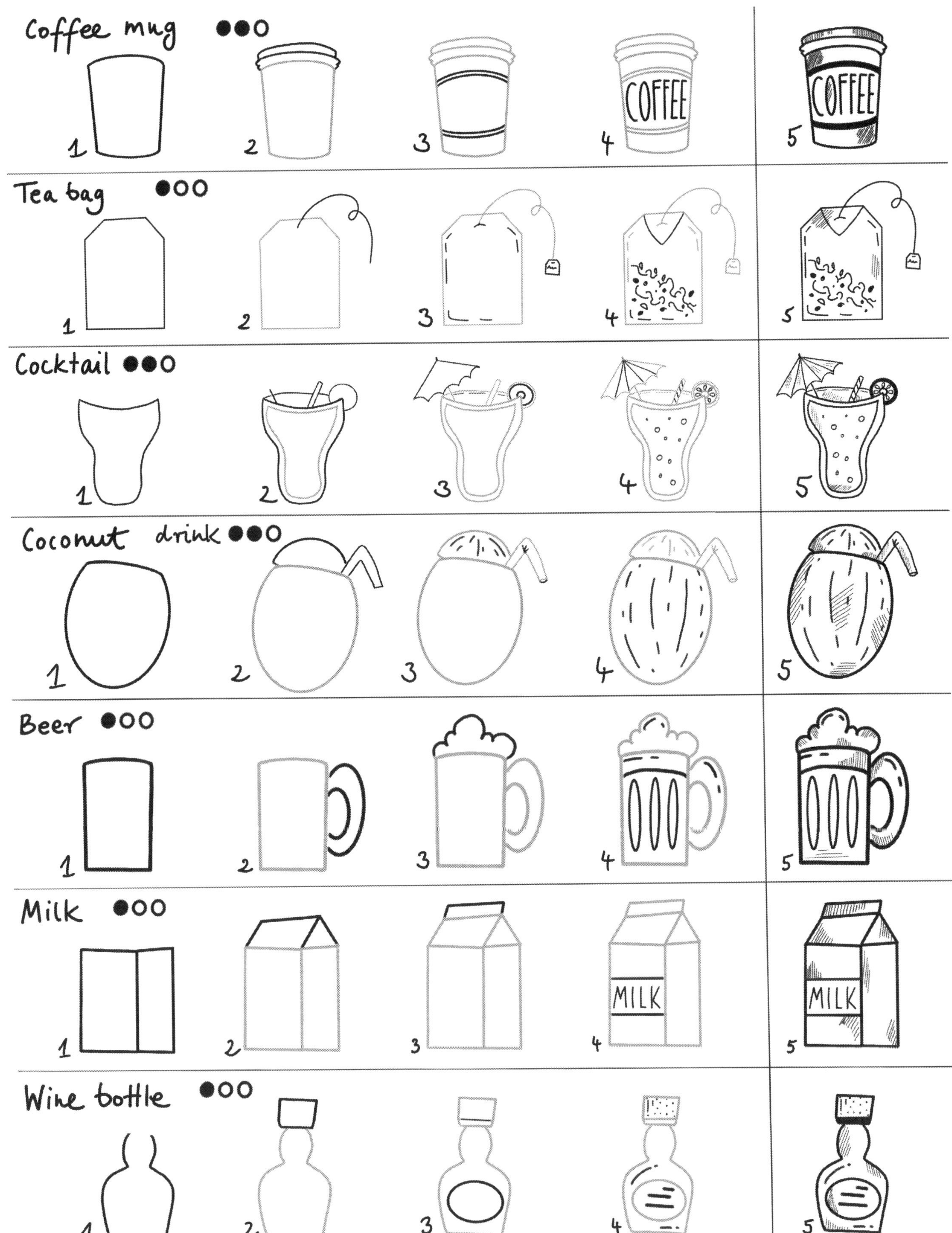
Coffee mug ●●○
1
2
3
COFFEE
4
COFFEE
5
Tea bag ●○○
1
2
3
4
5
Cocktail ●●○
1
2
3
4
5
Coconut drink ●●○
1
2
3
4
5
Beer ●○○
1
2
3
4
5
Milk ●○○
1
2
3
MILK
4
MILK
5
Wine bottle ●○○
1
2
3
4
5

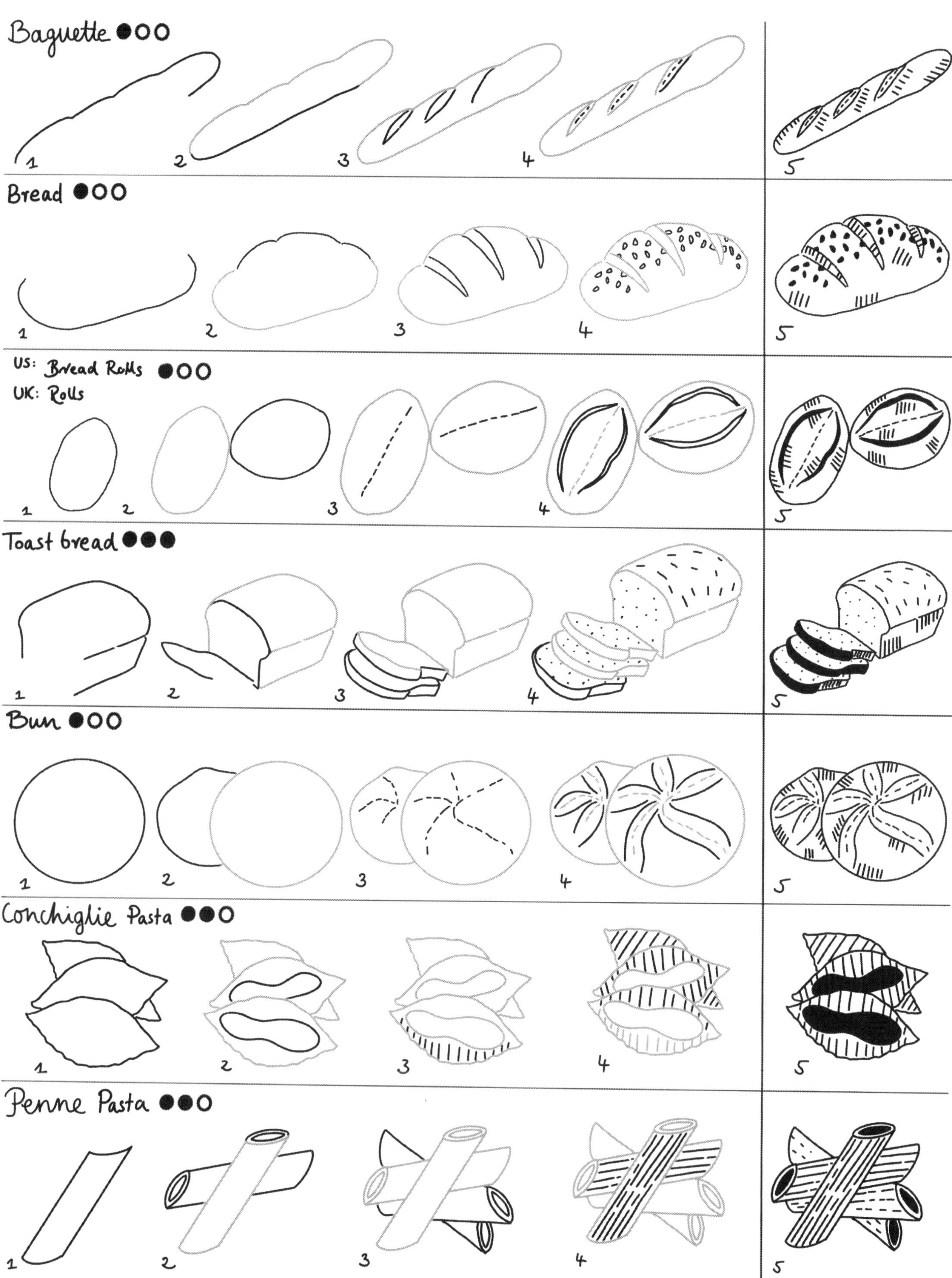
Baguette ●○○
1
2
3
4
5
Bread ●○○
1
2
3
4
5
US: Bread Rolls ●○○
UK: Rolls
1
2
3
4
5
Toast bread ●●●
1
2
3
4
5
Bun ●○○
1
2
3
4
5
Conchiglie Pasta ●●○
1
2
3
4
5
Penne Pasta ●●○
1
2
3
4
5

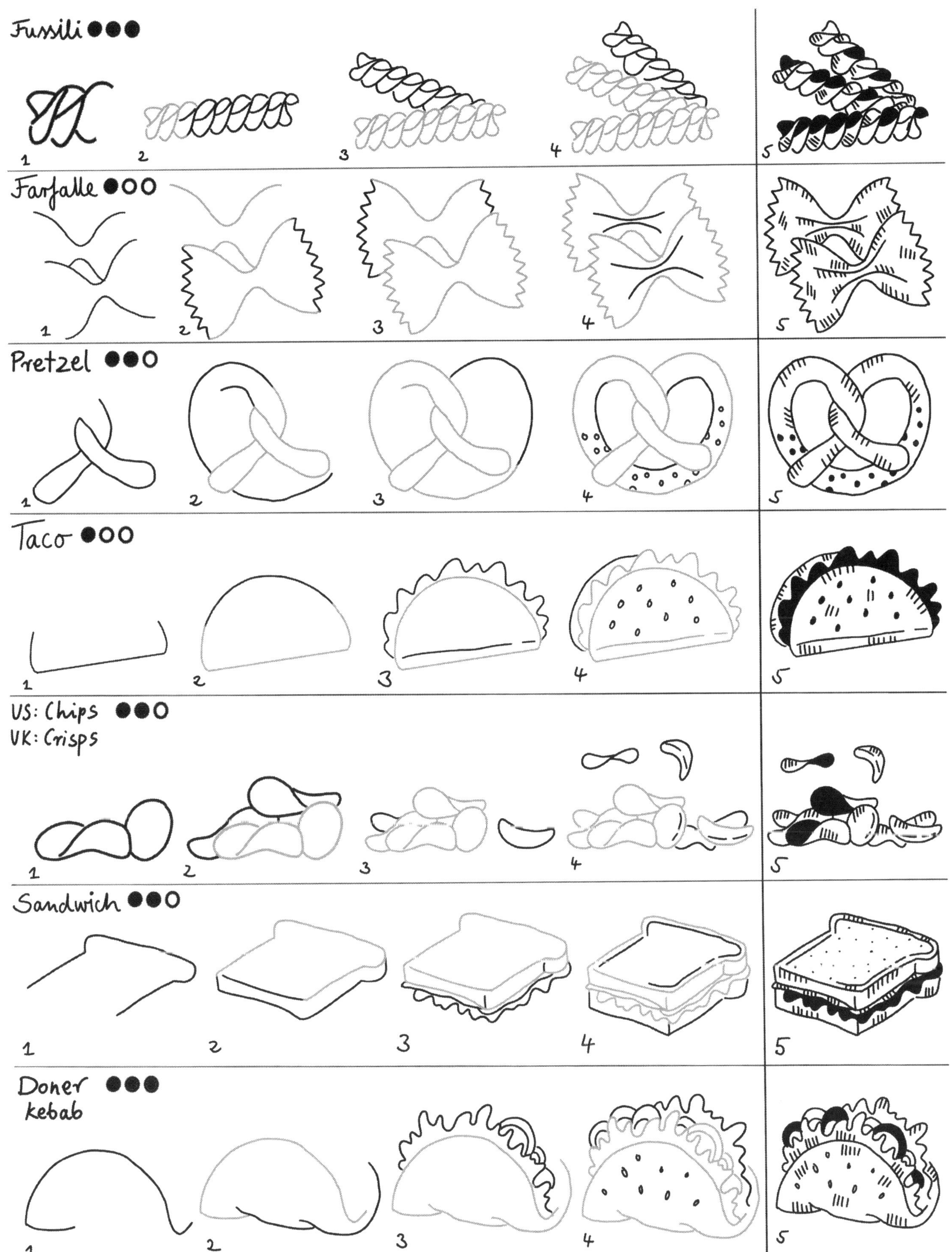
Fussili ●●●
1
2
3
4
5
Farfalle ●○○
1
2
3
4
5
Pretzel ●●○
1
2
3
4
5
Taco ●○○
1
2
3
4
5
US: Chips ●●○
UK: Crisps
1
2
3
4
5
Sandwich ●●○
1
2
3
4
5
Doner kebab ●●●
1
2
3
4
5

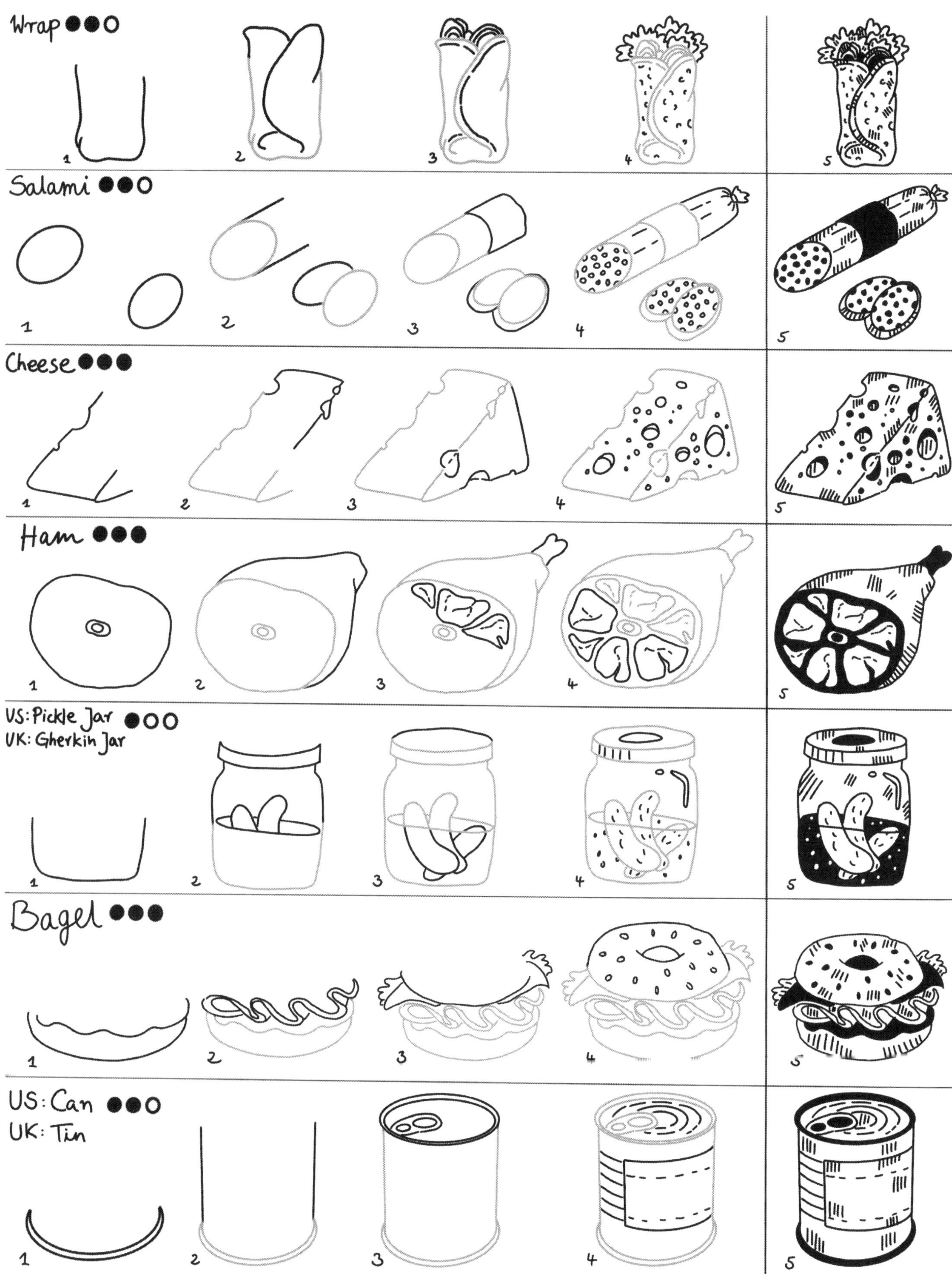
Wrap
1
2
3
4
5
Salami
1
2
3
4
5
Cheese
1
2
3
4
5
Ham
1
2
3
4
5
US: Pickle Jar
UK: Gherkin Jar
1
2
3
4
5
Bagel
1
2
3
4
5
US: Can
UK: Tin
1
2
3
4
5

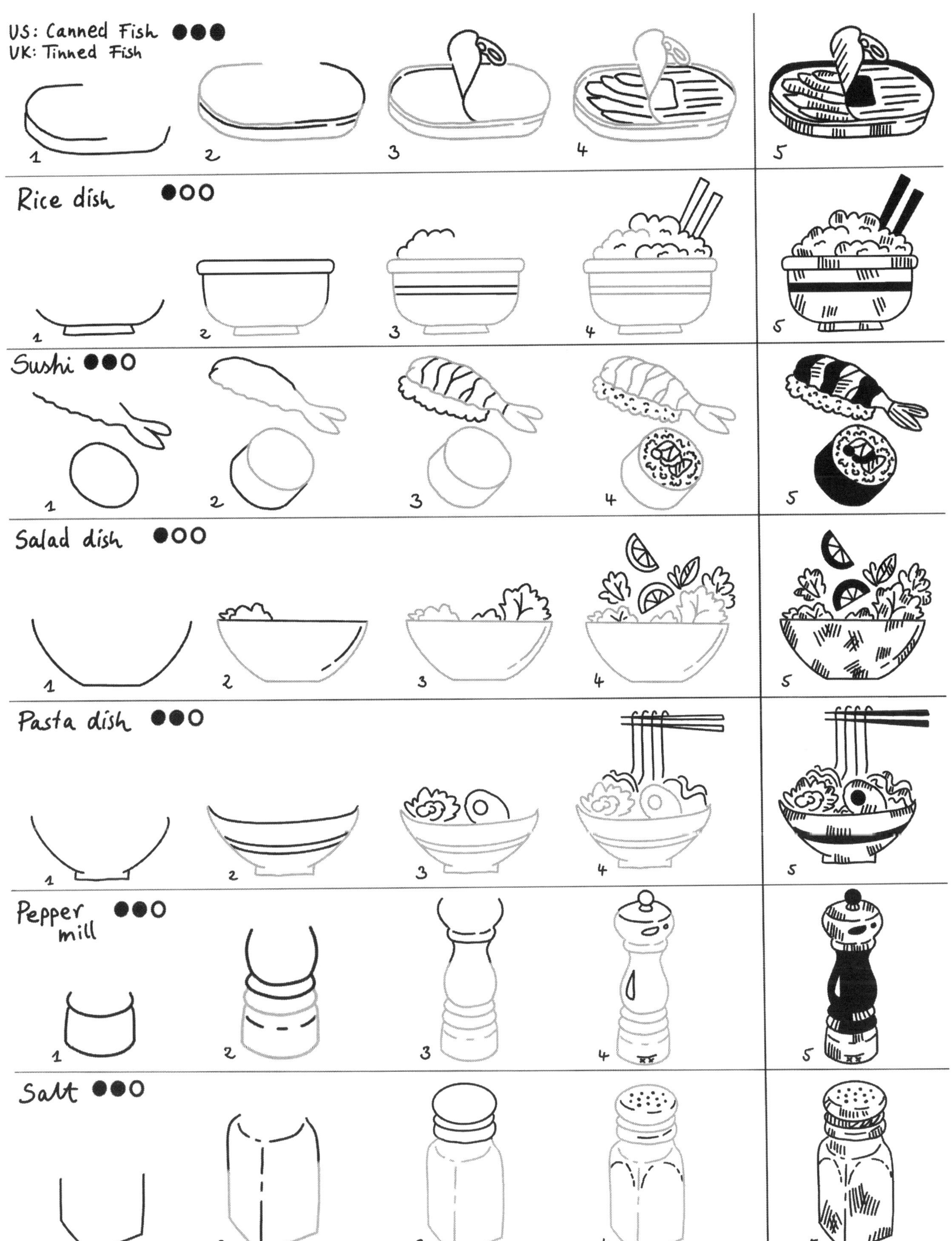
US: Canned Fish
UK: Tinned Fish
1
2
3
4
5
Rice dish
1
2
3
4
5
Sushi
1
2
3
4
5
Salad dish
1
2
3
4
5
Pasta dish
1
2
3
4
5
Pepper mill
1
2
3
4
5
Salt
1
2
3
4
5

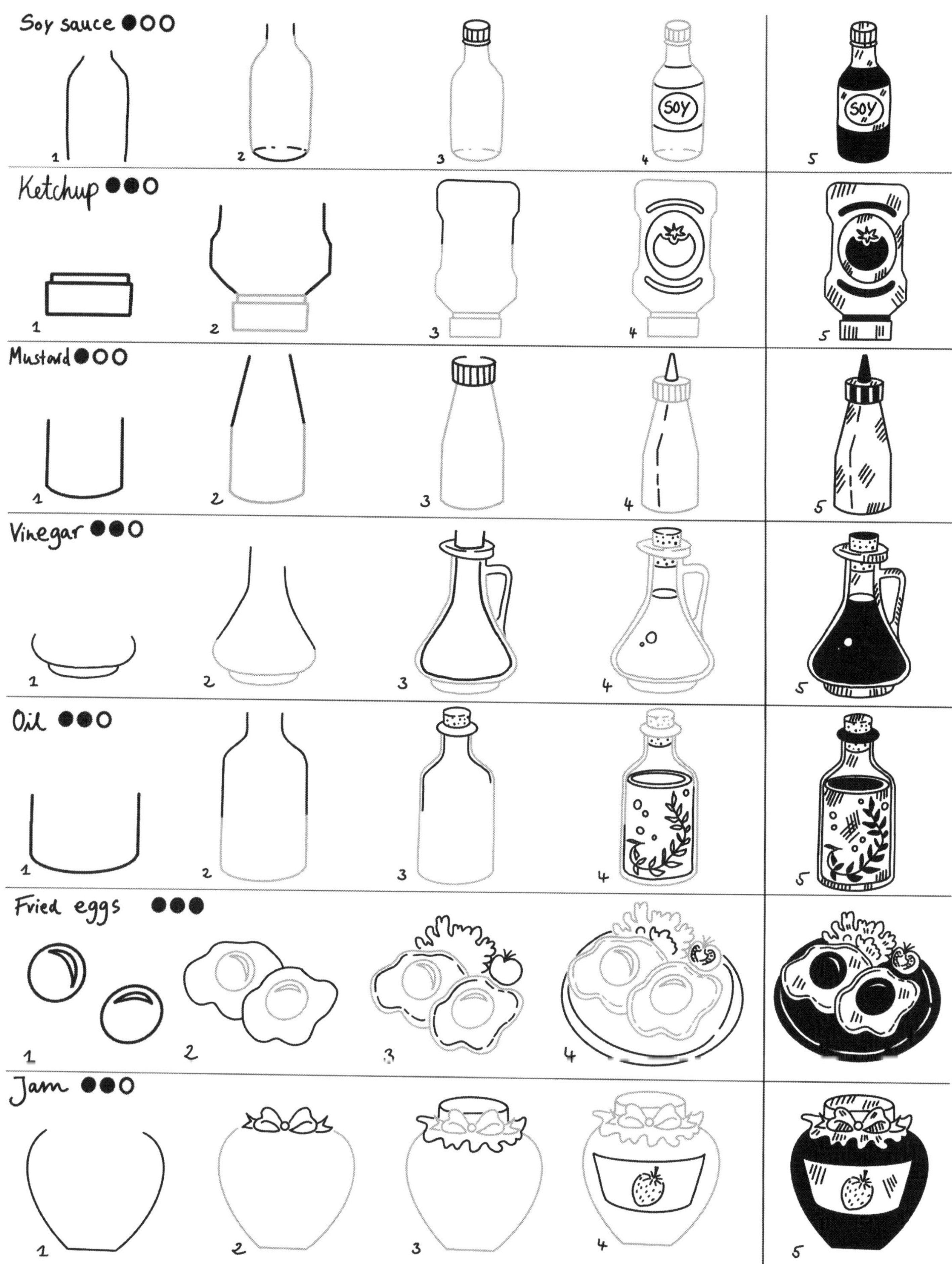
Soy sauce
1
2
3
SOY
4
SOY
5
Ketchup
1
2
3
4
5
Mustard
1
2
3
4
5
Vinegar
1
2
3
4
5
Oil
1
2
3
4
5
Fried eggs
1
2
3
4
Jam
1
2
3
4
5

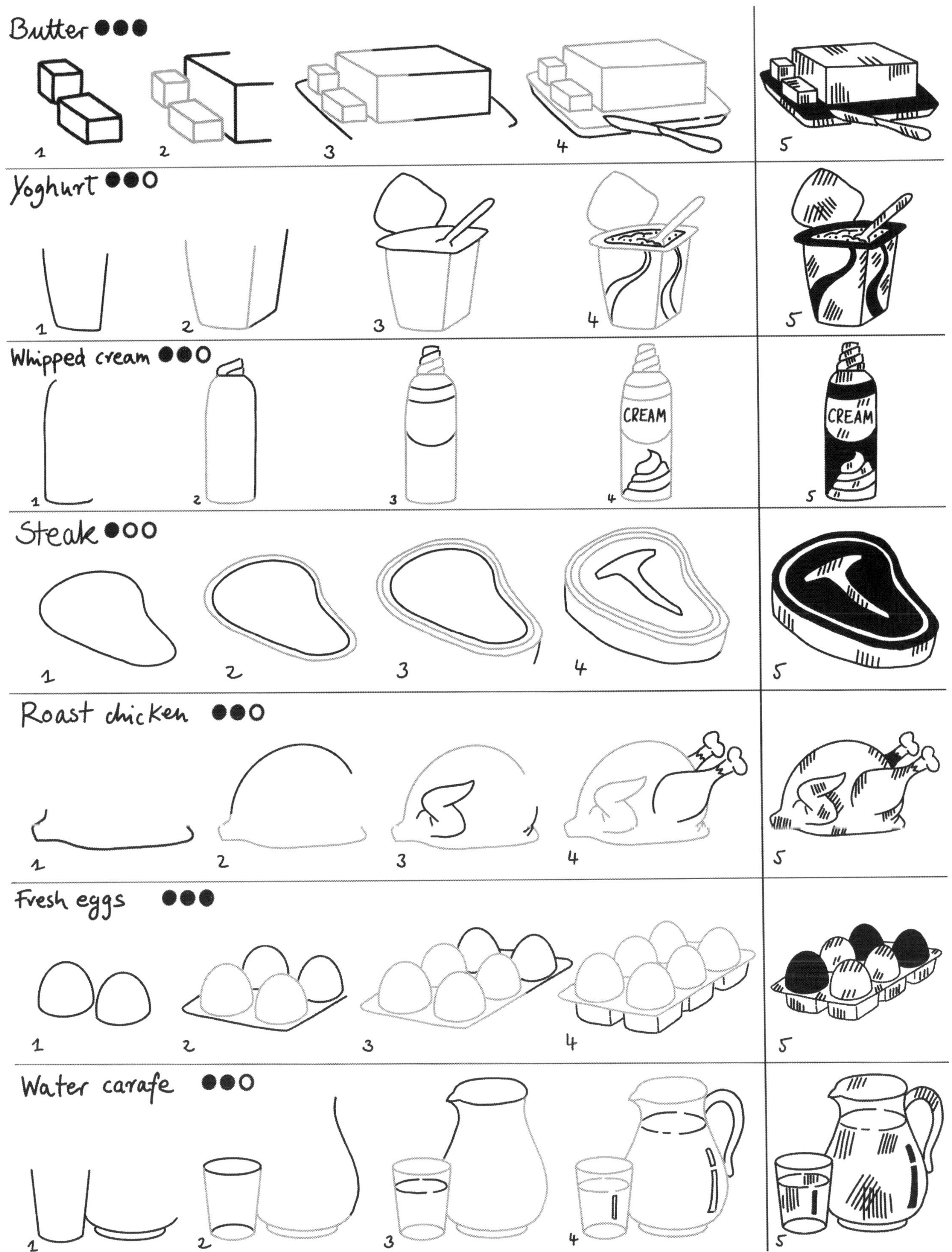
Butter
1
2
3
4
5
Yoghurt
1
2
3
4
5
Whipped cream
1
2
3
CREAM
4
CREAM
5
Steak
1
2
3
4
5
Roast chicken
1
2
3
4
5
Fresh eggs
1
2
3
4
5
Water carafe
1
2
3
4
5

# OUTDOOR

US: Mailbox
UK: Post Box
1
2
3
4
5
US: Dumpster
UK: Skip
1
2
3
4
5
Street sign
1
2
3
4
5
Streetlight
1
2
3
4
5
US: Crosswalk
UK: Pedestrian Crossing
1
2
3
4
5
Traffic light
1
2
3
4
5
Advertising pillar
1
2
3
4
5

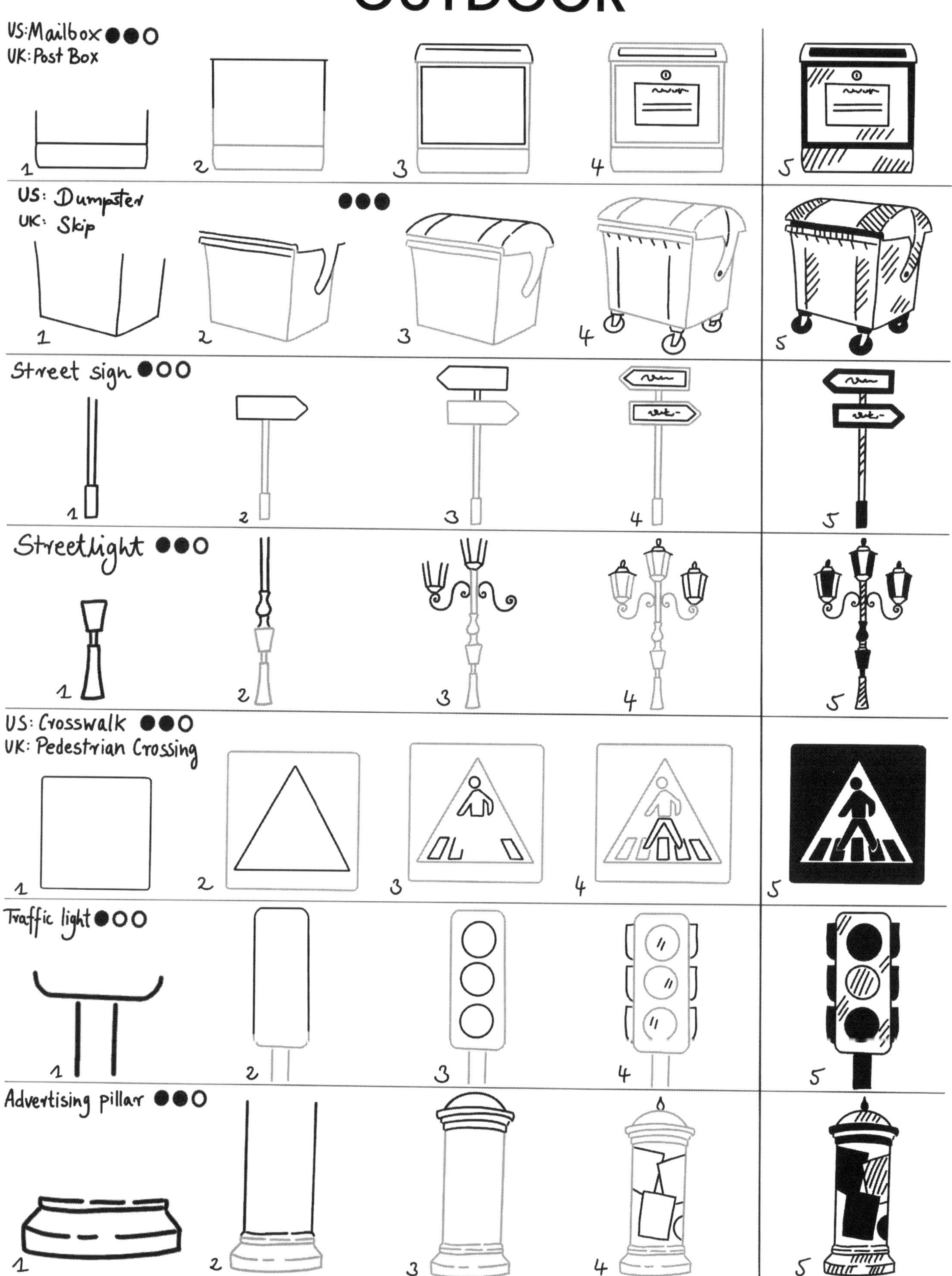

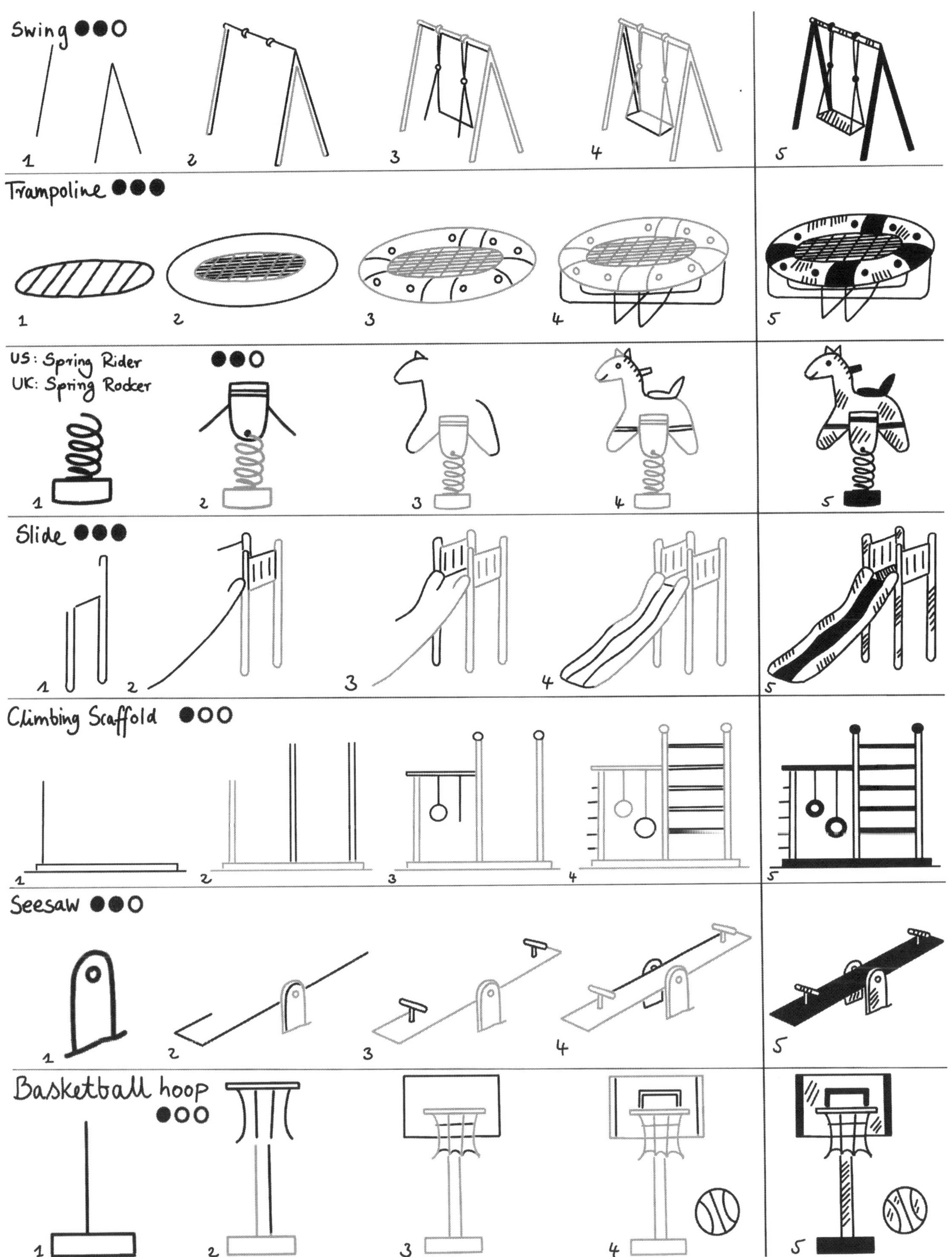
Swing
1
2
3
4
5
Trampoline
1
2
3
4
5
US: Spring Rider
UK: Spring Rocker
1
2
3
4
5
Slide
1
2
3
4
5
Climbing Scaffold
1
2
3
4
5
Seesaw
1
2
3
4
5
Basketball hoop
1
2
3
4
5

# VEHICLES

Bicycle ●●○
1
2
3
4
5
Motorbike ●●○
1
2
3
4
5
US: High-Wheel Bicycle ●○○
UK: Penny-farthing
1
2
3
4
5
Tandem Bike ●●○
1
2
3
4
5
US: Scooter ●●○
UK: Moped
1
2
3
4
5
Rickshaw ●●●
1
2
3
4
5
E-Scooter ●●●
1
2
3
4
5

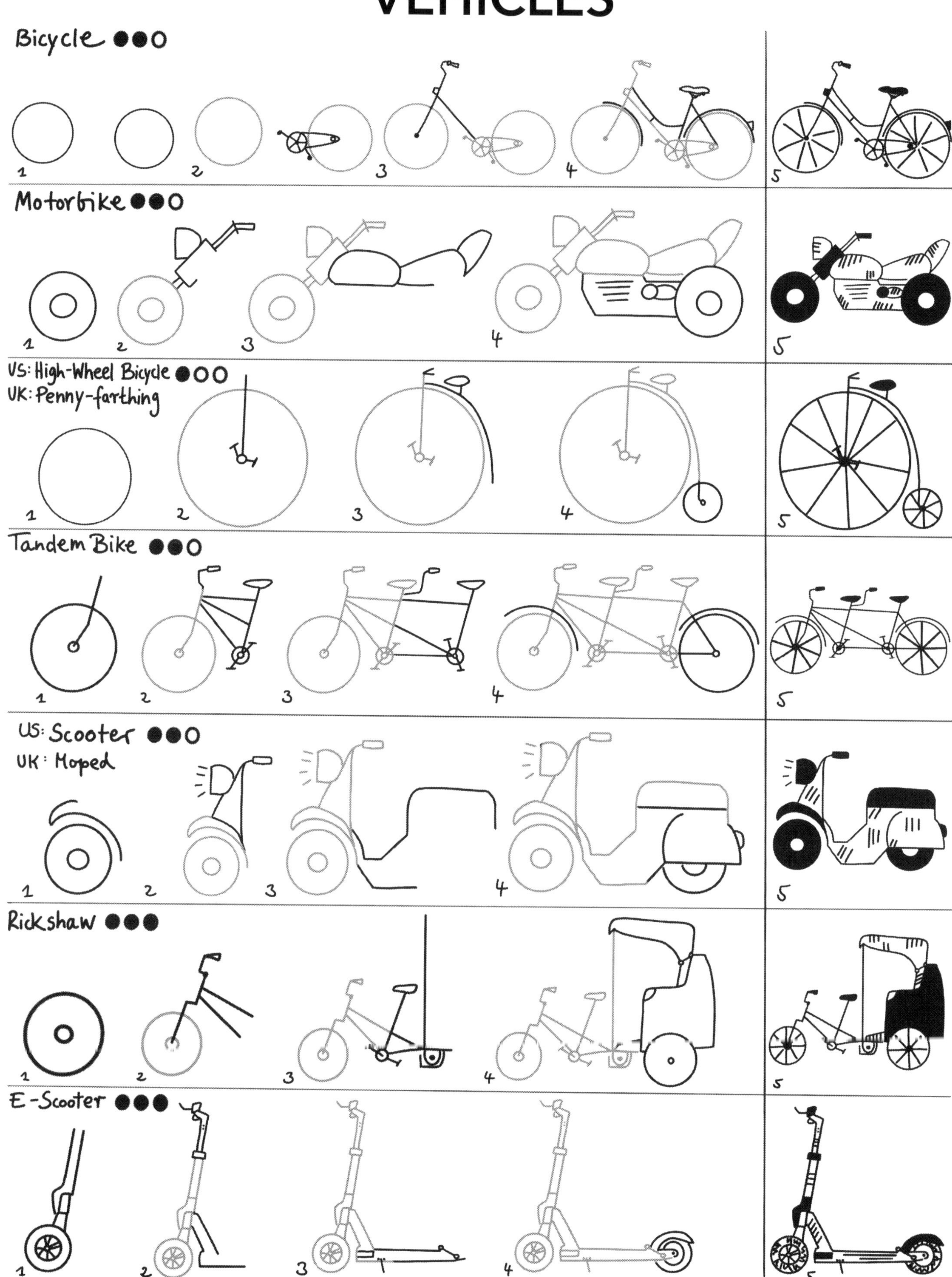

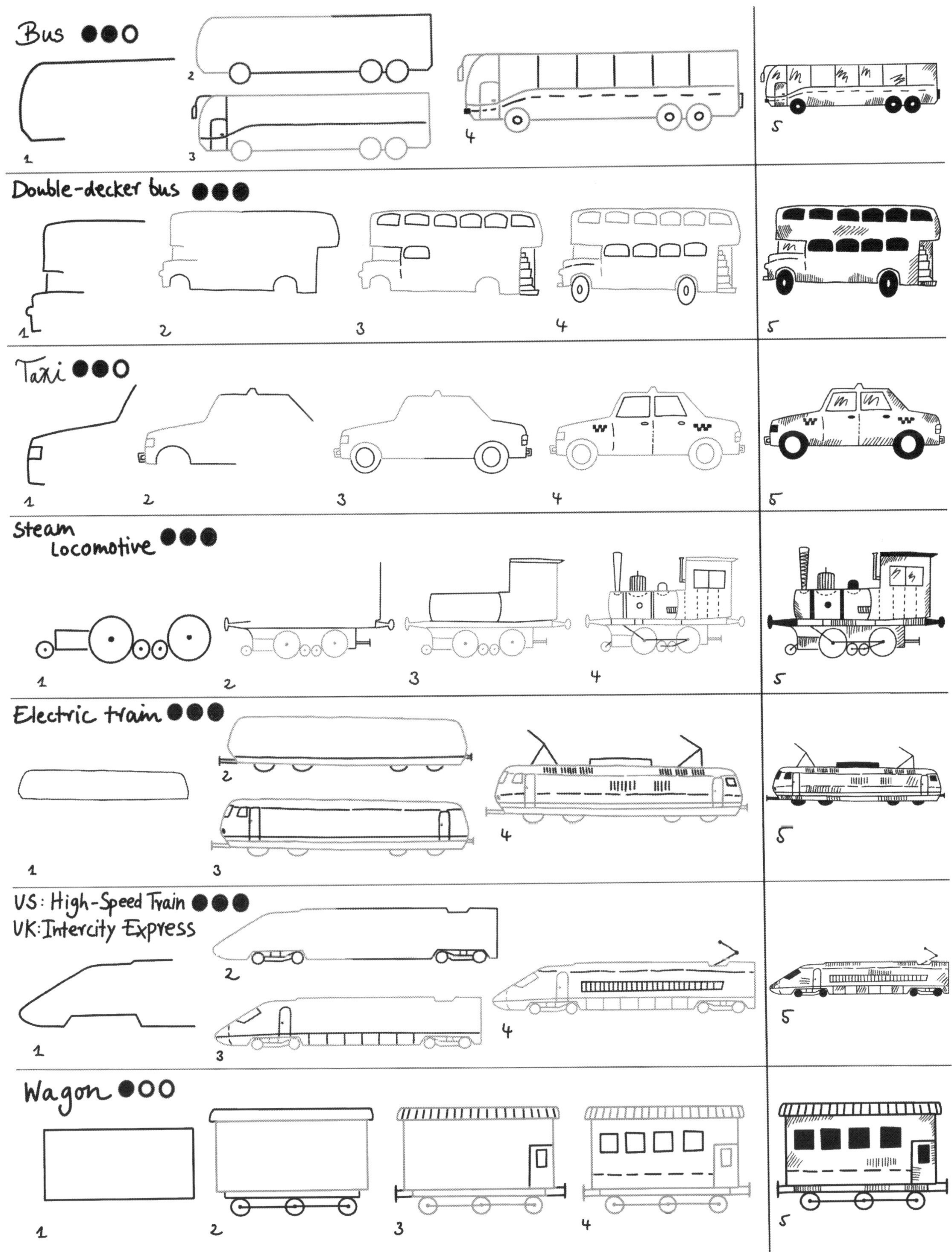

Bus
1
2
3
4
5
Double-decker bus
1
2
3
4
5
Taxi
1
2
3
4
5
Steam Locomotive
1
2
3
4
5
Electric train
1
2
3
4
5
US: High-Speed Train
UK: Intercity Express
1
2
3
4
5
Wagon
1
2
3
4
5

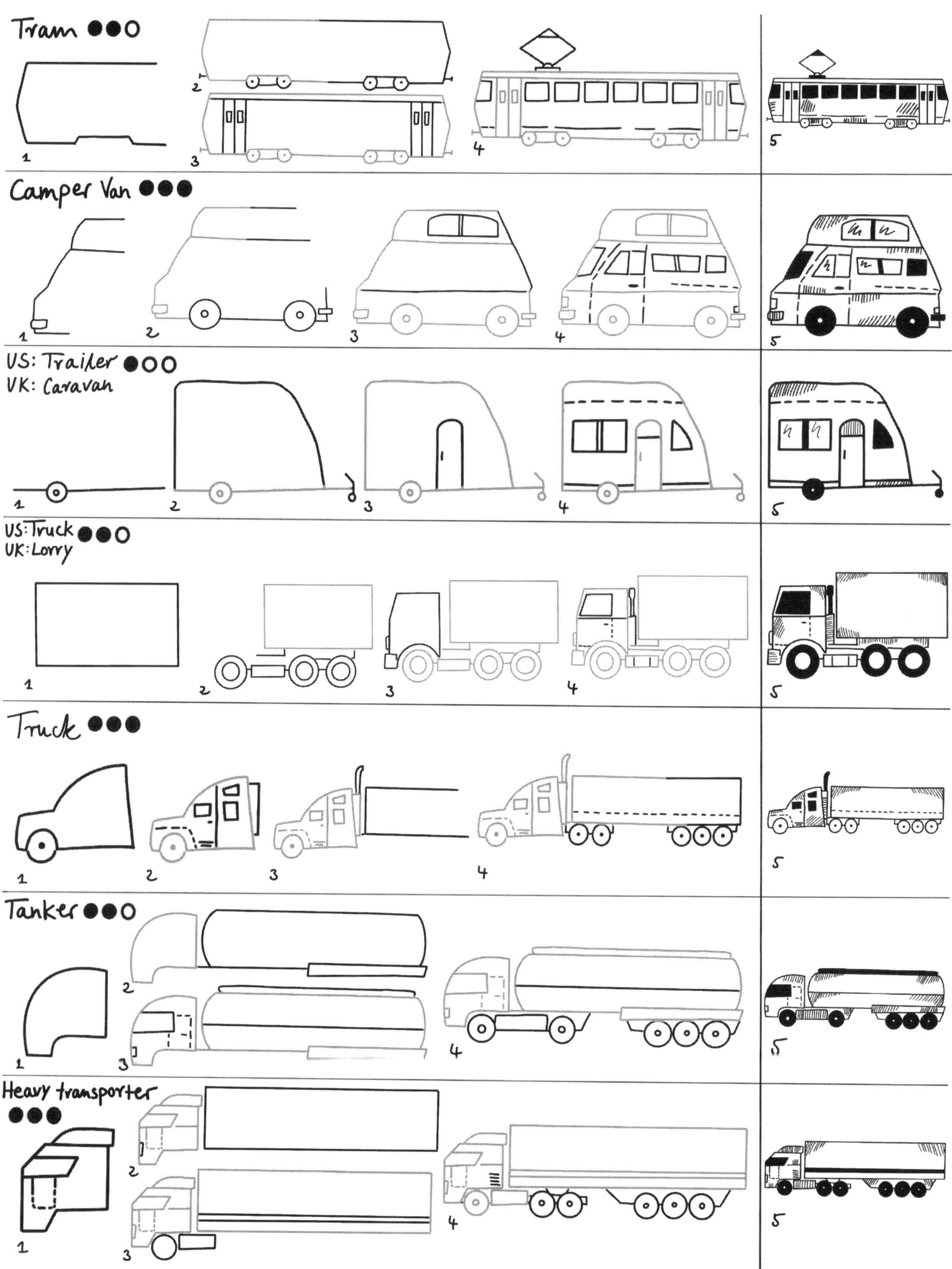

Tram ●●○
1
2
3
4
5
Camper Van ●●●
1
2
3
4
5
US: Trailer ●○○
UK: Caravan
1
2
3
4
5
US: Truck ●●○
UK: Lorry
1
2
3
4
5
Truck ●●●
1
2
3
4
5
Tanker ●●○
1
2
3
4
5
Heavy transporter ●●●
1
2
3
4
5

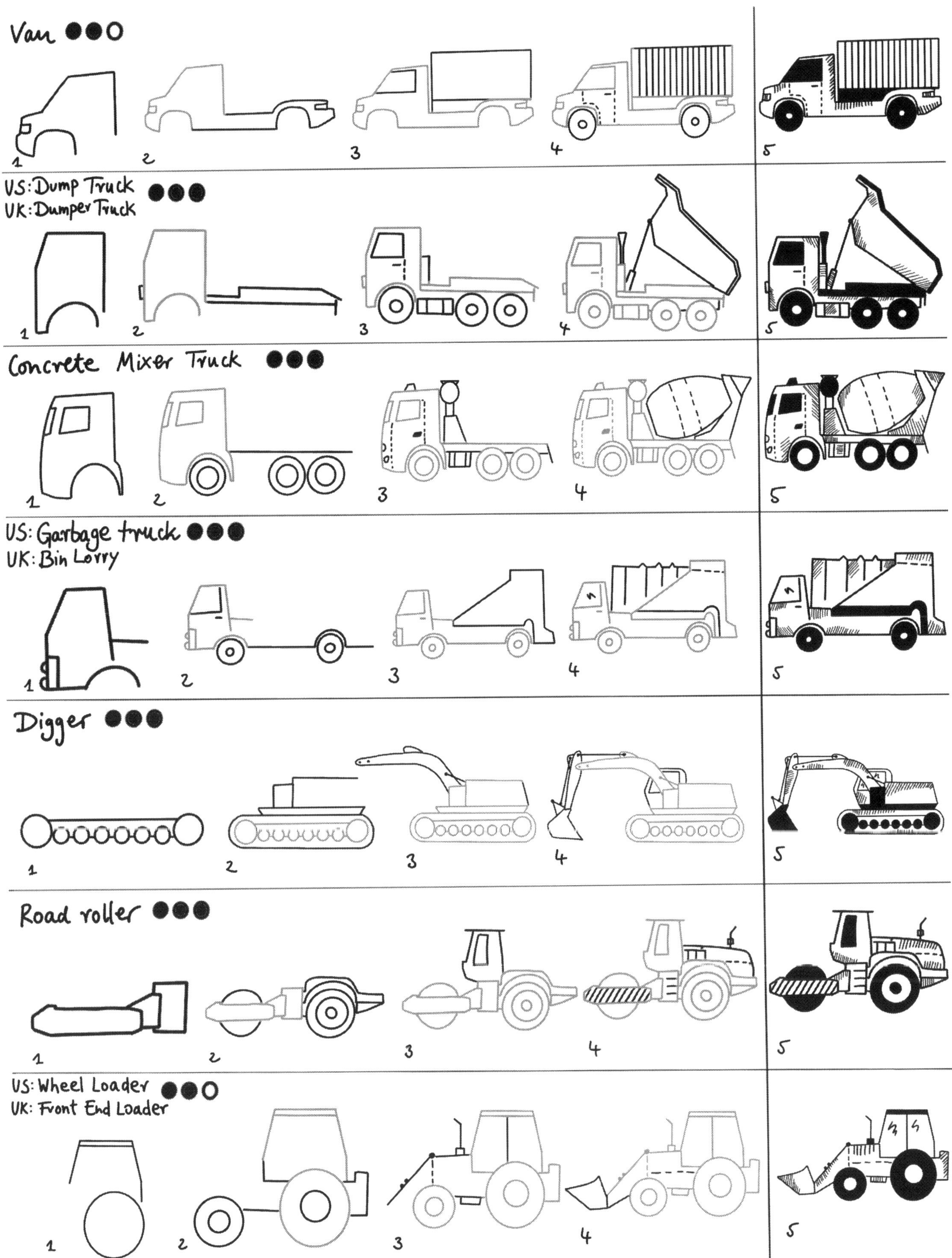
Van
1
2
3
4
5
US: Dump Truck
UK: Dumper Truck
1
2
3
4
5
Concrete Mixer Truck
1
2
3
4
5
US: Garbage truck
UK: Bin Lorry
1
2
3
4
5
Digger
1
2
3
4
5
Road roller
1
2
3
4
5
US: Wheel Loader
UK: Front End Loader
1
2
3
4
5

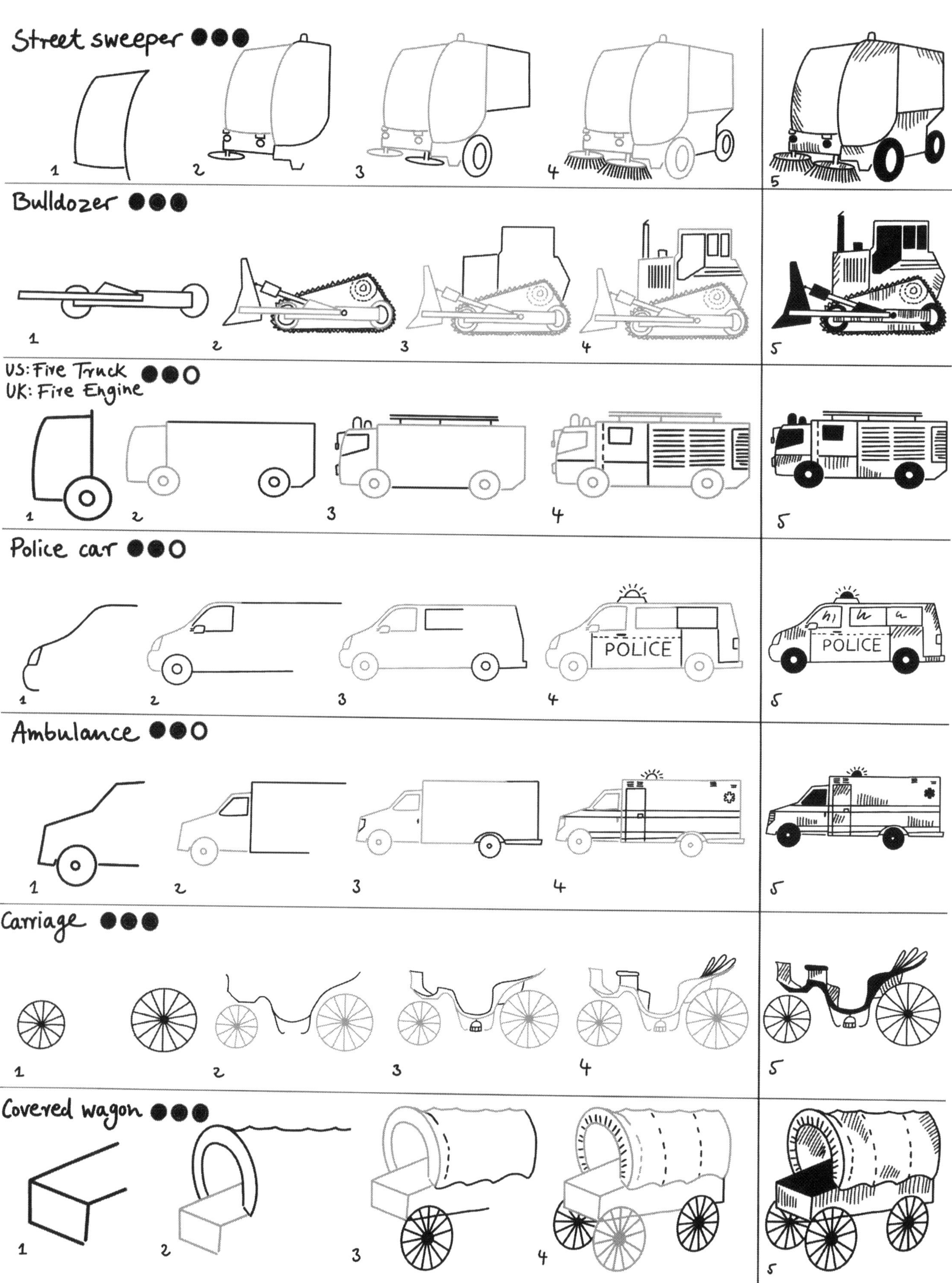
Street sweeper
1
2
3
4
5
Bulldozer
1
2
3
4
5
US: Fire Truck
UK: Fire Engine
1
2
3
4
5
Police car
POLICE
1
2
3
4
5
Ambulance
1
2
3
4
5
Carriage
1
2
3
4
5
Covered wagon
1
2
3
4
5

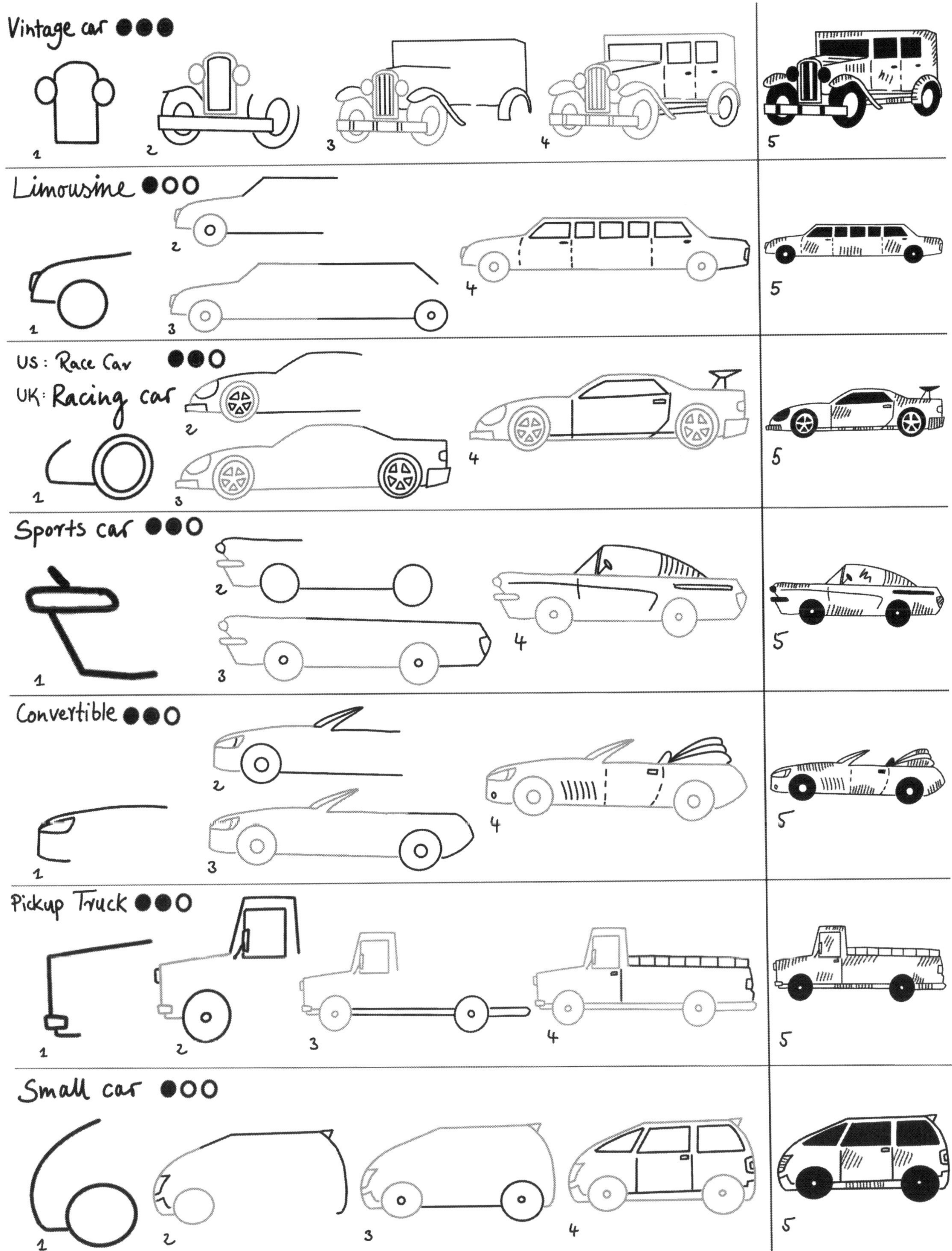
Vintage car
Limousine
US: Race Car
UK: Racing car
Sports car
Convertible
Pickup Truck
Small car

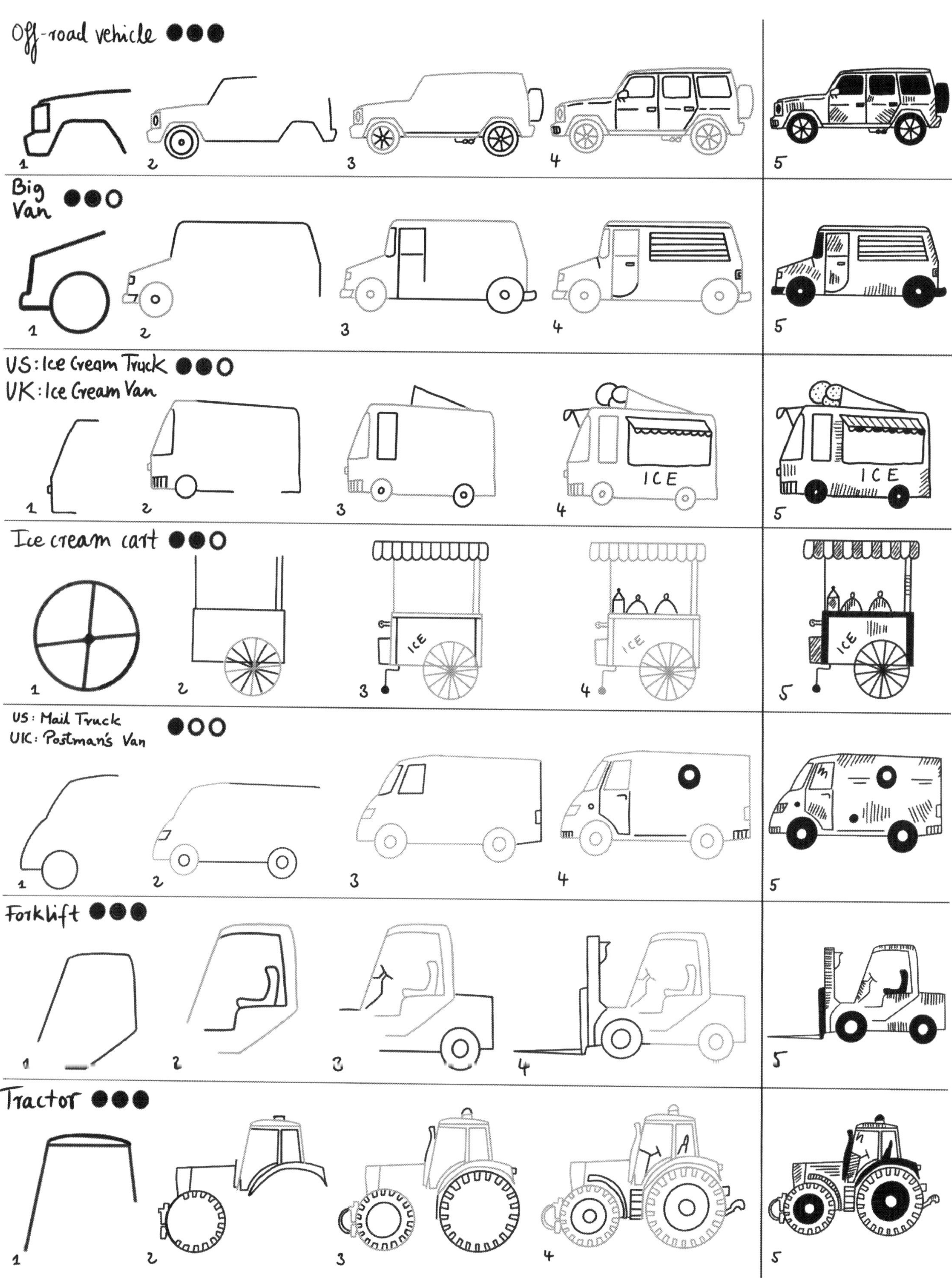
Off-road vehicle
1
2
3
4
5
Big Van
1
2
3
4
5
US: Ice Cream Truck
UK: Ice Cream Van
ICE
1
2
3
4
5
Ice cream cart
ICE
1
2
3
4
5
US: Mail Truck
UK: Postman's Van
1
2
3
4
5
Forklift
1
2
3
4
5
Tractor
1
2
3
4
5

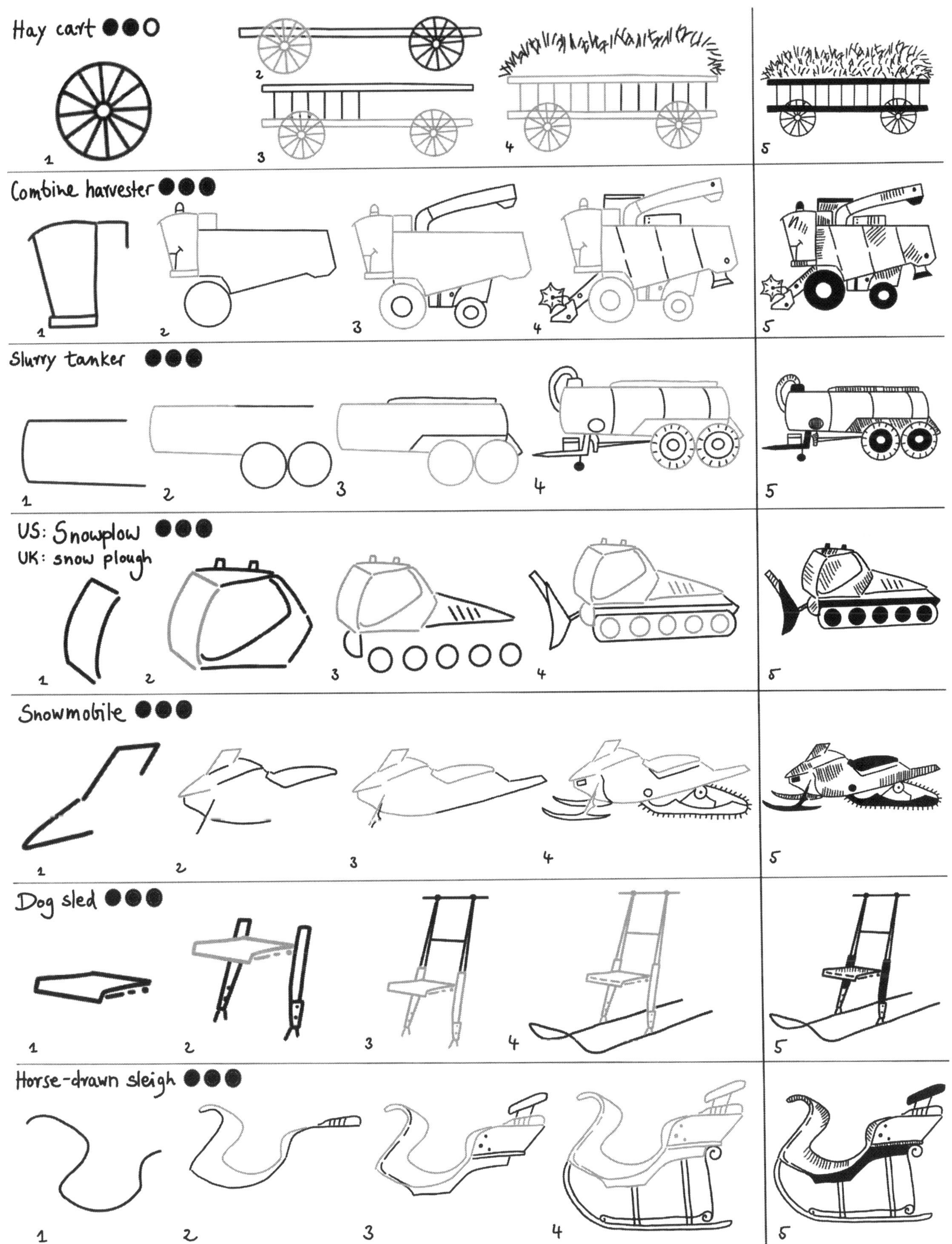
Hay cart
1
2
3
4
5
Combine harvester
1
2
3
4
5
Slurry tanker
1
2
3
4
5
US: Snowplow
UK: snow plough
1
2
3
4
5
Snowmobile
1
2
3
4
5
Dog sled
1
2
3
4
5
Horse-drawn sleigh
1
2
3
4
5

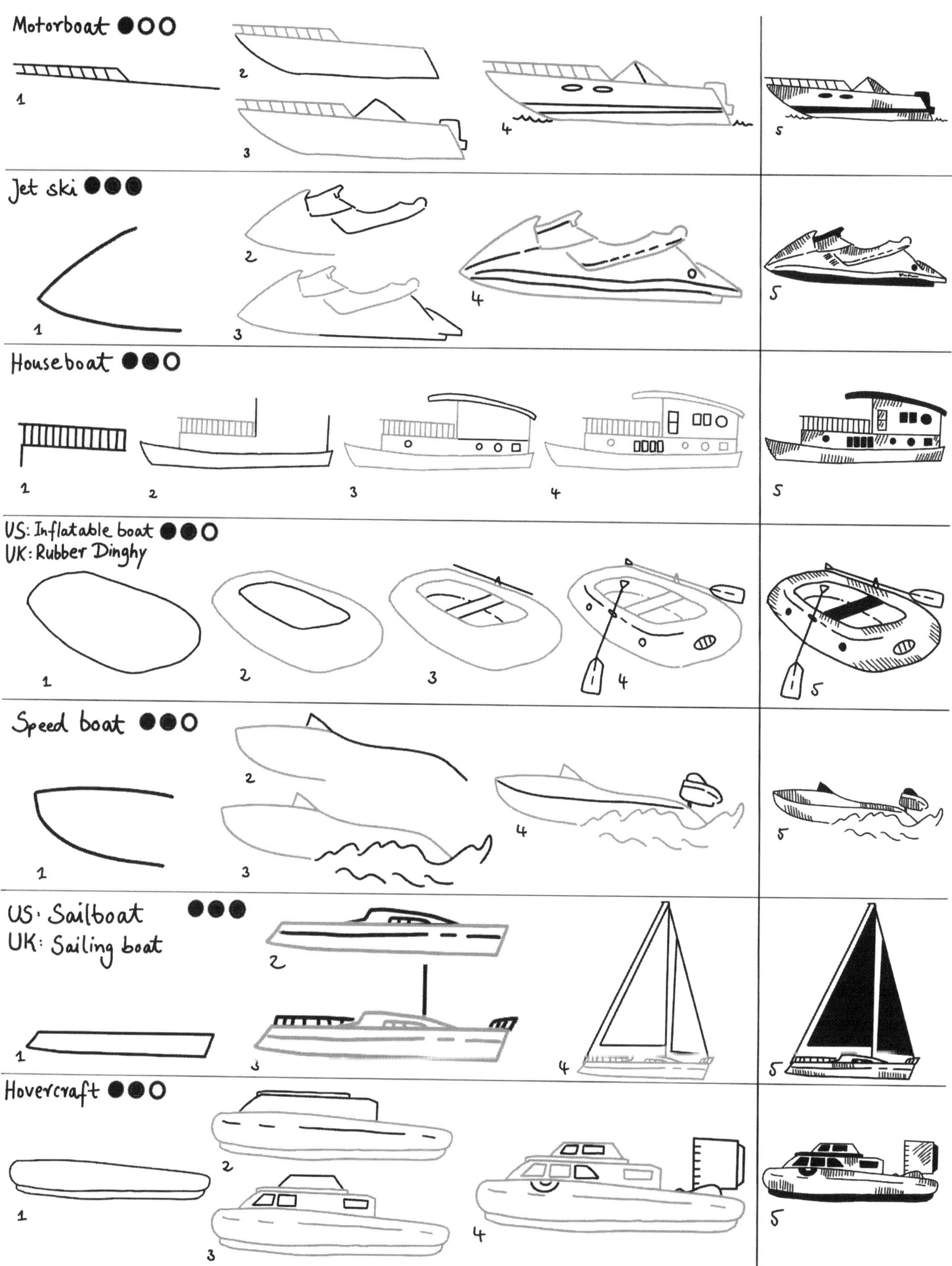
Motorboat ●○○
1
2
3
4
5
Jet ski ●●●
1
2
3
4
5
Houseboat ●●○
1
2
3
4
5
US: Inflatable boat ●●○
UK: Rubber Dinghy
1
2
3
4
5
Speed boat ●●○
1
2
3
4
5
US: Sailboat ●●●
UK: Sailing boat
1
2
3
4
5
Hovercraft ●●○
1
2
3
4
5

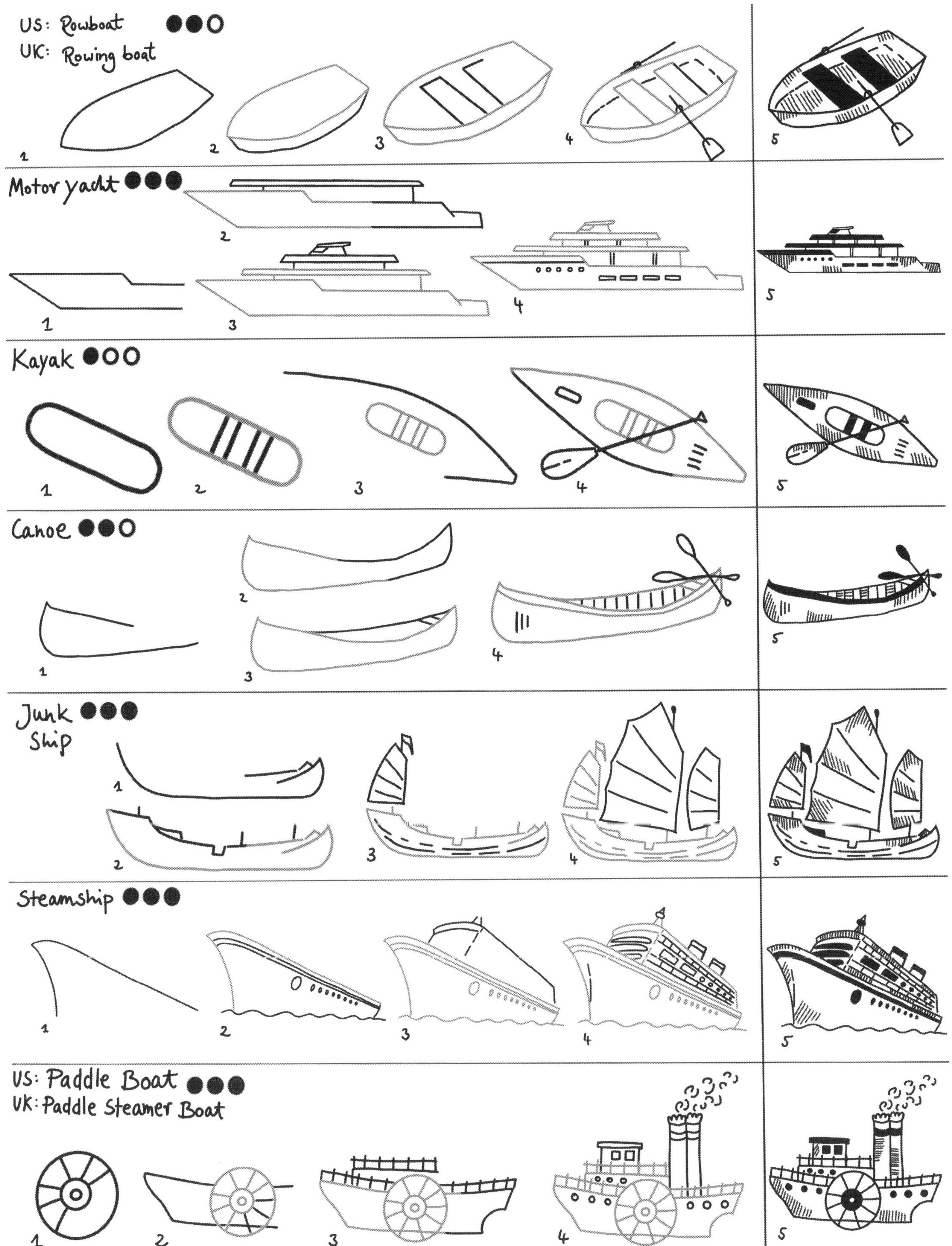
US: Rowboat
UK: Rowing boat
1
2
3
4
5
Motor yacht
1
2
3
4
5
Kayak
1
2
3
4
5
Canoe
1
2
3
4
5
Junk Ship
1
2
3
4
5
Steamship
1
2
3
4
5
US: Paddle Boat
UK: Paddle Steamer Boat
1
2
3
4
5

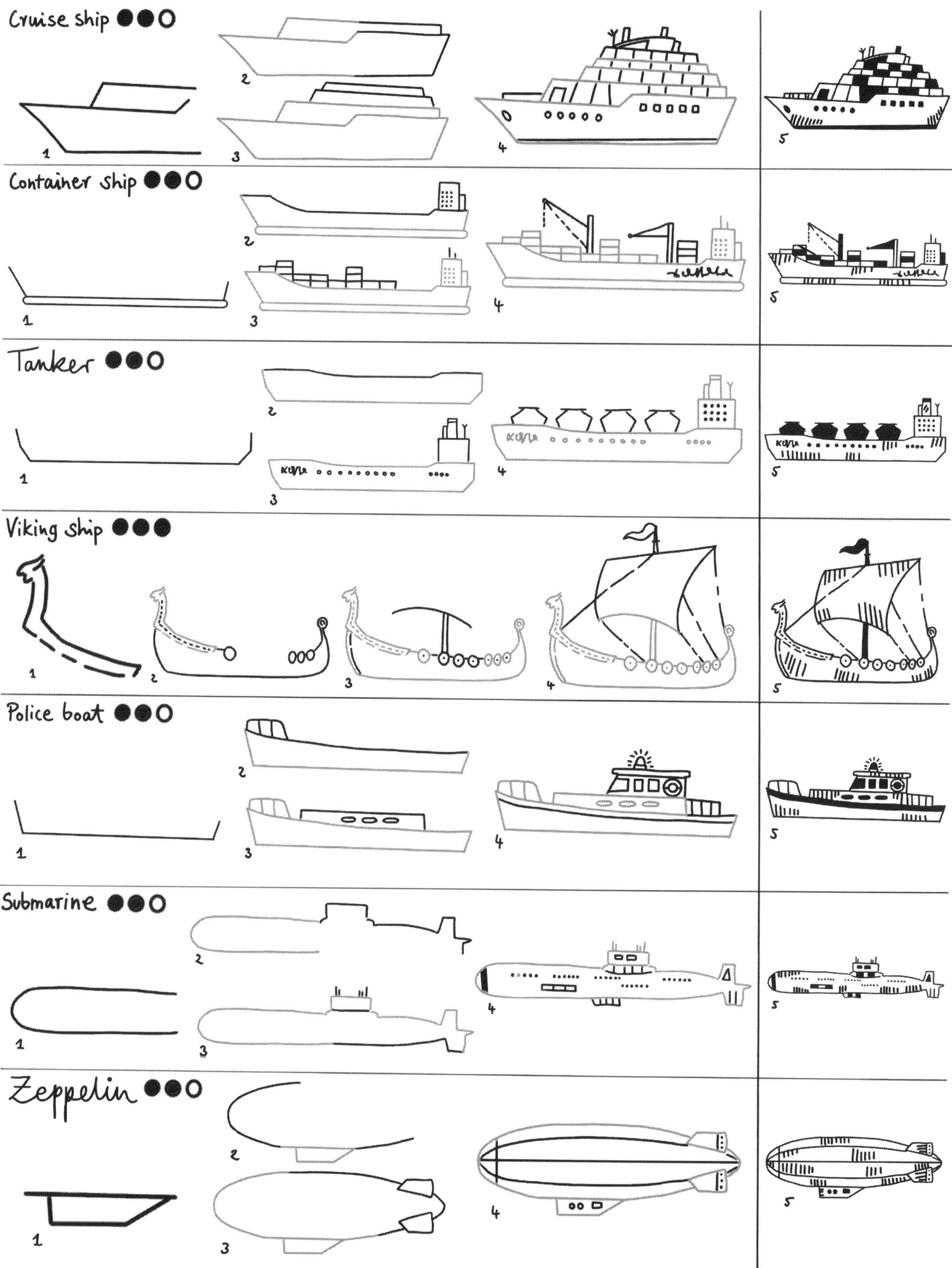
Cruise ship
Container ship
Tanker
Viking ship
Police boat
Submarine
Zeppelin

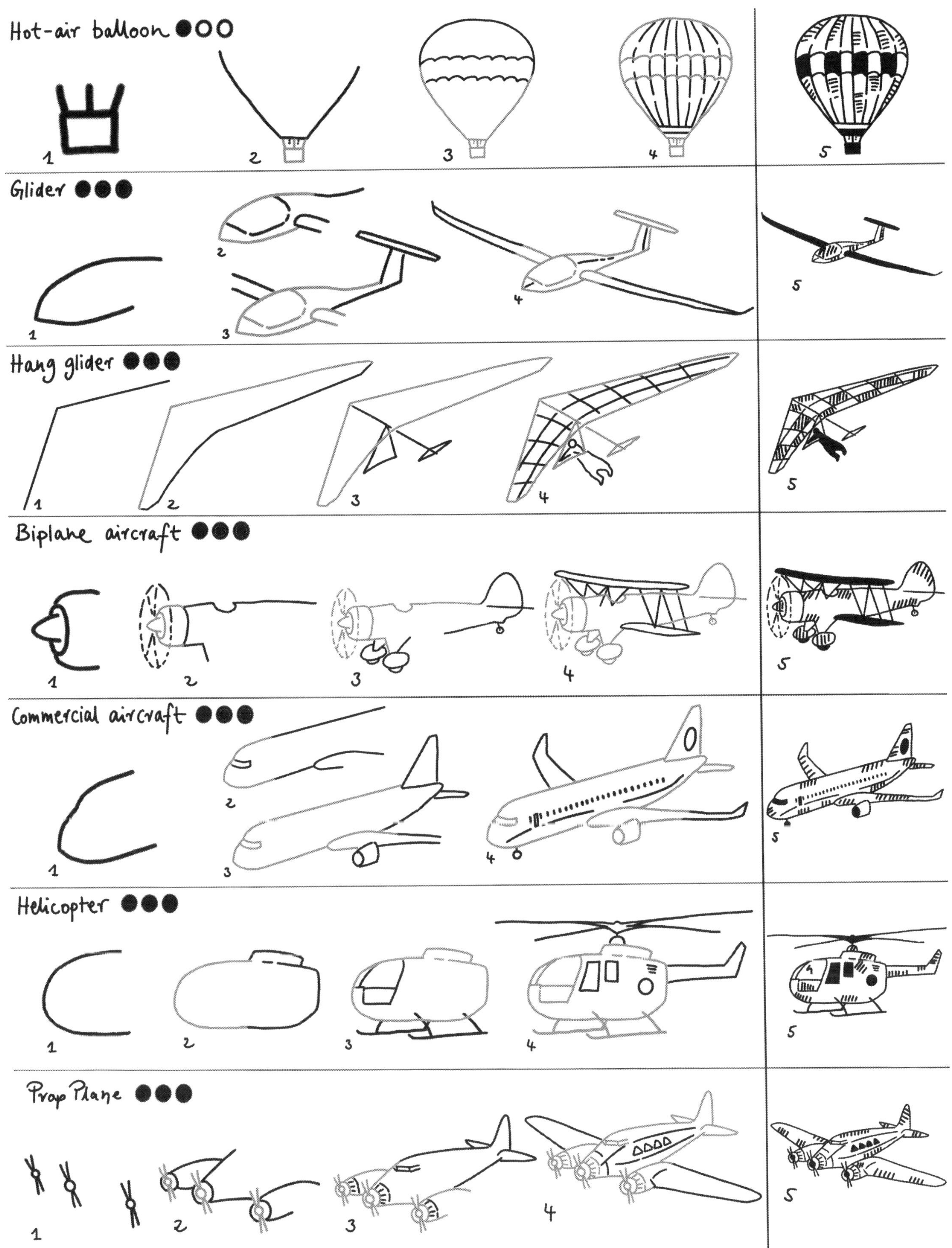
Hot-air balloon
1
2
3
4
5
Glider
1
2
3
4
5
Hang glider
1
2
3
4
5
Biplane aircraft
1
2
3
4
5
Commercial aircraft
1
2
3
4
5
Helicopter
1
2
3
4
5
Prop Plane
1
2
3
4
5

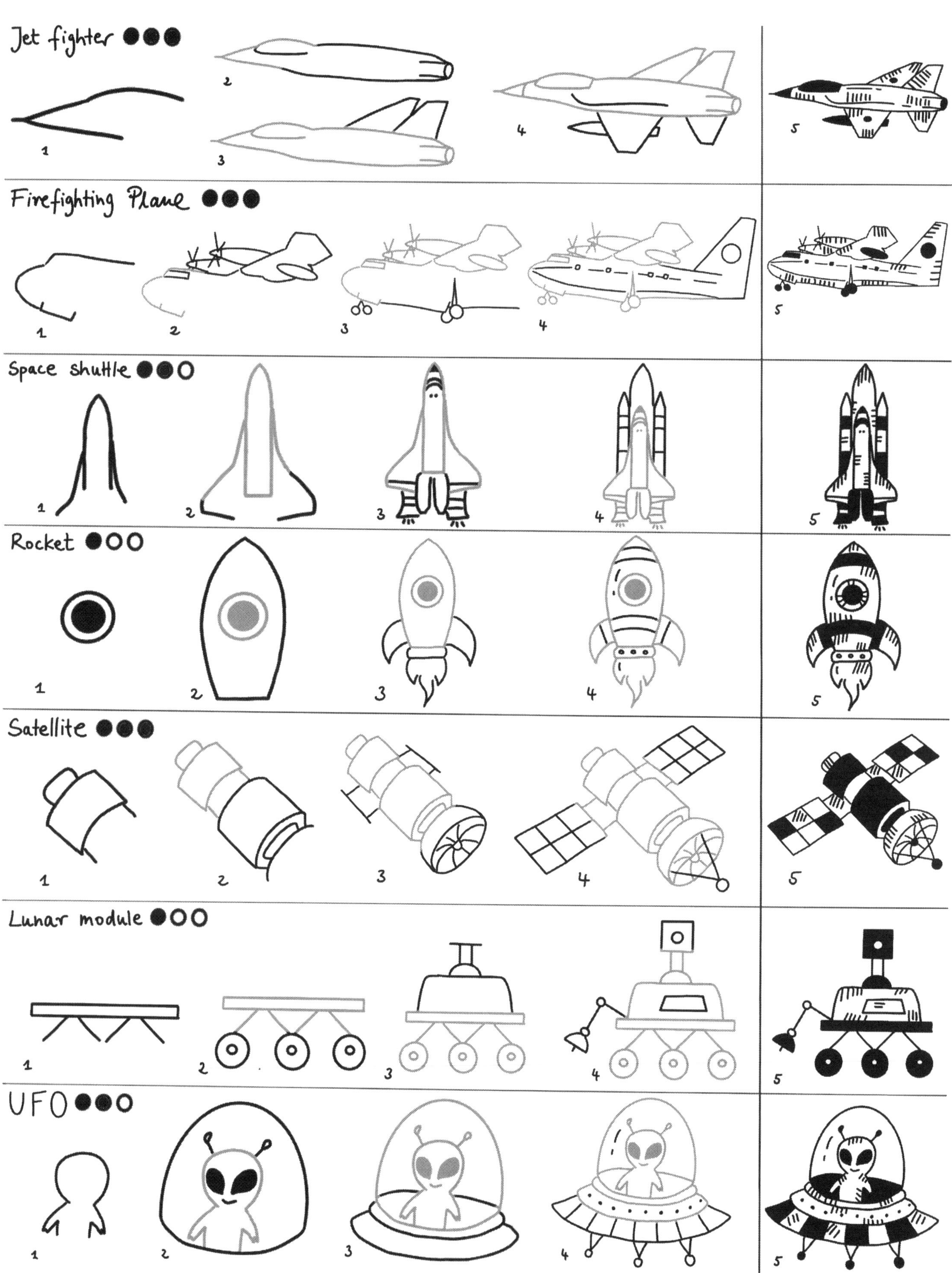

Jet fighter
1
2
3
4
5
Firefighting Plane
1
2
3
4
5
Space shuttle
1
2
3
4
5
Rocket
1
2
3
4
5
Satellite
1
2
3
4
5
Lunar module
1
2
3
4
5
UFO
1
2
3
4
5

# BUILDINGS & SIGHTS

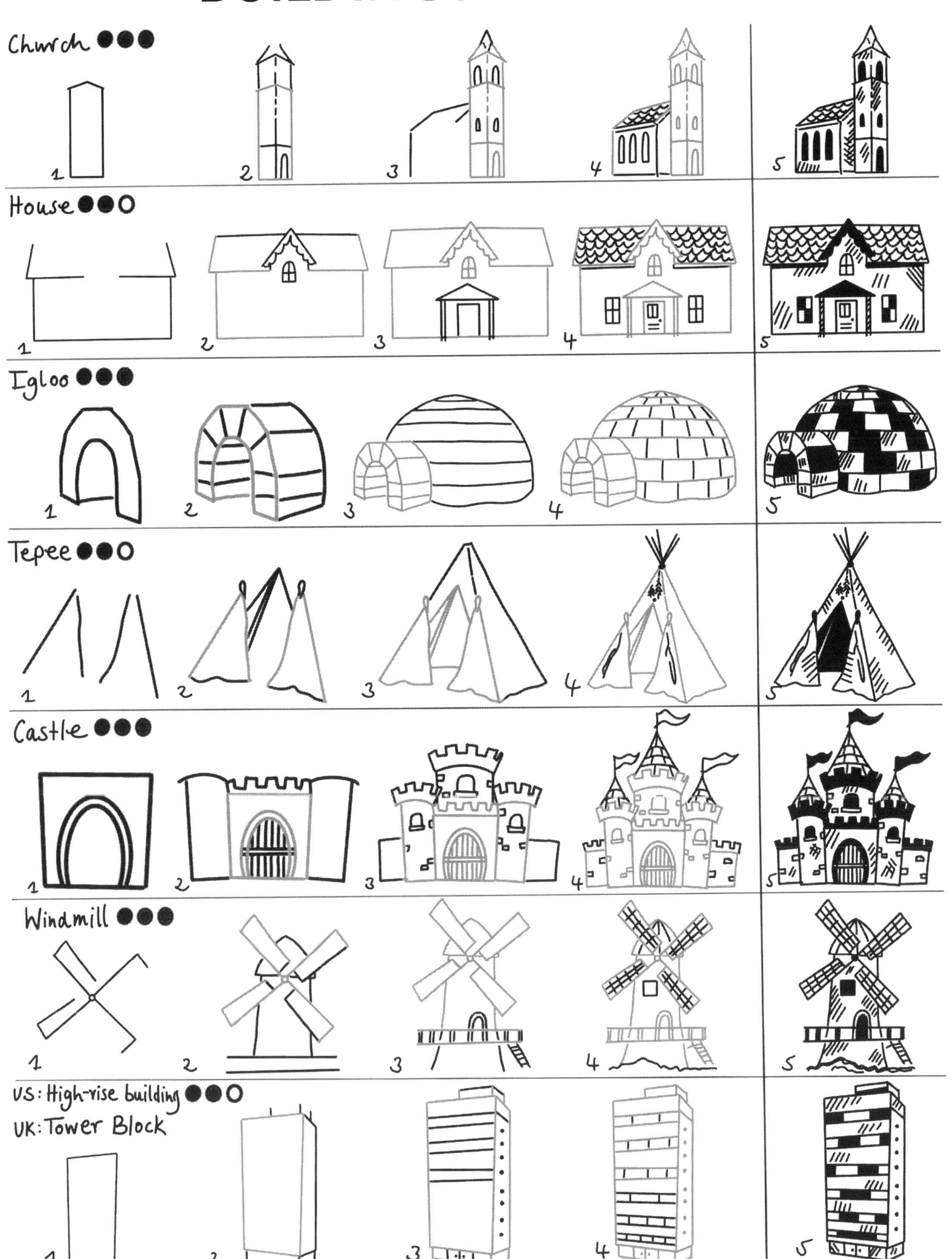

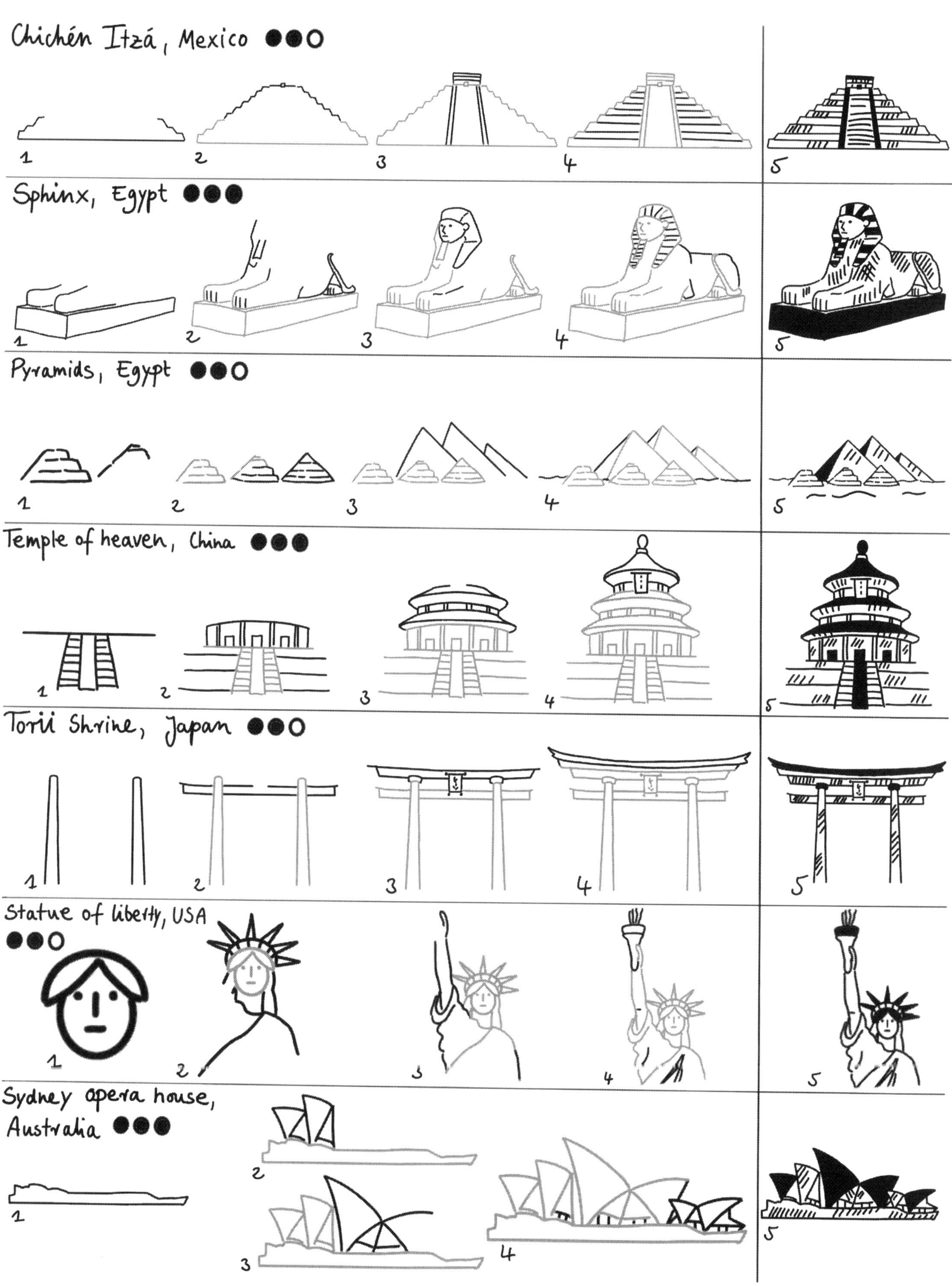
Chichén Itzá, Mexico
1
2
3
4
5
Sphinx, Egypt
1
2
3
4
5
Pyramids, Egypt
1
2
3
4
5
Temple of heaven, China
1
2
3
4
5
Torii Shrine, Japan
1
2
3
4
5
Statue of liberty, USA
1
2
3
4
5
Sydney opera house, Australia
1
2
3
4
5

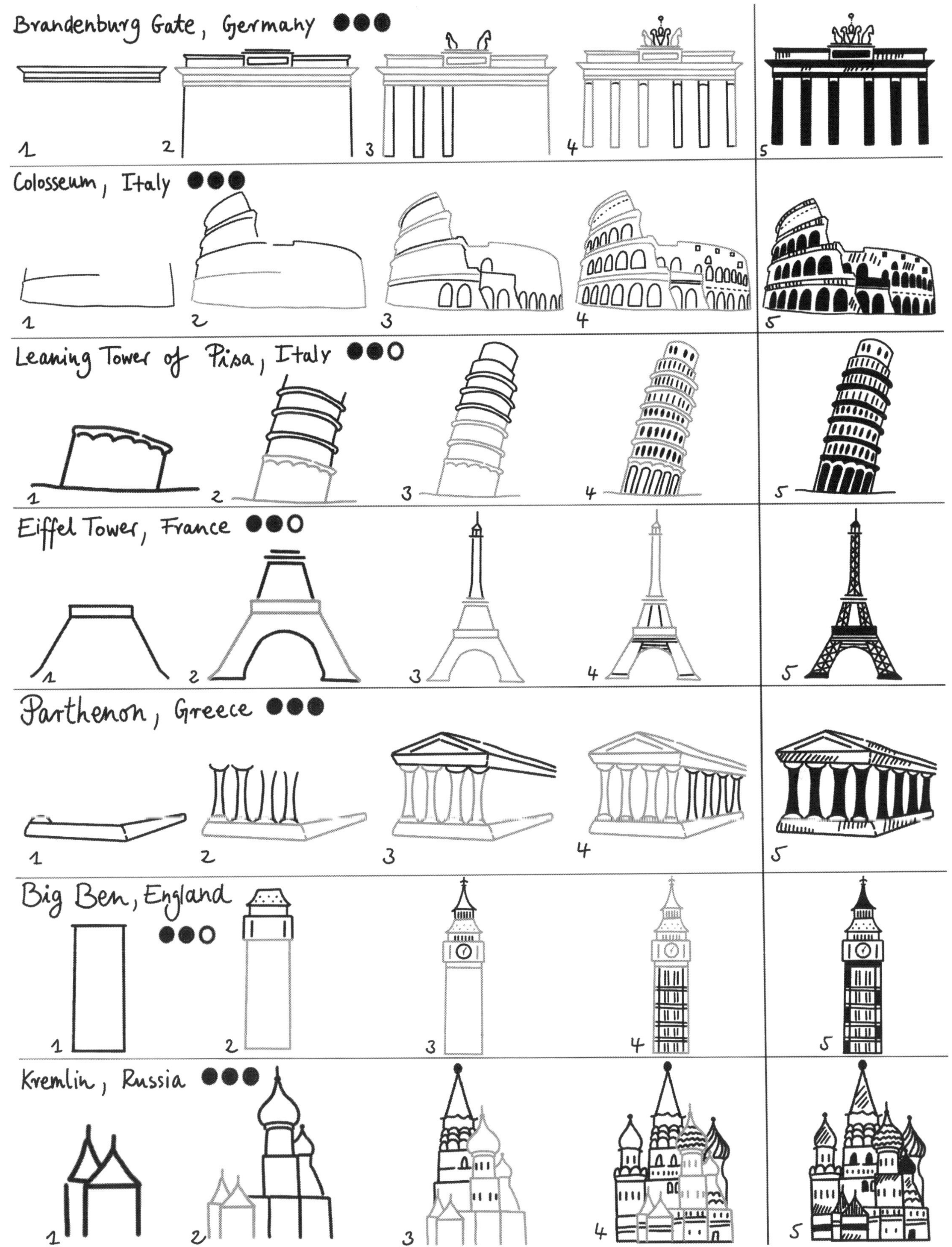
Brandenburg Gate, Germany
Colosseum, Italy
Leaning Tower of Pisa, Italy
Eiffel Tower, France
Parthenon, Greece
Big Ben, England
Kremlin, Russia

# OTHER

Laughing
1
2
3
Mean
1
2
3
Shh!
1
2
3
Angry
1
2
3
Embarrassed
1
2
3
Yawning
1
2
3
Crying
1
2
3
Eating
1
2
3
Sad
1
2
3
Thoughtful
1
2
3
Giggling
1
2
3
Kisses
1
2
3
Frightened
1
2
3
Eww!!
1
2
3

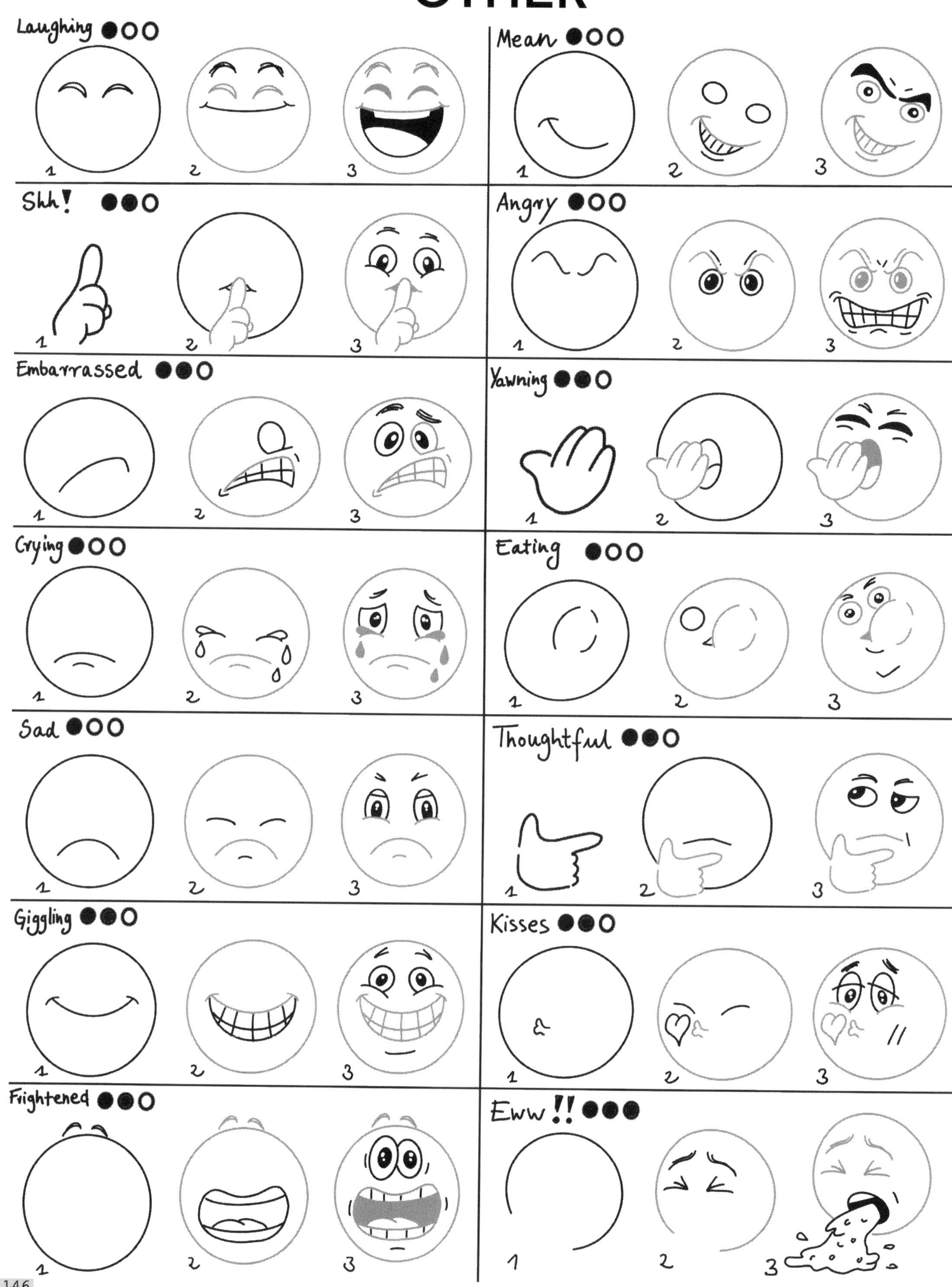

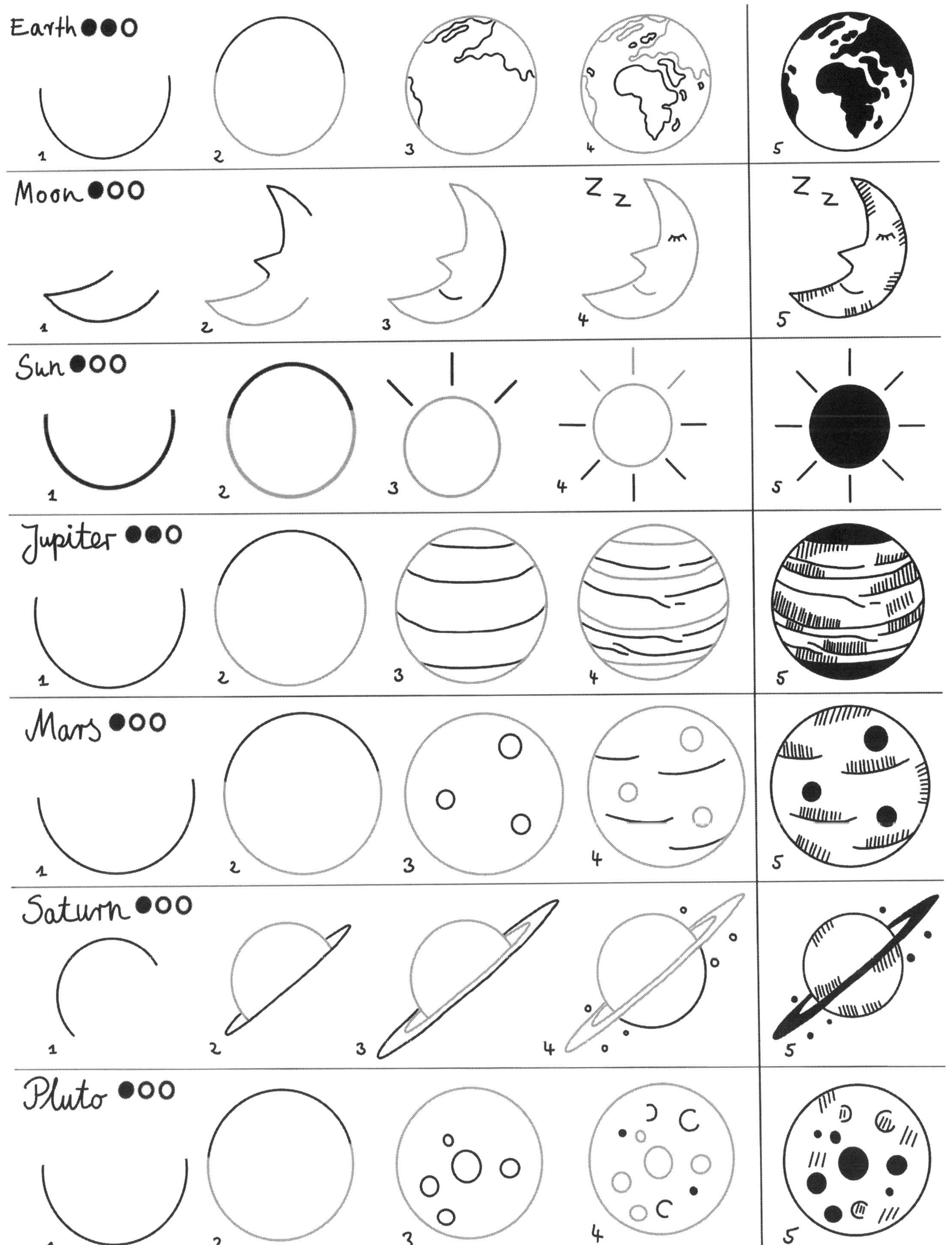
Earth
1
2
3
4
5
Moon
Z z
1
2
3
4
5
Sun
1
2
3
4
5
Jupiter
1
2
3
4
5
Mars
1
2
3
4
5
Saturn
1
2
3
4
5
Pluto
1
2
3
4
5

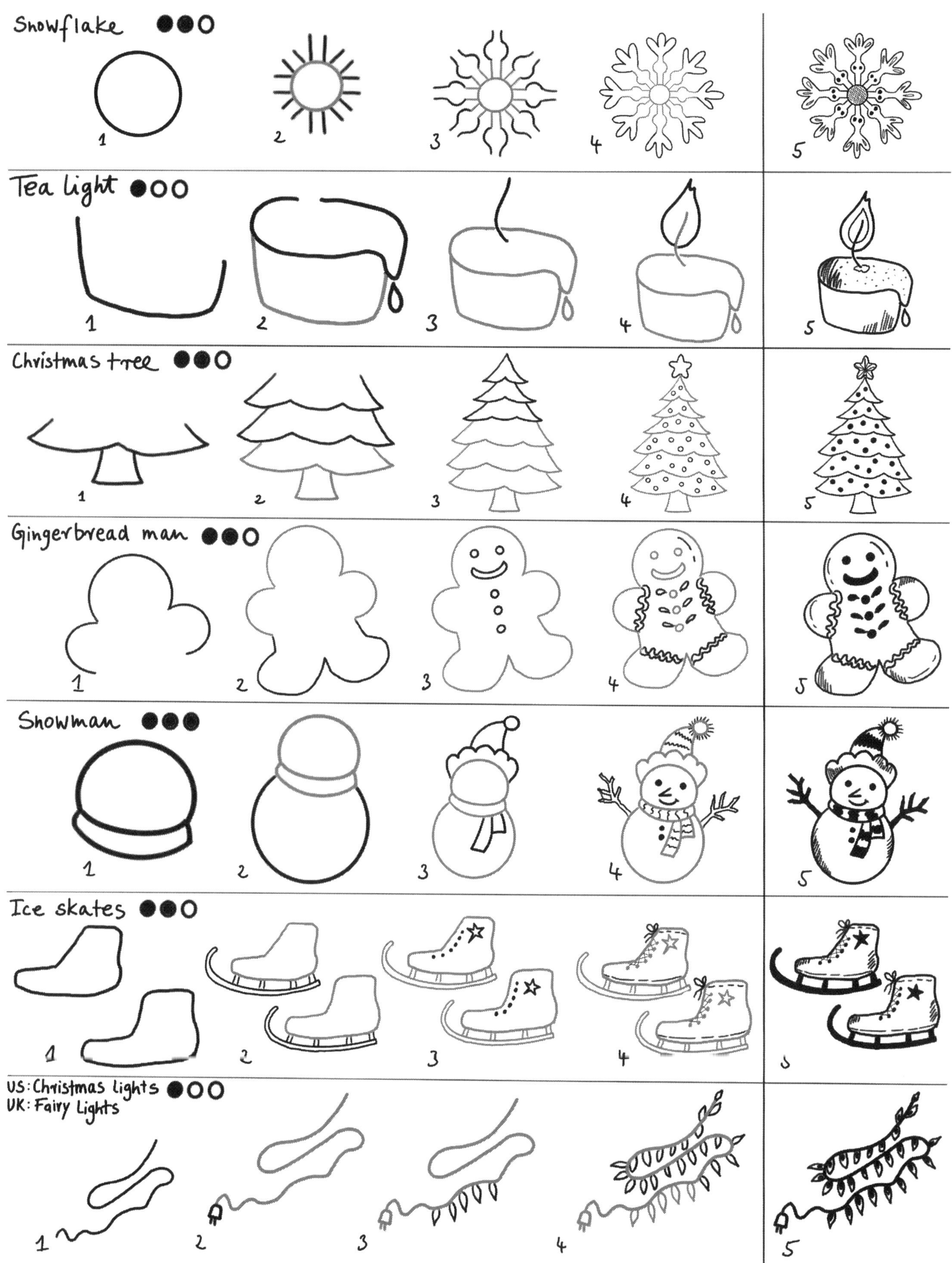
Snowflake
1
2
3
4
5
Tea light
1
2
3
4
5
Christmas tree
1
2
3
4
5
Gingerbread man
1
2
3
4
5
Snowman
1
2
3
4
5
Ice skates
1
2
3
4
US: Christmas lights
UK: Fairy Lights
1
2
3
4
5

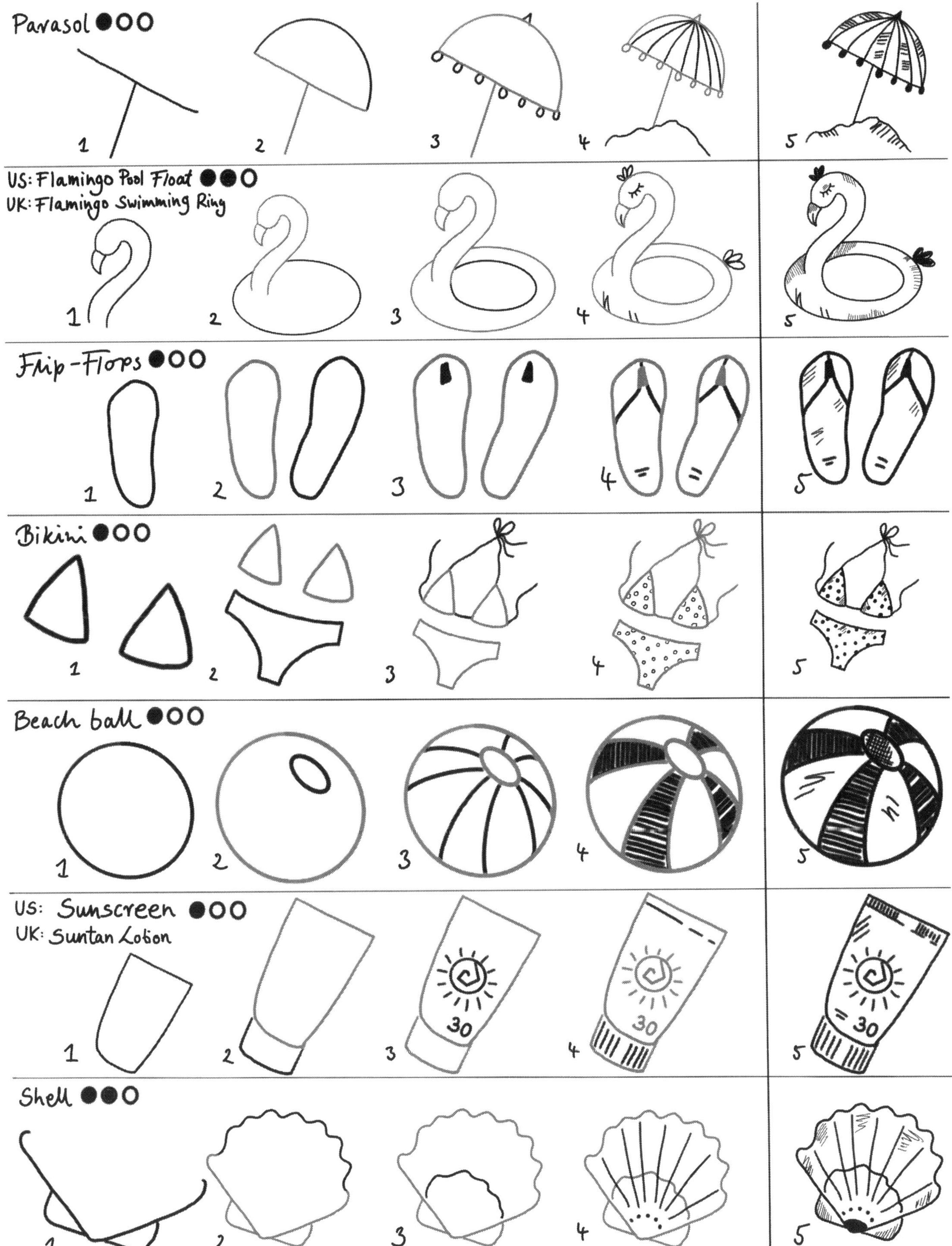
Parasol
US: Flamingo Pool Float
UK: Flamingo Swimming Ring
Flip-Flops
Bikini
Beach ball
US: Sunscreen
UK: Suntan Lotion
30
Shell

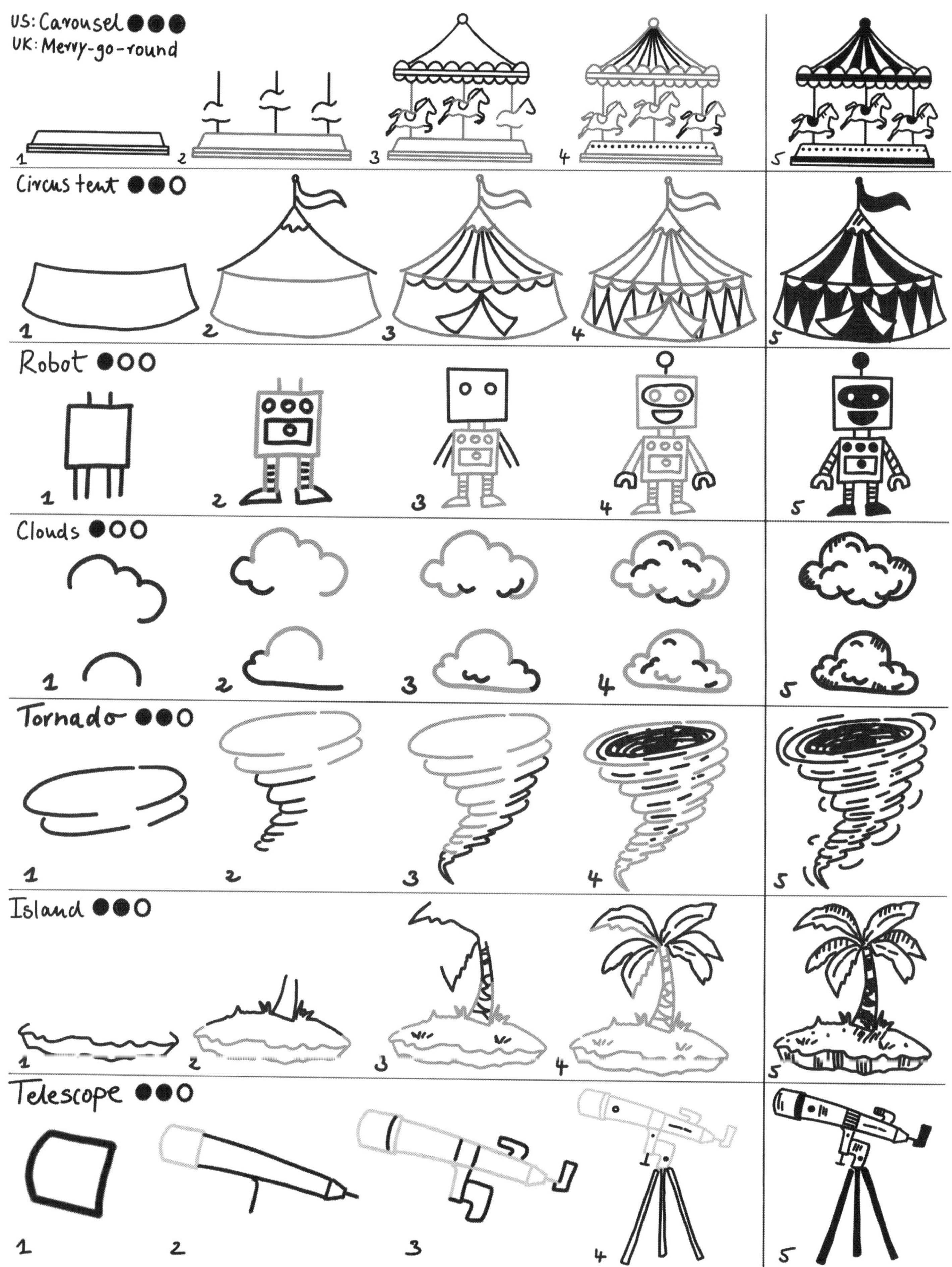

US: Carousel ●●●
UK: Merry-go-round
1
2
3
4
5
Circus tent ●●○
1
2
3
4
5
Robot ●○○
1
2
3
4
5
Clouds ●○○
1
2
3
4
5
Tornado ●●○
1
2
3
4
5
Island ●●○
1
2
3
4
5
Telescope ●●○
1
2
3
4
5

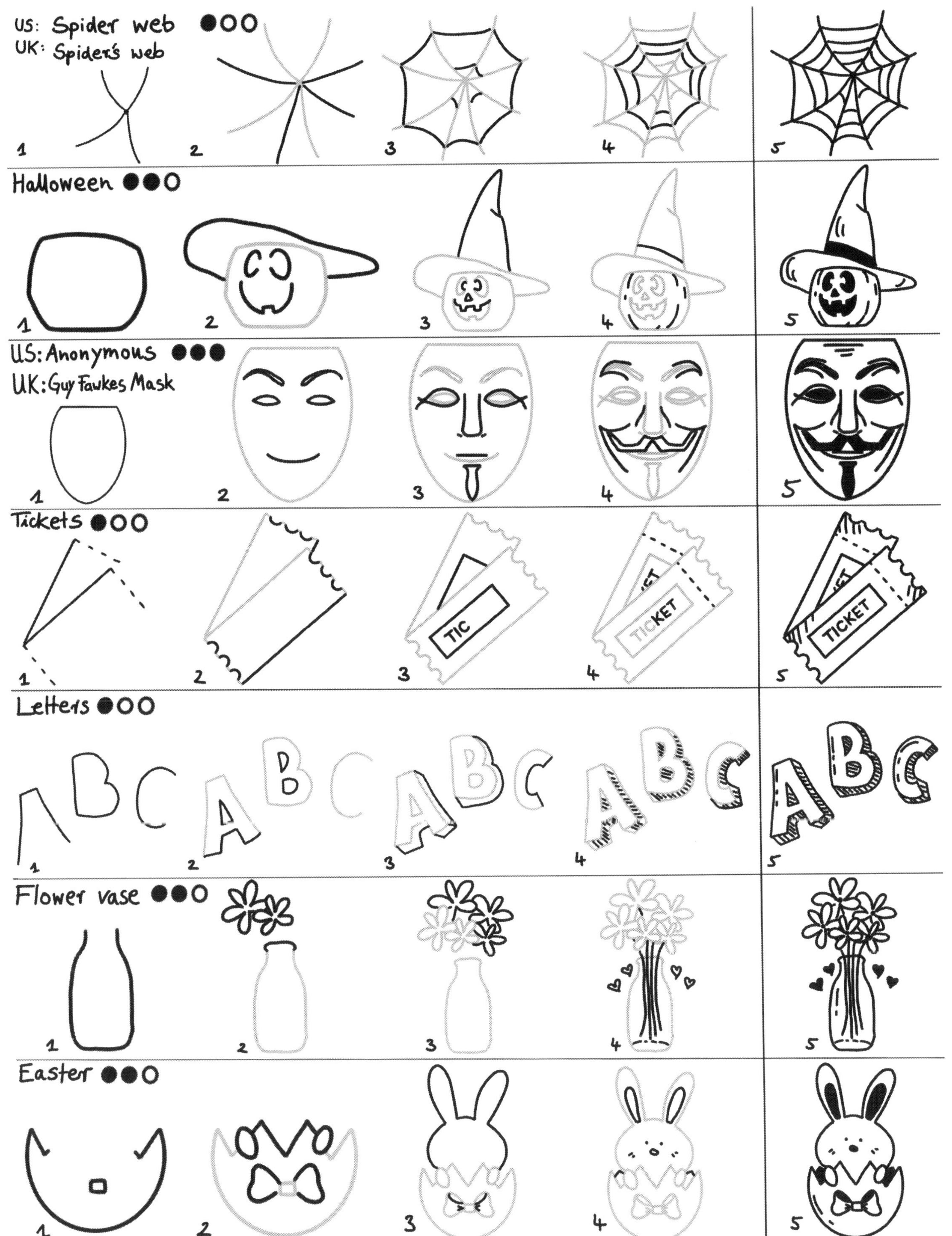
US: Spider web
UK: Spider's web
1
2
3
4
5
Halloween
1
2
3
4
5
US: Anonymous
UK: Guy Fawkes Mask
1
2
3
4
5
Tickets
TIC
TICKET
TICKET
1
2
3
4
5
Letters
1
2
3
4
5
Flower vase
1
2
3
4
5
Easter
1
2
3
4
5

# Register

# ABOUT THE AUTHOR

*„I am passionate about visual art and making art to make people happy." - Amanda Piniecka*

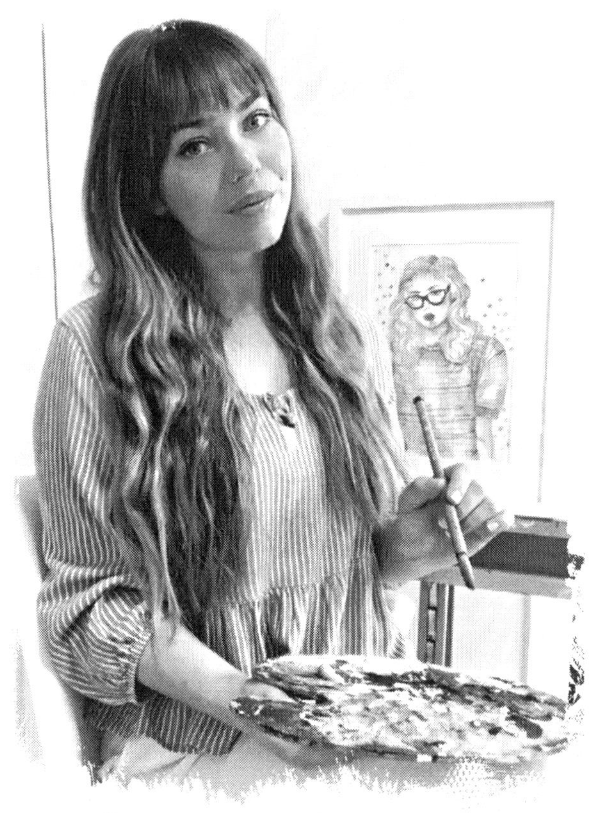

Amanda Piniecka was born in Poland in 1992.
She lives and works as a freelance artist in Freinsheim.
She started her artistic career as an illustrator. Later acrylic art and video works were added. In 2016 she graduated with a Bachelor of Arts in Mannheim, majoring in art education.
She made her first drawings on paper at the age of 5. Drawing has always been a great passion for her. Amanda is very active on the social media platform Instagram (@amy_pini) and enchants her fans with new artworks every day.

*„Over the past few years, I've started sharing my creative journey on Instagram. I hope you can learn something from it for your own artistic journey. See you there!"*

**Author:**
Amanda Piniecka
amandapiniecka@gmail.com

**www.amandapiniecka.com**
**Instagram: amy_pini**

*Thank you so much for choosing my book! I hope you have fun drawing and feel free to share your artwork with me on Instagram.*

***Instagram: amy_pini***

# IMPRINT

*ISBN: 978-9493264052*

**Publisher: Svim.Media**

***Svim.Media***
*N.P. Vogel*
*Zaanstraat 88*
*4388 TE Oost-Souburg*
*The Netherlands*

**Email: info@master.today**

**Telephone: +31628037010**

Made in the USA
Columbia, SC
14 November 2023